COMPANION

TO

MIDDLE ENGLISH ROMANCE

WITHDRAWN

COMPANION

TO

MIDDLE ENGLISH ROMANCE

edited by

HENK AERTSEN

and

ALASDAIR A. MACDONALD

VU UNIVERSITY PRESS

Amsterdam 1990

The illustration on the cover shows the wife of Sir Bertilak de Hautdesert visiting Sir Gawain in his bedchamber: BL MS. Cotton Nero A x, f.125.

CIP-GEGEVENS KONINKLIJKE BIBLIOTHEEK, DEN HAAG

Companion

Companion to Middle English romance / ed. by Henk Aertsen and Alasdair A. MacDonald. - Amsterdam: VU University Press.
Met lit. opg.
ISBN 90-6256-899-8
SISO enge 852.7 UDC 820"04/14" NUGI 953
Trefw.: Middelengelse letterkunde

VU University Press is an imprint of:
VU Boekhandel/Uitgeverij bv
De Boelelaan 1105
1081 HV Amsterdam
The Netherlands

isbn 90-6256-899-8
nugi 953

PREFACE

The editors of this book commissioned the following original essays on the Middle English romance, with the deliberate intention of offering the undergraduate reader a range of critical approaches and methodologies. It is, after all, improbable that a genre so voluminous and varied can be adequately studied from any single point of view. We hope that the book will be found both useful, in its provision of information, and interesting, in its attempt to stimulate new understandings of these fascinating texts.

We take this opportunity of thanking all colleagues, in the Netherlands and abroad, for their contributions to this volume.

Free University, Amsterdam
University of Groningen
July, 1990

Henk Aertsen
Alasdair A. MacDonald

CONTENTS

THE FRENCH BACKGROUND *

MARTIN GOSMAN

Although the concept of 'background', when seen in a literary perspective, is quite problematic in itself (not only does it suggest an optical relationship, but a causal one as well), with regard to the Middle Ages it should be employed with even greater caution than would be the case for modern times, where abundant biographical information normally enables one to establish—or at least make plausible—relationships between various literary and/or cultural manifestations. However, in periods where the author largely has a subsidiary status, and where he may even be hard to identify as an individual, the problem takes on different proportions altogether: there is no umbilical cord of copyright linking the literary artefact with the author who created it, as there is today. Once the work leaves the hands of the author, it becomes common property. It is of course possible for the author to derive some fame and honour from his creation, provided he has done the right things: alternatively, he can simply claim the honour, either directly or indirectly, as does Chrétien de Troyes in his *Conte du Graal*:

> Ki petit semme petit quelt,
> Et qui auques requeillir velt
> En tel liu sa semence espande
> Que Diex a cent doubles li rande;
> Car en terre qui riens ne valt,
> Bone semence seche et faut.
> Crestïens semme et fait semenece
> D'un romans que il encomence,
> Et si le seme en si bon leu
> Qu'il ne puet estre sanz grant preu   (1-10)

(He who sows little will harvest little. But he who wants to harvest something of value puts his seed in such a place where God returns him a hundredfold. Because in arid land every good seed will render nothing, Chrétien sows the seeds of a romance he will

---

* This chapter was translated by Wynzen de Vries.

begin now—and he sows them in such a good place that they cannot but fructify.)

In the Middle Ages and even in the Renaissance it is, therefore,
perfectly normal for authors to borrow both matter and techniques
from others without any acknowledgement. In the seventeenth century, Molière is able to say unblushingly: 'Je prends mon bien où je le
trouve.'
Literary material is there to be pillaged, or, should a milder
expression be preferred, it is 'available': borrowing and re-use are
normal. The essence of the creative achievement is the assimilation
of the extant material in circulation; this comprises the 'background',
usually of an intertextual nature. This is a problem in all periods.
There are differences, however, in the ways in which that 'background' is recognised as such (both by the author and his critic), or
seen as a separate entity. And this is where the shoe pinches, especially in the Middle Ages: every author draws on the material that is
available to him, and is able to do so without acknowledgement. If
there are acknowledgements, they may be there for several reasons:
they may constitute a simple *étalage de savoir* (where an author simply mentions the sources in his work); alternatively, and this is a procedure well known in discussions involving theological dogma, the
author may begin by giving full recognition to his sources in order
subsequently to use them as building-blocks for his own thesis; caution, after all, is what matters in theology, where the smell of brim-
stone is ever in the air. In literature (to which we limit ourselves
here), it is of course far from unusual to refer to one's 'sources', but
the material employed is always subject to aesthetic, social, and
emotional reconsiderations.
In the preceding I have silently assumed a linguistically un-
complicated relationship between artefacts: the author of one work
has no problems reading and integrating the work of his predecessor.
Of course the question becomes more complicated where there are
various linguistic registers, which may yield problems of communication between those who have insufficiently mastered them. When
one remembers that Chrétien de Troyes assimilates, in his romances,
matières of classical, biblical, Celtic, and even legendary origin, it is
clear that he was able to acquire these on the basis only of adapted,
i.e. translated, written or oral traditions. But Chrétien did not live on
an island; others on the Continent or in the British Isles had the same
material at their disposal and used it in a similar way, as far as basic
attitudes are concerned--or at least had the chance to do so (the

French master's procedure of assimilation being, of course, his own unique contribution). However, it will be clear that some caution is called for when one begins to speak of 'backgrounds' in general, and particularly with regard to the relationship between French literature and Middle English literature; it would be an untenable proposition to speak of a 'French' medieval literature as a monolithic block which (a) consisted entirely of original material, and (b) was therefore 'typical' as such. Here, too, there is compositeness. The same goes for literary production in Middle English.

There is, of course, a very special relationship between French and English literature in the Middle Ages. Apart from the the availability of 'sources' that constitute the European literary-cultural heritage, dealt with above, there was in post-Conquest Britain a double linguistic register (that is, if we leave Latin out of consideration). French, the language of the conquerors, functioned as a superstratum, and at the courts of the nobility supplanted English. This change was never complete and was certainly not permanent: at no time did literary production in the language of the defeated nation come to a complete halt, and in the fourteenth century English regained its lost position.

During the two centuries when French (or rather Anglo-Norman and, later, *Francien*, the language of the Ile de France, where the French royal power had its seat) had the upper hand in England, not only were translations and adaptations made from French, but writers in England also adapted themselves to the intellectual and literary traditions of French literature. At the end of the day, the patrons either still had a French bias, or it was *bon ton* closely to associate oneself with the prestigious literature. In both cases the command of French gave access to the dominant clique, and provided both the author and his product with the required legitimation (Bourdieu, 1989:97-8). This resulted in: translations and poetic adaptations of French material (which is what Laȝamon did in his version of the *Brut*); the fairly accurate adoption of French model texts (examples that spring to mind are the translations of Guillaume de Deguileville's work, or Caxton's *Eneydos*); or the composition of French texts by Englishmen (a typical example is Gower's lengthy *Mirour de l'Omme*). Scores of other examples could be quoted (Malone and Baugh, 1967:265, 288).

It may sound like a paradox, but the French 'background' is in fact—and this is the reason why I have already pointed out that the concept is optically misleading—as much referential background as breeding ground. At first it functioned as a model (this was inevitable, as the descendants of William the Conqueror were the ones in charge); later it became a source of inspiration for English literature, once the latter had started slowly to gain a consciousness of its own status. Even after English literature had taken on a clearly defined shape of its own, borrowings from French and other linguistic registers did not cease; Shakespeare, too, began by utilising French material, or texts that had earlier undergone French adaptations, and treated themes which had been expressed there in an artistically interesting fashion (or at least in a fashion that he found useful). Here the matter of Troy is illustrative: various adaptations (among them, that by Chaucer) stand between Benoît de Saint-Maure's French translation and the great dramatist's acquaintance with the story. What is essential is the function that French literature fulfilled in passing on the general European cultural heritage. It continued to do so for a long time, but there was also a period of keen rivalry between French and Italian literature (which, by the way, at certain times found itself in an identical position relative to the linguistic regions surrounding it: Italian too, moreover, derives much from French and Occitan literature).

It is not my intention in this introduction to give an enumeration of all possible relationships between French texts and English 'users'. Such a thing would be a typically nineteenth-century inventory of sources, not providing any insight into what characterises the literary achievements in the linguistic registers under consideration. The user of the present book will, I believe, profit more from an introduction to some characteristic texts, or groups of texts, that are dealt with in the following chapters. It will then be possible to compare the French characteristics, sketched only in broad outline, of course, with the Middle English ones. In this light, I shall pay attention to the epic (dealing with Charlemagne), the 'classical' romances (notably the ones about Alexander the Great), the *lais* and romances of Marie de France and Chrétien de Troyes, largely set in a 'Celtic' context, and one particular dynasty-novel (*Gui de Warewic*).

In what follows, the emphasis will be on what could be called the utilitarian aspects of these texts, since in the period concerned literature has an ancillary task, tending to preserve the social *status quo*. I shall limit myself to French texts from the twelfth and thirteenth centuries, since these are at the basis of the Middle English literature that begins to take shape at this time. Although in the fourteenth and fifteenth centuries, as pointed out above, there is still borrowing from French literature (the position of French lyric poetry is a relevant case in point: cf. Charles d'Orléans) and re-use of the narrative material and techniques found in French literature, there is a steadily growing distance between the literature that supplies and the one that receives. When, moreover, one realises that Chaucer had both a French and an Italian 'period', it is clear that a chapter on the French background of Middle English literature in that later period (the fourteenth and fifteenth centuries) would not only have to be different in substance, but would also have to be written from a different perspective.

Like most vernacular literatures, French literature also starts off by committing the past to record. A number of reasons can be given for this: not only does the past stand warranty for a certain purity (Christianity consistently sees the world in a perspective of *degradatio*), it also contains a socio-political motivation which, when respected, guarantees a preservation of the *status quo*, the Augustinian *ordo naturalis*, where theological and politico-philosophical argumentations converge. On a purely literary level this finds expression—at this time conformism is a *conditio sine qua non*—in a typological interpretation of socially codified characteristics, i.e. characteristics motivated in the 'historical' fiction: the hero's embodiment of a particular virtue, vassal's loyalty, self-sacrifice, and so on.

The first form in which the incipient French literature expresses itself, if we leave out of consideration a small number of religious texts more or less directly inspired by the traditions of the Latin Church, is the epic, which on the one hand provides the historical motivation already mentioned, and on the other both psychologically and functionally separates the ruling castes of society (*bellatores* and *oratores*) from the *laboratores*. Two elements are involved here. In the first place, the ideal model of the *agens*, the noble warrior, in its tendency to exclusivity—underlined not only by this noble warrior's dedication to the cause of the caste, but also by his functional indispensability—determines the way in which the past is perceived. In the second place—and this seems a paradox, since at this time society was feudal in character, and the king ought therefore to be regarded as a mere *primus inter pares*—literature is largely preoccupied with the ruler, who is the focus of interest and is seen as the exponent of a divinely ordained socio-political structure. Although the *narratio* may frequently concentrate on another *agens*, it is the king (or the system that he represents: at this time it is not possible to make a clear distinction between the two aspects of power, *institutio* and *persona*) who remains the centre of the action. It is not relevant whether the *agens* temporarily determining the action is an *adjuvant* or an *opposant*: what matters in both cases is the negation or confirmation of the *same* royal power. Examples here are the part played by the Saracens in the *chanson de geste* (negation) and that played by the Christian king's fellow-warriors, such as Roland and his fellow paladins (confirmation). In the Arthur legend Mordred and Gawain fulfil the same functions respectively.

This manner of thinking of the past finds its literary culmination in the epics around Charlemagne. Written at least three centuries after the emperor's death (the *Chanson de Roland* was composed c1100), these epics depict a 'historical' situation which is in fact an ostensibly contemporaneous one, since at this time no need was felt for a modern historical approach to the past: the setting (the fabula) is the past, the plot is contemporaneous. In the *Roland* and certainly in the *Couronnement de Louis* (1137-40) twelfth-century problems play an important part. The past is—and this is where the fascinating ambiguity comes in—both excuse and aim. The struggle against Islam, for instance, is an acute problem in the eleventh century (one recalls the preaching of Urban II at Clermont); what the *chanson de geste* does here is to suggest an approach which would, in view of the ideal political structure of the past, guarantee a solution: Charlemagne's power was represented as unchallenged (and how could it have been challenged when panegyric characterised the emperor as a ruler *gratia Dei*, and even as an *alter Christus*? See Kantorowicz, 1957:46, 82-3). On two different levels Charlemagne's warriors embody the ideal contract: the secular contract between a vassal and his liege, and the religious contract between a Christian and his God. The result is a fusing of the interests of the ruling *ordines*, a fusing, incidentally, that is to have many sequels in both literature and society (examples being the fighting monastic orders like the Knights Templars and the Hospitallers, Bernard of Clairvaux's *nova militia*).

The French epic defends both 'nationalist' values and general Christian ones, in that it appeals to themes that are functional only in the context of the French feudal structure (in the eleventh and twelfth centuries this only applied to the king's patrimony, roughly the region surrounding Paris and the feudal estates nominally connected with it) and of the 'Christian community', within whatever was left of the *Ecclesia* within Europe. Of course the literary character of a *Chanson de Roland* can be related to a background of well-known Germanic epic traditions, but the way in which it ultimately achieves its significance as a literary work is locally determined (this means that the way is cleared for anachronism). Despite the local 'colouring' the common European good is involved, defended by the Franks (the struggle against Islam); and yet, by means of the inescapable anchoring procedure—it is a French epic written for a French-language audience, living in a French-language context and frame of reference (Charlemagne is *their* king)—it functions as an illustration of a pioneering achievement. Seen in this light, it strikes one that the German *Rolandslied* views the battle at Roncesvalles not from a French perspective but very much from a general Christian one, and represents the part played by the French as merely subsidiary and instrumental (Wesle and Wapnewski, 1967:xii-xiii; Wentzlaff-Eggebert, 1960:78-81).

One particular consequence of the centripetal mode of thinking in the *Chanson de Roland* is that around 1100 (after the First Crusade, significantly) a generally acknowledged concept like the Christian warrior's duty to fight against Islam under the colours of the Church is modified into a French philosophy of *natio*: in contrast with the Curia's policy concerning fighters for the faith (which sought to turn *milites Christi* into *milites sancti Petri*), the combatants in *Roland* are exclusively *milites Christi*, that is, warriors who choose to dispense with the Curia's intervention, let alone its guidance. This means that the power of decision has been shifted (if the image is a permissible one) from Rome to Aachen (one of the places where, along with Paris and Laon, Charlemagne spent most of his time, when he was not out on expedition). The result is that Charlemagne, and not the pope, functions as *vicarius Christi*; via the Archangel Gabriel Charlemagne himself has direct links with the Lord. The fact that after his victory over the Saracen Marsilius, and later over Baligant, the emperor together with his army returns to *dulce France* (Gosman, forthcoming) points to an assimilation-process that displays aspects of territorial sentiment, and sufficiently illustrates the local thinking that characterises the *Chanson de Roland*.

One last element: what is essential is the way in which the panegyric on the heroes is worked out. This is true of every epic, but here we are faced with a remarkable combination of vassal's duty, caste-consciousness, warrior's honour (it would go too far simply to call Roland and Olivier 'knights', like Chrétien's heroes), religious trust in the ultimate victory of Christianity, and—very importantly—Christian self-sacrifice: the fighting takes place in a perspective that is strikingly close to what Bernard of Clairvaux was to formulate clearly: 'it is better to be defeated than to win'. From a religious point of view Roland's death is a triumph, even though feudally and personally it is a catastrophe. Seen in this light, the enigmatic Turoldus, who "*declinet*" (1.4002) the *Chanson*, presents a basic model for later portraits of knights.

Between roughly 1150 and 1180 there came into being in French the so-called 'classical' romances or *romans* (texts in *romanice*, the vernacular), which translate and adapt the narrative matter that developed, during classical antiquity, around Alexander the Great, the struggle at Thebes, the siege of Troy, and the resulting adventures of Aeneas. In addition—an example to demonstrate that the re-use of classical material is not limited to the four areas mentioned—an author like Ovid is frequently made use of, both in lyrical poetry and in narrative texts.

The 'classical' romances are extremely interesting, not only because of the fact that they enrich the French cultural heritage with new narrative material and motivations (in later ages Troy was in most European states regarded as the ideal socio-political structure; it is difficult to think of a royal house the fate of which is not in some way linked with that of Aeneas), but also because the reuse of that narrative material from a non-'national' past (but one often considered 'historical') entails a clarification of the author's status (though not of his personal interests). Leaving aside the well-known image of the Middle Ages as walking forwards while looking back (i.e. to the past, which contains the serene picture of an imperturbable *ordo naturalis*), there still is a perceptible gap between the author of the source text and the translator/adaptor of the target text: there is a consciousness of progression relative to that past. With regard to the epic, based as it is on oral traditions, this distance is of course no longer measurable. Also, the idea cannot be isolated from the feeling of superiority that causes Christianity to see the heritage of Greek and Roman antiquity as *spolia* with which the victor can do as he pleases.

Here we come to what is essential about the 'classical' romances. They are placed in a perspective of utility ("*chose digne por ramenbrer*": *Roman de Thèbes* 1.12: 'a thing worthy of remembrance') and especially of historical reliability: Homer, who according to Benoît was writing only one century after the fall of Troy, could not possibly have known everything ("...*onc n'i fu ne rien n'en vit*": *Roman de Troie*, 1.56: 'he was never there, nor did he see anything'), and moreover the fact that he depicted the gods as fighting with mortals had already even in his own time got him into trouble:

Dampner le voustrent par reison,
Por co qu'ot fait les damedeus

Combatre o les homes charneus.   (60-3)

(They were right in wanting to condemn him, because he made the
gods fight with mortal men.)

Benoît sets out to tell us exactly how things really happened. The account as given by the 'historical' source is adapted so as to bring
about a certain conformity with the twelfth-century norm (Benoît
did not realise that his 'eye-witnesses', Dares and Dictys, were writing a long time after the beginning of the Christian era and that
therefore their texts were also influenced by contemporary habits of
writing and perception, with the result that their picture of the events
is likewise a purely literary one). Apart from developments on the
psychological and on the sentimental plane, this process of adaptation
is the most fascinating aspect of the 'classical' romance; anachronism
runs rampant as a creative instrument (the Greeks and the Romans
are, for instance, depicted as medieval knights whose religious notions are of an extremely hybrid nature: it is unclear whether they
are Christians or pagans). It would not be right to regard the
anachronistic thinking of the Middle Ages as 'misguided'. On the
contrary, it is both the instrument of and the very evidence for what
has been called 'positive assimilation' (Köhler, 1977:12-3)—the
openness of a literary tradition to information from without, in such
a way that, through shifts and combinations, the content-characteris-
tics of 'genres' cause new horizons to be opened up, creating a new
aesthetic distance (Jauss, 1970:70).

It is not the matter only that is subject to modification. As far
as narrative technique is concerned, the 'classical' romances lie between the *chansons de geste* and, for instance, the romances of Chrétien de Troyes. The *Roman d'Alexandre* has the design and organisation of an epic, and is in rhymed *laisses* (stanzas of irregular length).
The epic itself, based upon a perception of the world that strikes one
as Manichean (good against evil, Christianity against Islam: *crestien-
té* against *païenie*), had combined this with the heroic code of Germanic tradition: knightly honour, self-sacrifice, group-conscious-
ness, and, most of all, loyalty to the principles and the interests that
concern that group, these are the concepts which in fact determine
the dedication displayed by heroes like Roland and Olivier, who,
because of their status, belong to the *magnates* among the nobility. Of
course it is a small step to a situation where knightly ethics and birth
coincide. The medieval, theoretical way of thinking in *ordines* fa-
vours the *bellatores*, and this attitude decisively conditions the description of the heroes in the *chansons de geste*. In Benoît's *Roman de*

Troie (c1160) this is already a fact (in the earlier *Le Couronnement de Louis*, it is still possible—although already exceptional—for a brave man to be made a knight even if he does not belong to the ruling caste (ll.1644-50). But in literature social status soon becomes what matters most: in order to be made a knight, one has to be of noble birth. The twelfth-century Trojan heroes are all either princes, or come from otherwise exalted backgrounds (as was the case with Homer's characters, incidentally). They remain epic heroes, however: the many scenes of fighting are prominent, and little attention is paid to emotional matters. In view of its special formulaic technique, the epic in its original form had been able to express emotional and psychological aspects in an exclusively physical way only: overwhelmed by grief at Roland's death, Charlemagne faints; to express the powerfulness of his feelings, the text repeats the event three times (*Chanson de Roland*, ll.2870-2908), as if it were a musical motif. Benoît, too, is unable to break free from this technique altogether, although he is capable of more effectively preparing events like this. Exploiting the medieval feeling for what is deviant, he makes it perfectly clear, in the purely physical portrait that he draws of Briséide (in English to become first Criseyde and then Cressida), that there is a flaw in her character: the fact that her eyebrows are set too closely together mars the ideal image of female beauty, and functions as a strongly connotative signal (ll.13261-866). The reader or listener contemporary with Benoît knows all he has to know, and will not really be surprised: despite the tears over her beloved Trojan Troilus, the heroine will soon deceive him with the Greek Diomede. This example already suggests that Benoît's handling of the psychological apparatus has still about it very much the technique of the epic, and that he is as yet unable to put himself in the shoes of his characters, as it were, so as to analyse their feelings. Despite his merits, Benoît did not succeed in getting the approximately 30,000 lines of his work completely under control: heroes who die in the first part (inspired by Dares) are still fighting lustily in the second part (derived from Dictys): Benoît—probably obsessed with his 'eye-witnesses'—has simply forgotten that they had died already. What is essential in his text—and this goes equally for other 'classical' romances—is the fact that the heroism depicted is no longer related to a metaphysical norm: people simply fight for their own interests. The Christian epic no longer seems to offer an all-embracing frame of reference, and literature now begins to concern itself rather with Man.

The socio-political relations of the time form an aspect that is now worked out with a certain degree of subtlety. Even the *Chanson de Roland* had already placed Ganelon's treachery in a feudal perspective, by its representation of situational details, and suggested several explanations for it. This is not the place to comment on the epic but on the romance, where the same problems play a part, although in a different way. The *Roman de Thèbes* (c1150), which deals extensively with the difficulties that face a vassal serving two lieges, is a case in point. The problem comes out clearly in the case of Daire le Roux: having had a quarrel with one liege, Daire chooses the side of the other (who has quite opposite interests). During the proceedings instituted against his vassal by the aggrieved party (I shall not go into the legal casuistry that characterises the passage in question), the judgement is influenced positively by the amorous feelings of the lord for a fair maiden (Petit, 1985:126-53). The passage is all the more interesting because in it the feudal state of affairs is made subordinate to the influence of the fair sex—an important step on the way that will lead to Lanval and Lancelot.

But before moving on to Marie de France and Chrétien, I should like to say something about one of the most seminal and yet underestimated French texts, which is usually referred to collectively as the *Roman d'Alexandre*. Around 1184, Alexandre de Paris compiled a number of Alexander stories, adding not a little from his own pen. The result is the *Roman d'Alexandre*, which in its more than 17,000 lines gives a complete picture of the Macedonian hero's life, from birth till death. Towards the end of the twelfth century, this conglomerate was enlarged with texts describing the revenge taken on Alexander's assassins; in the following centuries all kinds of adventures were added (in the thirteenth century, his journey to the Earthly Paradise, among other things; in the fourteenth, the Peacock texts: *Voeux du Paon* [Casey,1956], *Restor du Paon* [Carey, 1966], and *Parfait du Paon* [Carey, 1972]).The whole had by then assumed twice its original size. Apart from the continental Alexander texts, there is also an important Anglo-Norman text, the *Roman de Toute Chevalerie*, ascribed to one Thomas of Kent (Foster and Short, 1976-7). These texts are particularly interesting because of the ideal portrait that they draw of the rulers. It is not really surprising that all the Great Ones of the Earth see themselves as second Alexanders (or are compared to him, to their advantage):

C'est li quens Phelipes de Flandres
Qui valt mix ne fist Alixandres.   (*Conte du Graal*, 13-4)

(It is count Philip of Flanders, who is far superior to Alexander.)

This is because this very Macedonian, with his immense military successes, was the prototype of the *rex utilis*, the aggressive, expansion-
ist ruler who succeeds in realising his policy thanks to his vassals'
unconditional loyalty. And in the Middle Ages that was exactly the
great problem facing all kings. Leaving out of consideration all
Alexander's exotic adventures in the 'Orient', feudal relations play
the leading part. But there are differences: the continental romance
pictures a harmonious relationship between Alexander and his
twelve peers (cf. Charlemagne's twelve paladins), who will succeed
him after his death. It is exclusively thanks to the unconditional loyalty of these *magnates*, who have grown up with Alexander and have
been knighted along with him, that the king can achieve his successes.
He himself behaves in turn like one of them. No appeal, therefore,
that he makes to their availability for military action ever meets with
objections:

> Touz jorz vesquirent d'armes, itel fu lor labor.
> Par ceus et par les autres conquist il mainte honor,
> Car de par toute terre le tint on a seignor.
> *(Roman d'Alexandre*, I, 247-9)

(Every day they battled; such was their labour. With them and
with the others he conquered many a kingdom, because throughout the whole world people accepted him as their master.)

Of course this is an ideal image: in twelfth-century France royal authority was really only effective in the region surrounding Paris, and
not until the reign of Philippe Auguste does it attain consolidation
and expansion. The Anglo-Norman *Roman de Toute Chevalerie* (approximately 8,000 lines), written between 1175 and 1185, shows
more affinity with feudal reality. It may be assumed that the insular
situation, which allowed the royal power to think more in hierarchical terms (the nobility, only recently installed after all, commanded little influence), brought about a certain degree of realism; when
Alexander convenes his vassals, he does so in unmistakable terms: if
they shirk their duties, the king's wrath will manifest itself *de facto*
(Gosman, 1988:338-9). A peculiarity of the fourteenth-century interpolations is Alexander's ever increasing absence. On the one hand
this is logical, as the invention of new adventures for the hero was
difficult to justify 'historically' (the available Latin sources, such as

Curtius Rufius, clearly did exert a certain limiting influence), on the other hand the distancing of purely royal presence does correspond to the actual development of power as it took place in the Middle Ages: from a ruler joining his fighters in battle, the king became a commander at some remove. This was a slow development, but a steady one; it became too risky to have the king himself fighting alongside his men (the example of Jean II, who was taken prisoner by the Black Prince in 1356, is illustration enough). Power became abstract and able to be delegated: this already begins to emerge in Thomas of Kent's version. Although modest, the part played by Olympias, Alexander's mother, is indicative: when her husband is absent, she replaces him and receives the honours that are due to her status. Royal power is already on its way to becoming an *institutio*.

In the earliest texts women play a fairly limited role. Olympias is mentioned in the rumours surrounding her son's illegitimate birth: the queen had been allegedly seduced by an Egyptian sorcerer, Nec–tanebus by name. Disguised as the god Ammon, he is said to have fooled the queen into believing that the god himself slept with her, and that he had begotten a child (Alexander) upon her. In a dynastic perspective, illegitimacy was of course an extremely problematical issue, and it is therefore not surprising that the textual tradition shows many variations here: in some versions Olympias is innocent, in others she is well aware of what has happened, and appears to have consciously co-operated (Gosman, 1985:334). The most important element of the passage in question, however, is the deification of Alexander. This comes out clearly in another text, the thirteenth-century *Roman d'Alexandre en prose*, a translation *cum* adaption of the twelfth-century *Historia de Preliis* (Ross, 1988:54-7) which, although its description of the Macedonian is far more negative than that given by the other traditions, does not reject Alexander's divine status. In the first Alexander texts (which, as far as formal aspects are concerned, draw heavily upon the epic) the part played by women is, generally speaking, a limited one. Some Continental texts accord women so little status that, when Alexander is having an affair with queen Candace, one does not even know whether he is or is not married to Roxane, daughter of the defeated Darius III (Gosman, 1981:173-4).

In the fourteenth century this situation changes drastically. The *Voeux du Paon* shows the influence of courtly love: on top of the citadel of Ephezon lies the *Chambre de Vénus*, the ladies' bower where only occasionally the knights are admitted. From its windows, the ladies watch the battle and comment on the technical skills displayed by the knights who have sentimental ties with the spectating ladies. At the end of the story, Alexander (who most of the time does not engage in the action, but, like a kind of *dominus mundi*, observes the proceedings from the high bank of the river that separates him from the scene of the battle, and who is involved in the affair for no other reason than his desire to make good the injustice that he unwillingly committed at a much earlier stage) sees to it that each of the lovers gets the partner he or she wants. Love and war have become inseparable. Even the Alexander texts which deal exclusively with military affairs have herewith also succumbed to the smiles of the fair.

Clearly, the Middle English Alexander literature seeks part of its inspiration from the French tradition: the thirteenth century *Kyng Alisaunder* is a derivation from Thomas of Kent's text; John Gower takes over the story about Nectanebus and queen Olympias; and an unknown Middle Scots poet (formerly believed to be John Barbour) uses complete texts, among them the *Voeux du Paon*, for his Middle Scottish *Buik of Alexander* (see the survey by Bunt elsewhere in this volume).

This is very different, of course, in the twelfth-century texts that take their inspiration from the *matière de Bretagne*, like Marie de France's *lais* and Chrétien's romances. Under the powerful influence of the troubadours' tradition of *fin' amor* (these singers frequently crossed the Channel: Bernard de Ventadour spent a good deal of time at the court of Eleanor of Aquitaine), the heroes' actions soon begin to be determined by love. In each of the twelve *lais* that are ascribed to Marie (there are also others which are anonymous), one particular case is focused on: adulterous love (*Equitan*); a man between two women (*Eliduc*); love that takes away all sense of proportion (*Deus Amans*); self-sacrifice and loyalty (*Fresne*); love between a mortal man and a fairy (*Lanval*); etc. The last two are interesting here because of their Middle English adaptations, *Lay le Freine*, *Sir Landeval*, and Thomas of Chester's *Sir Launfal*. I shall briefly indicate some elements of *Lanval* here, and then pass on to Chrétien's work.

The essential characteristic of the 'Breton' tradition is the existence of an Otherworld, which seemingly (empirical description is of course not possible) is subject to a normative system of its own, just like the mortal world. As far as the appreciation of, for instance, knightly ethics and religion are concerned, this system of norms is at right angles to that of the Christian world of men: there is so much that is needlessly complicated. Confrontations with representatives from that Otherworld (usually ladies, although men can also play a part: cf. the anonymous *lai* of *Tydorel*, ed. O'Hara Tobin, 1976) always partake of the nature of a conflict, and can occur only if that 'monster of independence', the fairy, approves. This is where we touch on the psychological mechanism of the compensatory function that literature has. The Church's strict conjugal ethics subordinated the sentimental and erotic aspects of love-relationships to the Christian's duty with regard to populating the world: Be fruitful, and multiply. (Genesis 1:28). Desires not in keeping with this norm could be realised only in literature. Hence the erotic adventures of Alexander's men with the flower-girls (Armstrong *et al.*, 1937, iii.3325-544), hence also the welcoming gesture made by the fairy in Lanval, who will not allow pledges of loyalty or solemnisations (Rychner, 1969: 45-73) Yet there are norms too, quite simple ones, supported by a ban on transgression. The Celtic *geis* (a taboo or prohibition imposed from the Otherworld) is the essential instrument which, in case of disobedience, brings the amorous mortal back to his imperfect status. For the Otherworld is superior. This is evident at the end of *Lanval*, when the fairy intervenes to save her beloved from a certain death: the well-prepared arrival of the fairy, in which ever more beautiful maidens prefigure the culminating beauty (and therefore, superiority) of their mistress, serves to make the norm-system of the mortal world ridiculous. Moreover, nowhere do either the characters in the text or the author suggest that something unnatural is going on. It is only the nervousness of Lanval's horse (cf. l.46: *tremble forment* 'trembles greatly') that suggests the presence of something curious. Everything is plausible. In this we glimpse the most important side-effect of the integration of different cultural patterns: the world presented resembles, but is yet different from, that of the European knights in their feudal context. The heroes who live in the distant past or in inaccessible or vague places (the Greek and Roman heroes, for instance, or those from the world of Arthur) merely display an idealised and codified model attitude, which only *en passant* evokes the norms of human society (plausibility also has its claims: without the joy of recognition, no text is functional).

What is most striking is the fact that there is a confrontation between two worlds of make-believe: Arthur's world (fictitious) is placed alongside the Otherworld (unreal). Human reality as it actually exists has receded into the background altogether, even though the reader is convinced that there still are familiar points of reference for him to recognise; but this is where the poet's brilliant creative power manifests itself. An interesting example, which critics have

found difficult to deal with, is the famous passage from Chrétien's
Yvain: in the castle of *Pesme Aventure*, 300 young girls are forced to
make garments, under miserable circumstances: their guards are two
devils, who kill every knight who makes an effort to liberate the
maidens (ll.5101ff). The motivation is literary and unreal, but narra-
tively functional. Chrétien is certainly not depicting here the social
misery of the Flemish textile industry. What our author does do is to
paint, within the argument of his narrative, a recognisable, plausible
situation that gives the hero, Yvain, a chance to rehabilitate himself.
Although the situation there is less 'realistic', the same goes for the
Green Knight, whose head is first chopped off and later replaced.
The only thing that counts is the model action, of which the hero (in
this case Gawain) is nothing but a typical representation (Barron,
1974:417ff). The system of norms on which the action is based is that
of Arthur's court, which in its turn is the culminating ideological
centre whose task it is in all cases to guarantee the norm. Hence the
sacrosanct status of *coustume*. The traditional thinking in *ordines*
that is typical of thee higher layers of medieval society also finds its
literary self-confirmation here. It is interesting to see, incidentally,
that in the Arthur romances the part played by the clergy is usually
limited to *religiosi* living outwith the system—hermits and monks;
prelates are practically absent, even though it does take a bishop to
solemnise the royal marriage in *Erec et Enide* (ll.6794-807). Stability is what counts. This also appears in a different context, vividly
described by Huizinga—the oaths of knighthood worked out on a literary plane in the *Voeux du Paon*. It is the Burgundian sensitivity to
codified (and stage-managed) exteriorisation of the system of norms
that brings the latter to its culmination, and, at the same time
(because no higher gradations are left), leads to a rigid and ultimately fatal formalism (Doutrepont, 1906).

The code—which is never defined in any detail (it should be
remembered that any reference to *coustume* renders discussion of
content redundant)—determines the life of the participants, regard-
less of their origin (antiquity; the world of Arthur or Charlemagne;
etc.). Literature anyway is the apanage of the upper *ordo*, whose interests do not (and cannot) change. The argumentation with regard to
the usefulness of the code is circular, and that in two ways. Firstly,
Arthur's court is not only the (continually shifting) centre of the
ideal world, it is also the beginning and end of every *aventure*: the
knights usually receive their mission at the court itself (sometimes in
the form of a challenge manifesting itself on the spot, as in the case of
Meleagant in the *Conte du Graal*, who kidnaps Guinevere and

challenges the knights of the Round Table (ll.44-79), and having fulfilled the mission they return to the court, already laden with *pris et los*. Secondly, their behaviour is an enactment of the code observed at the court (again, no exhaustive description is ever given): the knights apply it in their adventures, and the success they meet with is automatically credited to that code. On the receptive plane, that of the medieval readers and listeners, another process of confirmation takes place: their caste has an essential function, distinct from that of the other two, and which serves to protect society.

This brings us to another essential phenomenon in the literature of that time: the knight has—and the code insists on this—a socio-political function. In Marie de France's *lais* this is not really important, since her subjects are case-studies of love, which in her writings sometimes manifests itself at the cost of the surrounding society: in *Deus Amans* lack of *mesure* leads to a tragedy; *Equitan* ends in the death of the adulterous woman and her royal lover; in *Eliduc* everybody retreats into the cloister. *Fresne* and *Guigemar*, on the other hand, offer solutions that tie in with the social feeling for order. Chrétien, however, takes a great step forward. His *conjointure* (a variant of the technique of *dispositio*) means that the material he adduces is subordinated to a central thesis. In *Erec et Enide* (1170), the spouses' passion, which makes them oblivious of everything else, leads to a reproach of *recreantise* (failing to live in accordance any longer with the code). In order to free himself of his disgrace, Erec together with his wife goes out into the world, and after many adventures, in which their love is very much put to the test—but this time in a social context—the couple are able to solve problems in an harmonious way. The most important adventure is the *Joie de la Cort*, an ironic designation for a pleasure-ground where a knight, bound by a sterile oath (the notorious '*don contraignant*'; Frappier, 1973:225-64), must obey his lady and challenge every knight who passes by. Many casualties are the result of this. After having defeated the knight (the injustice is now gone), Erec spares his life and takes him and his own beloved Enide to Arthur's court, where the couple, having lived hitherto in isolation, are now integrated into society. Of course the *Joie de la Cort* is an architectonic duplication of Erec and Enide's own situation: by living for themselves only, they were sterile too, thus breaking the code. Once they have realised their mistake, they are capable of actually governing a society. Erec, a prince, is crowned and returns to his kingdom. His royal robe, richly embroidered with the subjects of the quadrivium, symbolises the harmonious fusing of *chevalerie* and *clergie*, knighthood and

knowledge (acquired during the *quête*), the ideal combination in a
perfect ruler (ll.6672-747). It is at Arthur's court that the ceremony
takes place, which lends the Arthurian norm a kind of universal
validity: it is therefore not a coincidence that all knights, all the chal-
lengers from the most remote corners of the world, present themselves there. As long as the code is respected, harmony is guaranteed.
When that is no longer the case, the world collapses: Guinevere's
adultery with Lancelot, once it becomes known, leads to ruin: *La
Mort le Roi Artu* (?1230) paints the end of the Arthurian *ordo
naturalis*.

In the *Chevalier de la Charrete* (1179) mention is also made of
adultery by Guinevere. And that is all the more curious because, for
Chrétien, sexuality in principle belongs to the domain of matrimony.
His *Cligès* (1175) is an 'anti-Tristan'. Yet the central event of the
Chevalier de la Charrete is functional in the context of the romance's
central proposition, which is the knight's complete subjection to the
lady he adores. Having overcome his initial scruples, Lancelot is prepared to subordinate his knightly honour to the wishes of the lady,
Guinevere, and thus he steps on board the vehicle of disgrace, the
charrete. The conditioning influence of the lady has here reached its
climax. We shall never know whether Chrétien approved of this (the
romance was finished by Godefroy de Lagny), but it does not really
matter. What counts is the way in which the protagonists have been
situated in the literary reality controlled by the omniscient author,
and as long as there are no stylistic meta-elements which mitigate
things or place them in a different light, the factual details of the text
are all that the modern critic can work with.

In other words, the part played by women begins to take shape.
But, before we go into this, it is necessary briefly to discuss a key
figure from the world of Arthur: Gawain. Every heroic action, as
has been pointed out, is inspired by the norm and confirms it. The
problem is, however, that the norm cannot be described, at least not
completely. Nevertheless—and this is where the paradox lies—it
does function. The medieval author's solution for making the code
tangible and real is to give a representation thereof—not in an allegorical sense (which I shall not go into here), but in a theatrical
sense: Gawain, the king's nephew, is the incarnation of the ideal
knight, and every young man who presents himself at the court will
attempt to attain Gawain's level of knighthood and courtliness. Arthur's nephew is the touchstone with which the behaviour of others is
assessed. His very person inspires and conditions, but his perfection
leads to sterility (Busby, 1980:387). With Chrétien this becomes con-

spicuous: Gawain is capable of bringing Perceval out of his ecstasy (others had no success in this: cf. *Conte du Graal*, ll.4164-505), but he will never be able to find the Grail. When the *Conte du Graal* (1181) breaks off (Chrétien was unable to finish the text), the eternal womaniser finds himself somewhere in a miraculous castle, surrounded by 300 ladies. The number here symbolises both the impossibility of a deep personal relationship (Gawain limits himself to 'courtly' behaviour and, every now and again, a short affair with no real consequences), and the social sterility of the type of courtier he incarnates. Gawain is a mere catalyst. Of course he, too, can fight and eliminate injustice, but he will never reach the lonely heights of a Perceval or of a Lancelot, who sacrificed his knightly honour for a lady. For Gawain is the living embodiment of the canonised code; he lacks the imperfection of a knight who fails fully to adapt himself. In his ideal status there is no grain of sand to make the machine come to a standstill, or anything which might lead him to do unexpected things. Gawain does not break fresh ground. His triumph over the Green Knight is praiseworthy, of course, but it remains a personal, technical triumph: the world is not fundamentally changed. In the story of the Green Knight he is the puppet of others, who impale him on his own code. His adventure, in fact a relative fiasco, is merely another confirmation of that code. The circular movement that characterises the adventures in Arthur's world—not just intra-textually (within each text) but also inter-textually (with the same heroes returning all the time; in this respect the Arthurian romances are a prefiguration of Balzac's *Comédie Humaine*)—is visible here as well: Gawain confirms the code that he himself incarnates.

The works of Chrétien de Troyes established a permanent position for the Arthurian matter, of which the setting had been determined by Geoffrey of Monmouth and Wace. The results, as is known to everybody, are immensely significant: the thirteenth-century *Continuations* (cyclically organised) by Manessier and Gerbert de Montreuil, and the additions dealing with Merlin's adventures, by Robert de Boron and various anonymous authors, all serve further to perfect the image of the model ruler and his society. After taking a great many turns, English literature culminates here in Malory's Morte Darthur.

The part played by women has been mentioned more than once already. It is an extremely complicated one: not only is there, hermeneutically speaking, a text-inherent aspect to it (how one interprets the woman as *agens*), it is also rooted in the perspective of idealisation that I have mentioned. Literature—and of the romance this is

certainly true—creates a true picture of an untrue situation: in other
words, the plausibility of the formulation masks the unreality of the
literary situation. The fairies and the wizards, the giants and the
monsters are acceptable (in the fiction) as long as they either behave
in accordance with the accepted and recognisable norms, or express-
ly reject them (which means that, indirectly, the prevailing system of
values is acknowledged as functional). With regard to the part played
by women, who in many texts are the dominant figures, we need of
course have no illusions. It is true that under the influence of the
Church, which in the twelfth century made an effort to mitigate the
terms of matrimonial law, women were offered a certain amount of
protection, yet—and this is even more true of the later centuries,
when Roman Law manifests itself not only in the field of political
philosophy but also in that of matrimonial law—it is hard to define
the actual social space left to the weaker sex in practice. 'Define' is
the key term here, since of course a wide range of variations is met
with. There is a world of difference between Alda, the fair lady who
silently takes in the message of Roland's death, before dropping dead
on the spot, and Liénor in Jean Renart's *Guillaume de Dôle* (c1210),
who takes full control of all things, since the male protagonists
(otherwise depicted as model knights) are either unable to act or are
totally apathetic. This is also to pass over the differences between
Nicolete in the otherwise unique *chantefable* (a unique combination
of prose and verse), *Aucassin et Nicolete* (?c1250), where the young
girl has to take all the initiative in order to rescue her love for Aucassin, and also the ladies in the fabliaux, who ridicule their husbands.
The narrative matter of the latter genre, more international even
than that which we find in the stories of Arthur, culminates in the
Decameron (1349-51) and the *Canterbury Tales*. There is no need to
go into these here.

It is curious to see—and here literature is very definitely
'compensatory'—that an independent and distinctive part is played
not only by some of the highplaced ladies (such as Queen Guinevere
and Jean Renart's Liénor) but also by young maidens, who had no
legal status whatsoever. In the *pastourelles* this is very clear: sometimes the shepherdess is a prey for the knight, but in most cases she is
able to fend him off, or indeed to make a fool of him. Nicolete and
Liénor find themselves in the same situation. But they never cross the
border defined by Christian society. This is a privilege that belongs
to 'oriental' beauties or Celtic fairies, and sometimes to Chrétien's
maidens. A case in point is Blanchefleur, who seems prepared to go

very far indeed in order to get Perceval to defend her interests (*Conte du Graal*, ll.1960ff).

In the long list of adventure-romances such as *Apollonius de Tyr* (?1148), *Floire et Blanchefleur* (1147), *Guillaume de Palerne* (?1223), and *Joufroi de Poitiers* (1273), where a series of events is associated with a particular person who can himself scarcely exert any influence on the incidents with which the author confronts him, there figure a number of texts that provide local noble families (whether actually existent or not) with a glorious past. In the epic this is already encountered: *Le Chevalier au Cygne* and *Godefroy de Bouillon* are related to an eponymous hero and his glorious dynasty. An extremely interesting text is the *Roman de Mélusine* (1393), where De Lusignan's claims to Cyprus are placed in an apparently 'historical' framework—with the fairies in control, however. Considerable variation is found in the degree to which things are worked out. Sometimes it is indeed a question of inserting into the romance a number of historically verifiable facts; sometimes the family's name is a mere excuse for the introduction of all sorts of rocambolesque adventures. The latter category is exemplified by *Gui de Warewic*, written between 1232 and 1242. The initial refusal by Felice, daughter of the Earl of Warwick, Lord of Oxford, to associate with the son of a social inferior who nonetheless adores her, generates a number of adventures in which the hero can prove his superiority:

> Dune estes vus iço Gui?
> Fiz estes al senescal Sequart;
> Mult vus tienc ore a musart,
> Quant d'amur m'avez requis;
> Trop estes certes hardis.   (334-8)

(Aren't you Gui? You are the son of the seneschal Sequart; I think you are a real fool to ask me for my love; that's what I'd call having a lot of nerve.)

Through his heroic deeds, which procure him the favour of both the German and the Greek emperors (the latter even offers him his daughter, and thereby also, after the emperor's death, the imperial crown), Gui also obtains the hand of the beautiful Felice. But that is not the end of the story. With no previous hints to suggest this unexpected turn, Gui, after fifty days of marriage, decides to dedicate his life to the service of God, and to travel as a pilgrim to the Holy Land—something which, incidentally, does not keep him from performing a great many further knightly deeds.

The romance is not a frame story proper, but there are many points of resemblance: the hero experiences the adventures, together with a number of loyal friends, but the events do not change his character. Every aspect of the hero's behaviour is determined by the situation: there is no psychological motivation or character development. Although of course the local aspect (the part played by the Warwick dynasty in the struggle against the Danes) is what sets the story going, the presentation of the struggle in England is not essentially different from that of the heroic deeds performed by Gui in the Middle East. The romance incorporates a number of motives which in the works of earlier authors were dominant. Thus, Gui has for a while as his faithful companion a lion that he rescued from a snake (the motif comes from Chrétien's *Yvain*), whilst a treacherous seneschal sends him on a perilous mission—like Ganelon in *Roland*, taking a chance on Gui's sense of honour. What is also interesting (although it does not lead to a deepening of the *narratio*) is the theme of non-recognition: after his long stay in the Holy Land, Gui is recognised by neither his friends nor his wife. In the latter case we are indeed dealing with an adaption of the famous Alexius-motif (Storey, 1968:ll.211ff).

This text, as has already been said, is not part of a tradition of cyclically bound material, like that concerning Charlemagne or Arthur. As in these latter cases, however, here too the aim is the creation of an unquestionable framework in the form of a 'historical' context, which is made functional within the caste that constitutes the target group. In the cyclical texts the past is often used to authenticate 'national' interests and identities. Moreover, the desire to historicise specific local dynasties (in other words, to fit them into the glorious collective past) cannot but constitute, in a society where patronage (of whatever nature) is virtually the only stimulus for literature, an important step on the way towards individualisation not only of the dynastic senior and his interests but also of the author himself.

Here we touch a problem which so far has been dealt with only incidentally; namely, the question of the relationship between the author and the audience or patron. Despite my remarks, in the first paragraph of this paper, concerning the relationship between author and text in the Middle Ages, where scribes often interpret the possibility of intervention as a right or even as a duty (patronage can have considerable influence), it is acutally difficult to describe the patrons or the audience in any but the most general terms. Many dedications are rather vague: consider the way in which Chrétien begins his *Chevalier de la Charrete*:

> Puis que ma dame de Chanpaigne
> vialt que romans a feire anpraigne,
> je l'anprendrai molt volentiers
> come cil qui est suens antiers   (1-4)

(Because my lady, the countess of Champagne, wants me to write
a romance I, her loyal servant, shall be happy to oblige her.)

It cannot even be said with certainty whether this is actually Marie de
Champagne, daughter of Eleanor of Aquitaine, later queen of England. And what ought one to think of the beginning (a real prologue
it can scarcely be termed) of *La Mort le Roi Artu*? The author starts
off thus:

> Aprés ce que mestres Gautiers Map ot mis en ecrit des
> Aventures del Seint Graal assez soufisanment si com li
> sembloit, si fu avis au roi Henri son seigneur que ce
> qu'il n'avoit fet ne devoit pas soufire, s'il ne ramente-
> voit la fin de ceus dont il avoit fet devant mention et
> conment cil moururent.   (p.1)

(After master Walter Map had put into writing the adventures of
the Holy Grail as well as he could, King Henry, his lord, was of
the opinion that the story Walter had written would not suffice if
he did not tell of the last days of those he sang about, and did not
describe the way they died.)

Does this imply a commission by Henry II, or is it a trick of the author's? Also, many dedications change in the course of time, as texts
are sometimes retrospectively dedicated to a patron, without there
having been a previous commission (Firth Green, 1980:98; Bumke,
1979). Sometimes one can rely on text-internal signals concerning
the target group aimed at. Thus, Alexander de Paris' *Roman d'Alexandre* is clearly intended for those who are *de haut parage et ont
terre a baillir* ('of high social standing and who have countries to
rule'), the *gentil chevalier et li clerc sage et bon* ('noble knight and
the wise and virtuous clerks')...and the *dames* and *pucelles* ('young
noble ladies'; branche IV, ll.1631, 1652-3).

Of course there are also clues as regards content that suggest a
relationship with a particular audience, but here, too, caution is called for. Thematically speaking, and often organisationally as well (as
with the traditional poetry of the troubadours), the production of
texts in 'authoritarian' societies is subordinated to the principle of le-

gitimation, as I have already pointed out. In that kind of situation, every author has to adapt himself to the code of his target group in order to be accepted, and must utilise the accepted techniques in order to remain 'readable': a noble audience therefore demands noble adventures. This requirement is met by the epic, yet on the basis of its technique of presentation it cannot be claimed *per se* that, for instance, *Roland* with its élitist social ideology would also have functioned in an élitist way: the typical jongleur's technique suggests declamation in front of mixed companies, in the sense that it was also enjoyed by people outside the target group originally aimed at (the *bellatores*). The stylistic characteristics (parataxis, limited lexicon, and rhetorical simplicity; hyperbole and simile are the dominant figures of speech) contribute to the accessibility (and therefore the polyvalence) of such texts within the various social groups, which consist not just of the feudal lord's *familia*, but of all of his servants as well.

The romances are rather different. The same top layer of society is concentrated on, but the manner of presentation now seems to exclude the bottom layers of the 'clan': the *ornatus difficilis* ('the highly decorated style'), with its metaphors and figures of speech, and also the processes of psychologising, have the effect of limiting the audience. Furthermore, the heroes are no longer representatives of what formerly would have been the 'clan', but rather represent the prominent caste within it. With regard to that caste they defend and illustrate (in the strong sense of the word) the distinctive, élitist code. This provides a new legitimation, functioning more circularly even than in the case of the epic. Thus the caste determines the code (based on, among other things, previous literary productions), the code of literature extols the caste and its representatives, and the caste sees itself confirmed. As time goes by—and this is very clear in the *Voeux du Paon*—the nobility, compelled by competition from the middle classes and by changing military techniques, withdraws even more into itself: the *Chambre de Vénus* is a genteel earthly 'paradise', a *locus amoenus*, where only the élite can enter, to occupy themselves there with games (the 'King who does not lie', etc.) and—something very important—to indulge in what, a few centuries later, will be regarded as preciosity (*Voeux du Paon*, ll.1679ff). A hermetic use of language becomes a distinctive criterion for caste-distinction.

The Alexander romances as well as the prose-settings of the Arthurian texts clearly show this withdrawal on the part of the noble audience. Literature here follows the socio-economic developments, in the sense that, instead of being a mechanism of confirmation and an outlet (as was largely the case in the twelfth century), it now becomes a mere outlet and an escape. This can be seen clearly in the ceremonial of knighting: the Peacock oaths of Jacques de Longuyon's heroes are put into practice, and one is reminded of the Heron and especially the Pheasant Oaths, sworn at Philip of Burgundy's court at Lille in 1454, where the duke and his noblemen pledged themselves to go on a crusade. In this particular case, literature itself has become a code (Huizinga, 1955:251).

Occasional texts like the dynasty romances (for example, *Gui de Warewic*) are different yet again. Although probably conditioned by local wishes, it is on account of their weak and unmarked *narratio* (a *narratio* that can hardly be called personally-bound: Gui's adventures are mere derivatives of the canon determined by Chrétien and his successors) that they do not qualify as being in essence local creations. The 'historical' motivation, in this case the struggle against the Danes, required a hero, a local dynasty was able to supply one, and *ipso facto* literature has become an instrument of propaganda. This was also the case with regard to the pretentions of the Lusignan clique concerning Cyprus. That the Warewic/Warwick setting was a weak one, functioning as a mere starting point, is obvious from the fact that the Catalan Joanot Martorell, in his *Tirant lo Blanc* (completed in 1490), utilises elements of the Warwick tradition, with which he had become acquainted during his stay in England (cf. Riquer, 1964). If *Warewic* had really been a marked text, Martorell would not have been able so simply to do this.

It is clear that, in the space allotted to me here, I have not been able to sketch the French 'background' to Middle English literature, for which very much more space would be needed. In the above I have tried to highlight a few 'utilitarian' aspects which seem to me to be functional for texts related to the subjects to be dealt with in the following chapters. This modest contribution may give an impulse to further analyses of the relationships between the various literatures of different regions in the medieval period.

SELECT BIBLIOGRAPHY

Armstrong, E.C., D.L. Buffum, Bateman Edwards and L.F.H. Lowe (1937). *The Medieval French Roman d'Alexandre*. Vol. II: *Version of Alexandre de Paris. Text*. Princeton, N.J.: Princeton University Press.
Barron, W.R.J. (1974). *Sir Gawain and the Green Knight*. Manchester: Manchester University Press, and New York: Barnes and Noble.
Bédier, J. (1964). *La Chanson de Roland*. Paris: Piazza.
Bourdieu, P. (1989). *Opstellen over smaak, habitus en het veldbegrip*. Trans. D. Pels. Amsterdam: Van Gennep.
Bumke, J. (1979). *Mäzene im Mittelalter. Die Gönner und Auftraggeber der höfischen Literatur in Deutschland 1150- 1300*. München: Beck.
Busby, K. (1980). *Gauvain in Old French Literature*. Amsterdam: Rodopi.
Carey, R.J. (1966). *Jean le Court dit Brisebare. Le Restor du Paon*. Genève: Droz.
Carey, R.J. (1972). *Jean de le Mote. Le Parfait du Paon*. Chapel Hill, N.C.: University of North Carolina Press.
Casey, C. (1956). *'Les Voeux du Paon' by Jacques de Longuyon: an Edition of the Manuscripts of the P Redaction*. Ann Arbor, Mich: University Microfilms.
Constans, L. (1904-12). *Benoît de Sainte-Maure. Le Roman de Troie*. 6 Vols. Paris: Firmin-Didot.
Doutrepont, G. (1906). *Epître à la maison de Bourgogne sur la croisade Turcque projetée par Philip le Bon (1464)*. In: *Analectes pour servir à l'histoire ecclésiastique de la Belgique. Série III*. Vol. II:144-95. Leuven: Peeters.
Ewert, A. (1933). *Gui de Warewic. Roman du XIIIe siècle*. Paris: Champion.
Fewster, C. (1987). *Traditionality and Genre in Middle English Romance*. Cambridge: D.S. Brewer.
Firth Green, R. (1980). *Poets and Princepleasers. Literature and the English court in the late Middle Ages*. Toronto: University of Toronto Press.
Foster, B. and I. Short (1976-7). *The Anglo-Norman 'Alexander' ('Le roman de toute chevalerie') by Thomas of Kent*. 2 Vols. Anglo-Norman Text Society, 29 and 31. London: Westfield College.
Frappier, J. (1964). *La Mort le Roi Artu. Roman du XIIIe siècle*. Genève: Droz.
Frappier, J. (1973). *Amour courteois et Table Ronde*. Genève: Droz.
Gosman, M. (1981). L'élément féminin dans le 'Roman d'Alexandre': Olympias et Candace. In: *Court and Poet. Selected Proceedings of the Third Congress of the International Courtly Literature Society [Liverpool, 1980]*. ARCA 5. Ed. Glyn S. Burgess. Liverpool: Francis Cairns. 167-76.
Gosman, M. (1985). *Le Roman d'Alexandre en prose*: un remaniement typique. *Neophilologus* 69. 332-41.
Gosman, M. (1988). *Le Roman de Toute Chevalerie* et le public visé: la légende au service de la royauté. *Neophilologus* 72. 335-43.
Gosman, M. (forthcoming). La propagande de la croisade et le rôle de la chanson de geste comme porte-parole d'une idéologie non officielle. In: *Proceedings of the XIIth International Congress of the Société Rencesvals (Barcelona, 1988)*.
Huizinga, J. (1955). *The Waning of the Middle Ages*. Harmondsworth: Penguin. (First publ., 1924). (Translation of *Herfsttij der Middeleeuwen*. First publ., 1919).
Jauss, H.R. (1970). *Literaturgeschichte als Provokation*. Frankfurt am Main: Suhrkamp.

Kantorowicz, E.H. (1957). *The King's Two Bodies. Studies in Medieval Political Theology.* Princeton, N.J.: Princeton University Press.
Köhler, E. (1977). Gattungssystem und Gesellschaftssystem. *Romanische Zeitschrift für Literaturgeschichte* 1. 7-22.
Langlois, E. (1966). *Le Couronnement de Louis.* Paris: Champion.
Malone, K. and A.C. Baugh (1967). *A Literary History of England.* Vol.I: *The Middle Ages.* London: Routledge and Kegan Paul.
O'Hara Tobin, P. (1976). *Les Lais anonymes des XIIe et XIIIe siècles. Edition critique de quelques lais bretons.* Genève: Droz.
Petit, A. (1985). *L'anachronisme dans les romans antiques du XIIe siècle.* Lille: Centre d'Études Médiévales.
Raynaud de Lage, G. (1968-9). *Le Roman de Thèbes.* 2 Vols. Paris: Champion.
Riquer, M. de (1964). *História de la literatura catalana.* Vol. II. Barcelona: Ariel.
Roach, W. (1959). *Chrétien de Troyes. Le Roman de Perceval ou le Conte du Graal.* Genève: Droz.
Roques, M. (1970). *Les Romans de Chrétien de Troyes.* Vol.I. *Erec et Enide.* Paris: Champion.
Roques, M. (1965). *Les Romans de Chrétien de Troyes.* Vol.II. *Cligès.* Paris: Champion.
Roques, M. (1970). *Les Romans de Chrétien de Troyes.* Vol.III. *Le Chevalier de la Charrete.* Paris: Champion.
Roques, M. (1965). *Les Romans de Chrétien de Troyes.* Vol.IV. *Le Chevalier au lion (Yvain).* Paris: Champion.
Ross, D.J.A. (1988). *Alexander Historiatus. A Guide to medieval illustrated Alexander Literature.* 2nd ed. Athenäums Monografien Altertumswissenschaft: Beiträge zur klassischen Philologie 186. Frankfurt am Main: Athenäum.
Rychner, J. (1969). *Les lais de Marie de France.* Paris: Champion.
Storey, C. (1968). *La vie de Saint Alexis.* Oxford: Blackwell.
Wentzlaff-Eggebert, F.W. (1960). *Kreuzzugsdichtung des Mittelalters. Studien zu ihrer geschichtlichen und dichterischen Wirklichkeit.* Berlin: De Gruyter.
Wesle, C. and P. Wapnewski (1967). *Das Rolandslied des Pfaffen Konrad.* Tübingen: Niemeyer.

AN EXEMPLARY HERO: ALEXANDER THE GREAT

GERRIT BUNT

The Background

One of the most famous heroes of medieval romance was an un-
doubtedly historical figure, Alexander the Great. The story of his
life and conquests was one of the legacies of Antiquity which were
cherished in the Middle Ages. What attracted medieval writers and
audiences in the figure of the Macedonian conqueror was probably a
complex of factors. One of these must have been his association with
Aristotle, to medieval men the greatest of all philosophers, who was
for some time his tutor. Alexander as a philosophical king, who, in
the words of *Kyng Alisaunder*, "*dude by his maistres techyng*" (l.32:
'acted according to his master's teaching'), could serve as an exhortation to contemporary monarchs to be similarly guided by the advice
of wise and learned men. His successful campaigns against oriental
enemies must have appealed to medieval Europeans, who felt the
constant threat of the powerful and culturally often superior Moslem
nations of the East. The stories about Alexander could also be read as
sources on the geography and natural history of the distant countries
that Alexander had traversed on his campaigns. His meteoric career,
cut short by his untimely death leading to the disintegration of his
huge empire, made Alexander an ideal subject to exemplify the
transience of human achievement and glory. The daring and panache
of many of his exploits, his reliance on stratagem rather than brute
force, as well as the magnanimity and generosity for which he was
famous, made him an attractive hero, who could be held up as an
example worthy of imitation. On the other hand, the excesses which
some sources attribute to him, his occasional arbitrary cruelty and
his being, as one Latin account has it, "*victor omnium, sed ira et lux-
uria victus*" (*Historia de Preliis* I[3], cap. 130: 'victor of all, but overcome by wrath and lechery'), also made it possible to use him as a
warning against unlimited pride and lust for sensual gratification and
power. Stories about Alexander could be used in "Mirrors for
Princes", treatises which ostensibly instructed rulers as to their duties but also contained useful lessons for humbler readers. The Alex-

ander material was thus extremely versatile and allowed many lessons to be extracted from it.

Alexander was born at Pella, the "capital" of Macedonia, in
356 BC as the son of Philip of Macedon and Olympias. He succeeded
his father as king at the age of twenty, and two years later he crossed
the Hellespont at the head of a Greek army. In a series of battles he
defeated Darius III of Persia and conquered a vast empire which
included Egypt, where he founded Alexandria, and extended as far as
India. He married Roxane, a Bactrian princess, as well as Darius'
daughter Barsine. He impressed his contemporaries by his respect
for conquered nations and his ability to win their loyal allegiance. In
323 BC, when he was only thirty-two years old, he died of a fever at
Babylon. On his death his empire was divided among his generals.

This brief synopsis of Alexander's career is largely based on
the accounts of Diodorus Siculus (1st century BC), Plutarch (1st century AD) and Arrian (2nd century AD).[1] However, these authors
were unknown to medieval writers. The "historical" sources available to them were mainly Quintus Curtius Rufus' *Res Gestae Alexandri Magni*, Justin's *Epitome* of the *Historiae Phlippicae* by Pompeius Trogus and Orosius' *Historiae adversum Paganos*. But much
the best-known account of Alexander's career was a highly "legendary" one, the Hellenistic Alexander romance usually referred to as
Pseudo-Callisthenes. We should note at this point that the distinction
between "historical" and "legendary" sources is a modern one, and it
should cause us no surprise to find Pseudo-Callisthenes or later derivatives used as sources in professedly historical writings.

In addition to these two types of writings, and largely independent of them, there was also a vigorous anecdotal tradition in which
Alexander is held up as an example for the imitation of virtues or the
avoidance of vices. The best-known of these anecdotes is the story of
Alexander's meeting with the philosopher Diogenes, which is related, in a variety of versions, by John Gower (*Confessio Amantis* iii.
1201-1330), Ranulf Higden (*Polychronicon* iii, cap. 20), John Lydgate (*Fall of Princes* i.6233-6279) and by Sir Gilbert Hay in his *Buik
of King Alexander the Conquerour*. As Higden[2] tells the story, Alex-

---

[1] Modern biographies of Alexander the Great are too numerous to catalogue.
Among the more recent accounts are Green (1970), Fox (1973) and Renault
(1975). Mary Renault is also the author of several historical novels on Alexander
and his successors.

[2] Ranulf Higden (d.1364) was a monk of St. Werburgh's Abbey, Chester, who
became famous through his Latin universal chronicle *Polychronicon*, of which

ander comes upon Diogenes, who is sitting in a barrel which is con-
structed so as to enable him to face the sun at all times and seasons. He
offers the philosopher anything he may desire; but Diogenes merely
asks Alexander not to stand in his sun. Another famous anecdote was
that of Alexander and the Pirate. A pirate is brought as a captive before Alexander for the latter to pass judgement. The pirate argues
that his activities are of the same kind as Alexander's conquests; but
since he has only a small number of men under him he is considered a
pirate, whereas Alexander, who has a large army, is honoured as a
conqueror. Alexander sees the pirate's point and takes him into his
service. In English we find this story related by Gower in his *Confessio Amantis* (iii.2363-2437), Higden (*Polychronicon* iii, cap. 27)
and Sir Gilbert Hay; it is alluded to in Chaucer's *Manciple's Tale*
(ll.226-234).

   We can be fairly brief on the "historical" sources that were
available in medieval times. Paulus Orosius was a disciple of St. Augustine of Hippo, and wrote his *Historiae adversus paganos* at the
instigation of his master to refute the accusations of the pagans that
catastrophes such as the sack of Rome by the Vandals in 410 were a
punishment for the unfaithfulness of the Romans to the old gods. His
book sets out to prove that history had always been full of disasters.
Orosius treats Alexander, "*ille gurges miseriarum*" ('that whirlpool
of miseries'), as one of the catastrophes let loose upon the world, and
the picture of Alexander, as well as of his father Philip, that emerges
from his book is extremely negative. The translation of Orosius into
Old English which was made by or at the command of King Alfred
the Great contains the earliest account of Alexander's conquests in
the English language, and adds a brief reference to the Nectanebus
story (on which see below) which is characteristic of the "legendary"
tradition. Orosius' compendium of ancient history was a well-known
text throughout the Middle Ages, and it was repeatedly drawn on as a
secondary source.

   Quintus Curtius Rufus probably lived in the first century AD.
His *Res gestae Alexandri Magni* is a somewhat romanticised biography of Alexander which was widely known in medieval times. At an
early stage of its transmission, however, the first two of its ten books
were lost, and there are several lacunae in the surviving eight books.
In some manuscripts these gaps are filled by interpolations from
Justin (see below). Quintus Curtius was the chief source for the *Alex-*

---

more than 100 manuscripts survive. It was translated into Middle English by
John of Trevisa in 1385-87, and again by an anonymous translator in the fifteenth
century.

andreis by Walter of Châtillon, composed between 1178 and 1182 as a Vergilian epic. The *Alexandreis* was widely used as a school text, and became the source of several vernacular redactions (not in English, however).

Pompeius Trogus appears to have lived during the reign of Augustus. He wrote a history of the world in forty-four books, the *Historiae Philippicae*, which in its original form is lost. We do posess an epitome by a certain Justin, which also became a well-known text in the Middle Ages, and served as a source for Orosius. Most of the account of Alexander that Higden gave in his *Polychronicon* is also derived from Justin.

The Alexander story that our romances tell, however, owes much more to the "legendary" tradition, at the head of which stands a Hellenistic romance which is usually referred to as Pseudo-Callisthenes. This presents a confused and much romanticised account of Alexander's career, which in the course of time underwent a good deal of interpolation and modification. Alexander is here not the son of Philip, but of the last Egyptian Pharaoh, Nectanebo II, whose name in our sources is usually given as Nectanebus. He is skilled in the arts of magic, and when the Persian armies are threatening his country, he learns through magical means that they will be victorious. He decides to flee in disguise, and eventually reaches Macedonia, where he is much impressed by the beauty of Queen Olympias. While Philip is absent on a military campaign, he is able to persuade Olympias that the Libyan god Jupiter Ammon wishes to beget a son upon her who will conquer the whole world. Needless to say, Nectanebus, in the shape of a dragon, impersonates Ammon and thus becomes the father of Alexander. When Alexander grows up, he passes for the son of Philip, and Nectanebus becomes one of his tutors. One night, as Nectanebus is instructing him in astronomy, Alexander, who does not know that Nectanebus is his father, suddenly pushes him from a height, thus causing his death. Before he dies Nectanebus reveals that he is Alexander's father. This episode receives very varied treatment in later versions of the story; Gower, for instance (*Confessio Amantis* vi.1789-2366) tells the story as a warning against sorcery, for which Nectanebus' sudden death was a fitting punishment. Alexander's own death, according to Pseudo-Callisthenes and its derivatives, and indeed to nearly all medieval accounts of his life, is not due to a fever; instead he is said to have been poisoned by a trusted servant. Rumours that Alexander had been poisoned circulated at an early date, although Arrian firmly rejects them.

The earliest or α version of Pseudo-Callisthenes was translated into Latin by a certain Julius Valerius (early 4th century AD), whose work became better known in an abbreviated version which is usually referred to, from its editor, as the *Zacher Epitome*. In its numerous manuscripts the *Epitome* is often accompanied by another Latin translation from Greek, the *Epistola Alexandri ad Aristotelem*, the letter of Alexander to Aristotle on the marvels of India and his campaign against its king, Porus. In its standard or "vulgate" form the *Epistola* exists in numerous manuscripts. An incomplete Old English translation survives in the Nowell Codex (now part of MS Cotton Vitellius A XV), which also contains *Beowulf*. An extremely literal and almost unreadable Middle English translation exists in Worcester Cathedral MS F.172 of c1440.

The most important vernacular derivative of the combination of *Epitome* and *Epistola* is the Old French *Roman d'Alexandre*. This lengthy epic has a complex history. Its standard form is the work of Alexandre de Bernai or de Paris, who about 1185 combined and expanded several existing poems into a huge composite. One of these earlier poems, which as a separate text we know only through a Latin prose version, is the *Fuerre de Gadres*, a story of a foraging expedition during Alexander's siege of Tyre. A famous manuscript of the *Roman d'Alexandre* is Oxford, Bodleian Library MS Bodley 264, which is sumptuously illustrated; it was completed in 1338, probably in Flanders. There exist a good many later interpolations and continuations to the *Roman d'Alexandre*. One of these is *Les Voeux du Paon* ('the vows of the peacock', c1312) by Jacques de Longuyon, a poem of over 8,000 lines dealing mainly with amorous intrigue and courtly games. Its connection with the Alexander story is slight. In this poem we first find the Nine Worthies, three pagans (Hector, Alexander, Julius Caesar), three Jews (Joshua, David, Judas Maccabaeus) and three Christians (Arthur, Charlemagne and Godfrey of Bouillon). Alexander figures as one of the Nine Worthies in the Middle English *Parliament of the Three Ages*, where the brief synopsis of his life (ll.332-403) focuses on the stories of the *Fuerre de Gadres* and *Les Voeux du Paon*, and in the *Alliterative Morte Arthure* (l.3408). In all these poems the Nine Worthies are examples of the transitoriness of human achievement and fame.

The only other redaction of Pseudo-Callisthenes which is of importance for our purpose is the ∂ version, of which no Greek manuscript is known to survive. It exists, however, in Ethiopian and Syriac translations, and in a tenth-century Latin translation by Leo, archpriest of Naples. Leo's original translation has come down to us in only a very few manuscripts, but it was revised and expanded into what has become known as the first interpolated, or I^1, redaction of the *Historia de Preliis Alexandri Magni* ('the history of the battles of Alexander the Great'). It adds, among other material, the story of Alexander's visit to Jerusalem, and that of his correspondence with Dindimus, king of the Brahmans. The legend of Alexander's visit to Jerusalem is first found in the *Jewish Antiquities* of Flavius Josephus (1st century AD); from there it found its way into Peter Comestor's *Historia Scholastica* (c1170), a Latin paraphrase of the Bible interspersed with stories from ancient history, but the episode in the I^1 redaction of the *Historia de Preliis* appears to go back directly to a Latin translation of Josephus. The episode relates that Alexander sent messengers to the Jewish high priest Jadus to claim tribute, which was refused since Jadus felt that he owed allegiance to Alexander's enemy, Darius. Alexander then marched on Jerusalem in anger, but the high priest, acting on the advice of an angel, went to meet him in full pontificals at the head of a solemn procession. When Alexander saw the divine name inscribed on the high priest's breastplate, he knelt down in adoration. He was shown the prophecies of Daniel which had predicted that a Greek king would overthrow the power of the Medes and Persians (Daniel 8), and granted to the Jews the privilege to live according to their own laws.

The five letters interchanged between Alexander and king Dindimus of the Brahmans go back to a tract entitled *Collatio Alexandri Magni cum Dindimo* ('the conversation of Alexander the Great with Dindimus'), which is one of a number of texts dealing with Alexander's confrontation with Indian sages who live austere lives and go naked. The Brahmans of the *Collatio* are a nation of philosophers who live on an island, renouncing all possessions and comforts. Alexander begins and ends the correspondence, but Dindimus' two epistles are considerably longer than Alexander's three. They contain a vigorous attack on the Greek way of life and on Alexander's lust for conquest and power. Alexander, however, has the last word in favour of the Greek point of view. It is generally thought that originally the *Collatio*, unlike other tracts on the Brahmans, was favourable to Alexander, defending him against his detractors in the Cynic school of philosophy; but in medieval adaptations the ascetic views of Dindimus are usually given more prominence. In Higden's *Polychronicon*, for instance, Alexander no longer has the last word, and at the conclusion of the episode he ackowledges his utter defeat (iii, cap. 29). The *Historia de Preliis* I^1, however, gives the correspondence in its usual form, in which some sort of balance is maintained between Dindimus' asceticism and Alexander's defence of his own way of life.

Later, the I[1] redaction underwent further expansion and revision. Probably in the second half of the twelfth century the I[2] recension was made, in which numerous additions appear from Orosius and other sources; one of these was the *Liber Prophetarum* ('the book of the prophets') by Pseudo-Epiphanius, which supplied the story of the bones of Jeremiah. Alexander, wishing to found a city in Egypt, finds that the site is infested by serpents and other noxious creatures. He then buries the bones of the prophet Jeremiah at various points round the site as an effective protection against the serpents. The story is told in Hay's *Buik of King Alexander the Conquerour* (ll.2657-2666) and alluded to in *Kyng Alisaunder* (l.7998).

Another episode added in the I[2] version is that of Alexander's confinement of the evil tribes of Gog and Magog behind an iron wall or gate, from where they will burst forth at the end of time, causing much destruction and bloodshed. West-European retellings of this story are derived from the *Revelations* of Pseudo-Methodius, a text originally composed in Syriac in the late seventh century, when much of the Christian Near East was overrun by Moslem conquerors; it was soon translated into Greek and thence into Latin, and became a popular text throughout the Middle Ages. Pseudo-Methodius' account of Gog and Magog and of Alexander's confining their twenty-two nations behind an iron gate takes its cue from a few passages in the Bible, notably Ezekiel 38:1-39:16 and Revelations 20:7-10.[3] In the I[2] recension of the *Historia de Preliis* the names of Gog and Magog are not mentioned, but the evil habits of the nations enclosed are treated at some length.

The *Historia de Preliis* I[1] was again reworked between 1185 and 1236 into the I[3] recension, which is almost entirely rewritten and contains numerous interpolations. One of these is a brief summary of the *Fuerre de Gadres*; another is a brief passage which deals with the inclusion of Gog and Magog. Unlike the I[2] version, I[3] gives the names of Gog and Magog, together with the names of the twenty other nations that were enclosed with them. The episode is not only quite different in content from what we find in I[2], it is also inserted

---

[3] The Middle English translations of Pseudo-Methodius have been edited by d'Evelyn (1918) and Perry (1925). They go back to a shorter Latin version of the *Revelations* which omits the episode on Alexander and contains only a brief reference to the breaking out of Gog and Magog at the end of time.

at a different point in the story. It should be added that the I³ variant
of the Gog and Magog episode is also found in a number of I¹ manuscripts. Indeed, the manuscript tradition of all *Historia de Preliis*
recensions is highly variable. Many scribes treated it as a "living
text" which could be added to or abbreviated as they saw fit.

Many interpolations in I³ are of a moralising character. Thus
Darius' dying speech is much expanded with a warning against pride.
It is followed by a description of Darius' throne, which is set upon
seven steps each made of a different precious stone; the highest, however, is made of clay to remind kings that they are made of earth and
will return to its substance. In some manuscripts and incunables not
only of I³ but of all three versions we find the famous scene of the
philosophers at Alexander's grave, who each pronounce an epigram-
matic, if platitudinous, comment on the transience of human glory.

Two texts, both of Oriental origin, which present Alexander
as a philosophical king must be briefly mentioned. The *Secretum
Secretorum* ('secret of secrets') purports to contain the instruction
given by Aristotle to his pupil Alexander; but it is primarily a treatise on the art of government which also gives some encyclopaedic
information, and Alexander himself does not figure in it. It was
translated into Latin and thence into numerous West-European vernaculars. M.A. Manzalaoui (1977) has edited nine fifteenth-century
English translations for the Early English Text Society; and John
Lydgate and Benedict Burgh made another translation under the title
*Secrees of Old Philisoffres. The Dicts and Sayings of the Philoso-
phers* was originally composed in Arabic in the eleventh century; it
was translated into Spanish and then into Latin, reaching England
through the French translation by Guillaume de Tignonville of
c1400. The most famous English translation is that by Earl Rivers,
which was printed by Caxton in 1477; Bühler (1941) has edited
several other fifteenth-century English versions. The book consists
of a series of lives of philosophers, each biography being followed
by a collection of memorable sayings. One of the philosophers is
Alexander; his life is said to be based on the α recension of Pseudo-
Callisthenes, but shows many differences from the usual account.
Alexander is the son of Philip, and Nectanebus is not even
mentioned; his death is not caused by poison, but by a fever which
brings on a bleeding nose. The story does give a fair number of
letters which Alexander exchanges with various other personages,
including Darius and Porus. Following the biography there is a
series of brief anecdotes rather than a string of apophthegms. One of
these anecdotes is found, in the translation of Earl Rivers, in the

Dublin MS of *The Wars of Alexander*. In *The Dicts and Sayings* Alexander is presented as a wise and just king, and an implacable enemy of false religion.

The English Romances

In turning now to a discussion of the Middle English Alexander romances, we should give pride of place to **Kyng Alisaunder**. It is the earliest of all surviving Alexander romances, and the only one of which we possess a complete text; most importantly, it is the most attractive full-length treatment of Alexander's career in Middle English. *Kyng Alisaunder* is included in the famous Auchinleck Manuscript of c1340 (National Library of Scotland, MS Advocates 19.2.1, plus a number of fragments now in the university libraries of Edinburgh, London and St. Andrews); but most of the text is now lost and all the miniatures that once illuminated it have been cut out. A complete text of the romance is found in MS Laud Misc. 622 of the Bodleian Library, Oxford, and there is a very corrupt version which, probably as a result of some sort of editorial intervention, omits a long stretch of text, in Lincoln's Inn MS 150. There exists also a printed fragment of an expanded text.

    Kyng Alisaunder is an adaptation in four-stress rhymed couplets of the Anglo-Norman *Roman de toute chevalerie* by Thomas of Kent, of whom nothing is known; in its turn this romance uses the Julius Valerius *Epitome* and the *Epistola Alexandri* as its chief sources. Further material is taken from two late classical handbooks of geographical lore, one of which is Solinus' *Collectanea rerum mirabilium* ('collection of marvellous things') or *De mirabilibus mundi* ('on the marvels of the world') written soon after AD 200, in which much space is given to the marvels of distant lands and to places which Alexander is said to have visited; the other text is the *Cosmographia* by Aethicus Ister (4th century AD). These two texts, and the *Epistola Alexandri*, are important sources for the *mirabilia* ('marvels') which form a prominent ingredient of medieval Alexander traditions, and which appealed to a taste for the exotic and the marvellous. Othello's "Anthropophagi and men whose heads do grow beneath their shoulders" (I.iii.144-145) come from this same tradition, as do such texts as *Mandeville's Travels*, which also contains references to Alexander's campaigns. Fantastic though it may seem to modern readers, medieval writers regarded the geographical and natural-historical lore that they found in such sources as Solinus and Aethicus Ister as serious information which they saw no reason to view with scepticism. In *Kyng Alisaunder* the poet, following *Le roman de toute chevalerie*, carefully lists his authorities for the *mirabilia*, lest his audience should think he has invented them. It is precisely this list of authorities with much of the section on the *mirabilia* that is omitted in the Lincoln's Inn MS.

The *Roman de toute chevalerie* survives in three manuscripts, all of which contain interpolations from the *Roman d'Alexandre* that are not represented in *Kyng Alisaunder*. Its poet must, therefore, have used an earlier redaction of the *Roman* in which these interpolations had not yet been inserted. There is some evidence that the poet treated his source critically, and compared the story of *Le roman de toute chevalerie* with that in Walter of Châtillon's *Alexandreis*. In ll. 3506ff he discusses the divergent accounts of "*þe gest*" and "*þe latyn*"[4] of an incident involving the physician Philippoun and the baron Permenyoun; as Smithers points out (1952-57:ii.26), it must have been the discrepancy of the baron's death in the *Roman* and his later reappearance in the *Alexandreis* that worried our poet. In ll. 2195ff he tells us that he has drawn on "the Latin" for details concerning the names of knights and their deeds in battle:

> Þis bataile distincted is
> Jn þe Freinsshe, wel jwys.
> Þerefore [J] habbe [hit] to coloure
> Borowed of Latyn a nature,
> Hou hiʒtten þe gentyl kniʒttes,
> Hou hij contened hem in fiʒttes,
> On Alisaundres half and Darries also. (2195-2200)

(This battle is set apart (?) in the French, quite certainly. Therefore I have, to embellish it, borrowed a way of recounting it (?) from the Latin, what the noble knights were called, how they acquitted themselves in battles, on Alexander's side as well as on Darius' side.)

Smithers (1952-57:ii.16) has also identified details in *Kyng Alisaunder* which may imply that the poet knew a variety of other sources, such as Julius Valerius, the *Zacher Epitome*, the *Fuerre de Gadres* and the *Historia de Preliis* I[2] or I[3]. The allusion at the end of the

---

[4] "*þe gest*" ('the story') probably refers to the Anglo-Norman *Roman de toute chevalerie*, the source for *Kyng Alysaunder*; "*þe latyn*" has been identified as Walter of Châtillon's *Alexandreis*.

poem (ll.7996-8) to the legend of Jeremiah's bones may go back to
the *Historia de Preliis* I[2] or to Peter Comestor's *Historia Scholastica*
(see Pfister 1976:93-5).

Kyng Alisaunder opens with a prologue of forty lines, only
partly based on the *Roman*, in which Cato, that is, the collection of
maxims known as *Disticha Catonis*, is quoted to the effect that *"opere
mannes lijf is oure shewer"* (l.18: 'other men's life is our precep-
tor'). The poet wishes to exclude from his audience those

> Þat hadden leuer a ribaudye
> Þan here of God oiþer Seint Marie,
> Oiþer to drynk a copful ale
> Þan to heren any gode tale.   (21-4)

> (Who would rather hear a ribald story than hear of God or saint
> Mary, or drink a cupful of ale rather than hear a good tale.)

and invites us to

> heren noble geste,
> Of Alisaundre, þe rich[e k]yng,
> Þat dude by his maistres techyng.   (30-2)

> (Hear a noble story of Alexander, the powerful king, who acted
> according to his master's teaching.)

as well as *"þe wondres of worme and beest"* (l.37: 'the marvels of
serpent and beast'). After Alexander has finally conquered Persia
and has been accepted as king, the poet pauses to introduce *"þe opere
partye / Of Alisaundres dedes hardye"* (ll.4747-8: 'the second part of
Alexander's valiant deeds') with a brief summary to whet his audience's appetite, as well as the list of sources that we referred to
above.

While the poem thus falls into two major parts, shorter divi-
sions are equally well marked by the so-called head-pieces. These
head-pieces are insets of a lyrical and/or sententious character which
punctuate the narrative and frequently introduce a new section. Some
are evocations of the spring season, others present little vignettes of
court life, or occasionally of the life of a merchant, sometimes with
an ironic undertone; many are mainly a string of aphorisms, a frequent theme being that of the surprises of life, of mutability and transience. Most of the head-pieces occur in the first half of the poem; in
the second half, which is dominated by the *mirabilia*, they are less

prominent, although we do find them introducing important episodes such as the enclosing of Gog and Magog, the final battle against Porus and the poisoning of Alexander. Their length varies from two to eleven lines, the longest being the last, which stands at the head of the story of Alexander's death. Some of the head-pieces are mono-rhymed, with the single rhyme continuing into the resumption of the narrative, and thus connectinging the head-piece to the story. This is also the case in the last head-piece, in which the theme of mutability, which runs through the entire poem, is elaborated. Two obscure Greek heroes and the biblical Absalom are recalled to exemplify the shortness of life and the vulnerability of human existence, although the statement that all three were soon forgotten is belied (l.7825) by the poem itself. "*Aventure*" is said to have suddenly turned against Alexander.

The head-pieces are all but unique to *Kyng Alisaunder*; only in *Of Arthour and of Merlin*, which is often believed to be by the same author, do we find anything comparable in Middle English. Smithers (1952-57:ii.35ff.) finds their origins in Old French and ultimately in classical Latin epic. There is a very useful discussion of their content and function in L.M. Kitchel's, unfortunately unpublished, doctoral dissertation (1973:66-80).

Kyng Alisaunder contains only a brief passage on the Brahmans (ll.5904-27) and their simple, golden-age way of life; there is no exchange of letters and no debate between Alexander and their king. The five letters of the *Collatio* have no place in the *Epitome-Epistola* tradition to which *Kyng Alisaunder* belongs.

More space is given to Alexander's inclusion of Gog and Magog and the events leading up to this famous event. Immediately after conquering the land of the Brahmans (which he does not do in other accounts), Alexander receives a "*man ferlich*" (l.5937: 'an extraordinary man'), black as pitch, whose head "*was in his body yshote*" (l.5942: 'was thrust into his body'). This remarkable visitor warns Alexander that unless he subdues the wicked nations in the country of Taracun in the north, between Gog and Magog, his fame will be of no value. Alexander, after consulting his dukes, barons and knights, decides to march against them. He assembles a large army and sails northwards. His campaign has little success and many of his men fall victims to their cannibalistic enemies, whose evil habits are again emphasised. Then the Meopante, who possess contraptions rather like submarines, provide him with a bitumen with the aid of which he succeeds in blocking the sole passage to the country of his enemies. They will be confined there until Doomsday, when Antichrist will

overthrow Alexander's wall and the wicked nations will break out of
their confinement, causing much bloodshed.

Another episode which in some form or other is present in
most Alexander romances is that of our hero's involvement with
Queen Candace. We are told that

> She loued Alexander pryuelik,
> And he hire, sikerlyk.
> Ac non of hem had oþere yseie.   (6652-4)

> (She loved Alexander in secret, and he her, to be sure. But neither
> of them had seen the other.)

For security reasons, however, Alexander decides to avoid the
queen's country. She then sends messengers to him declaring her
love and offering rich gifts, in response to which Alexander sends
her a metal image of himself. After he has defeated and killed Porus,
Alexander helps Candace's son Candulek to recover his wife, who
had been abducted by a hostile king. Masquerading as his general Antygon, Alexander then meets Candace. His trick of disguising himself, which had worked well with Darius, fails to deceive Candace,
who now has him in her power and compels him to become her
lover. To the outside world his pretence of being Antygon is maintained, until another son of Candace's, who is married to Porus'
daughter, discovers Alexander's true identity, and the latter is obliged to leave the queen to escape the son's revenge. Although there is
a courtly element in the episode, the emphasis is on Alexander's
falling a victim to the wiles of a woman. There is a slight anti-feminist element in the story, and Candace even recites a conventional
catalogue of men similarly entrapped by women; yet she is by no
means bent on his destruction and actively helps him to escape revenge at the hands of her own son.

Alexander's death by poisoning is recounted quite briefly. The
king realises immediately that he has been treacherously poisoned; he
is brought to his bed and then makes his testament. A testament of
Alexander, in which he divides his lands among his followers, is included in many versions of the story, but not in the *Roman de toute
chevalerie* as the author of *Kyng Alisaunder* knew it. The Durham
MS of the *Roman* has interpolated the division of Alexander's empire
among his twelve peers from the *Roman d'Alexandre*; but the
testament that we find in *Kyng Alisaunder* is very different, and can
hardly go back to the *Roman de toute chevalerie*. Alexander names
only nine heirs instead of the usual twelve or more; several of these

heirs are unknown in other versions of the testament, and most of them are assigned other territories than they are given in the usual historical or pseudo-historical sources. One of the heirs, Sampson of Ennise, here makes his first appearance in the poem, and among the lands divided here there are several whose conquest is not related earlier in the poem. The testament is evidently not too well integrated into the narrative.

Whatever its defects, however, *Kyng Alisaunder* is a most attractive romance. Its rhyme and metre may not be perfect, frequently depending as they do on feeble tags, but the poem easily holds the reader's attention through its lively and varied style and its combination of a light tone and didactic seriousness. The story moves rapidly and is attractively punctuated at irregular intervals by the head-pieces, which in a general way comment upon the story and emphasise its theme and structure. Alexander emerges as a great hero, immoderate and rash at times, but a generous and magnanimous leader and ruler. However, he is not superhuman, but subject to the same inexorable laws of mutability and transience as other mortals; his untimely death brings his ambitions to nothing, and his empire disintegrates as soon as he is dead.

A number of Middle English Alexander romances are written in unrhymed alliterative verse. Unfortunately, none of them has survived in its entirety. *The Wars of Alexander* now exists in two manuscripts, Oxford, Bodleian Library, MS Ashmole 44, and Dublin, Trinity College, MS 213 (formerly MS D.4.12), both of which contain considerable gaps, but generally supplement each other; after 5803 lines, however, the poem finally breaks off when Alexander has established his throne in Babylon and is not far from his impending end.

Alliterative lines characteristically fall into two half-lines joined by alliteration on three or more syllables. The most recent editors of the poem, Duggan and Turville-Petre, believe that late Middle English alliterative verse conformed to quite strict rules, although scribal corruption has often misled critics as to its character; they consider it the duty of an editor to emend corrupted lines so as to restore proper alliteration and metre. In a series of articles (Turville-Petre 1980, 1987; Duggan 1986a, 1986b) they have given expression to these views, which they put into practice in their edition of *The Wars of Alexander*. Their text thus often differs from that in the earlier edition of Skeat (1888), which adheres much more closely to the often corrupt manuscripts. Alliterative verse requires a large number of synonyms to express such frequent notions as 'man', 'battle', 'horse', 'go', etc. This extensive and often recondite vocabulary often has a heightening effect, although we cannot always be sure that such an effect was intended by the poet. One way in which the text may become corrupted is by scribal substitution of more common synonyms for the more unusual word in the original; such scribal substitutions frequently betray themselves by their failure to alliterate. Such lines are, therefore, usually emended by Duggan and Turville-Petre.

The prologue with which the poem opens leads us to expect an entertaining story, and there are numerous lines which refer to a poet reciting his poem before a live audience. We should, however, not naïvely interpret these references as evidence of oral presentation on festive occasions; such evocations of a direct contact between poet and audience were more probably conventional elements, designed to call up a convivial atmosphere. *The Wars of Alexander* is a quite bookish poem, which is most likely to have been read privately or in small groups of readers and listeners.

Like *Kyng Alisaunder*, the poem falls into two parts. After Alexander has finally overcome Darius, there is a second prologue in which we are told that "*pe lattir ende of his lyfe*" (1.3600: 'the latter end of his life') is now to be recounted. The poem is also divided into *passus*, which have been shown to consist of multiples of twenty-four lines or "strophes". In addition, the lines fall into groups of four or "quatrains". This analysis is not uncontroversial, but Duggan and Turville-Petre (1989:xxiii) uphold Kaluza's earlier analysis of 1892.

The primary source of *The Wars of Alexander* is the I[3] recension of the *Historia de Preliis*. Hamilton's argument of 1927 that there is a fourth version of the *Historia de Preliis*, which he labelled I[3a], and which was said to underlie *The Wars of Alexander* and *The Prose Life of Alexander*, has been proved unfounded (see Ross, 1961, and Duggan, 1976). In fact, within the limits imposed by its poetic form, which frequently necessitates amplification, *The Wars of Alexander* follows the *Historia de Preliis* I[3] quite closely.

In the alliterative poem battle scenes are treated more briefly than in *Kyng Alisaunder*, but much more space is given to the letters which Alexander exchanges with various correspondents. Letters are exchanged between Alexander and his first opponent, King Nicolas, Darius, the Amazons, the Athenians, King Dindimus of the Brahmans, Queen Candace, Porus and others, and also between Darius and his mother and Darius and his dukes, and we are invariably given each letter in full. Letters had formed part of the Pseudo-Callisthenes tradition from its very beginning, and Merkelbach (1977:48-77) has

shown that among its sources there must have been a kind of epis-
tolary romance. In *The Wars* the letters contain much of the philosophical and moralistic material which is prominent in the *Historia
de Preliis* I[3] and its derivatives. Thus the theme of pride leading to a
fall is elaborated in the correspondence between Alexander and Nicolas and that between him and Darius, where it applies to Alexander's opponents, but the reader is made aware that Alexander is by
no means exempt from this sin. Pride is again a major theme in the
letters later exchanged between Alexander and Porus. Since the end
of the poem is lost, we do not know whether pride will also contribute to Alexander's downfall; but the drift of the poem does make
us anticipate such a conclusion.

Unlike *Kyng Alisaunder*, *The Wars of Alexander* tends to en-
dow its hero with heroic and even superhuman qualities. Omens and
prophecies occupy a prominent part in the story, and Alexander also
views himself as a man of destiny, who has been willed by the gods to
conquer the earth. Yet he is well aware that he is a mortal, and he
firmly rejects the divine honours offered him by the conquered Persians (ll.3583-7). We are, therefore, somewhat surprised to read in a
letter that Aristotle sends to his former pupil at the end of his
conquests, "*Sum grayne of godhede, I gesse, was growen ȝow within*" (l.5748: 'some grain of divinity, I suppose, had grown within
you), which faithfully translates the Latin of the *Historia de Preliis*
I[3], cap. 123. We shall return to this passage in our discussion of *The
Prose Life of Alexander* below.

Kitchel (1973:164ff.) remarks on a few cases where the poet
of *The Wars* runs into difficulties over narrative motivation and
plausibility. Thus he tells us that Parmeon (the baron who in *Kyng
Alisaunder* was named Permenyoun) is beheaded (l.2707), but he
reappears alive later in the poem (l.3240). We have seen that the
author of *Kyng Alisaunder* was more clearly aware of the difficulties
at this point, and refused to follow his source uncritically. Kitchel's
observations on other inconsistencies seem less convincing.

While the poem is not without its weaknesses, and does not
always succeed in avoiding a certain monotony, there is certainly
much to be enjoyed. It presents a heroic and philosophical Alexander, well aware that he is a mortal, and that pride is a constant danger, but yet succumbing to it himself; in short, a hero who may be
larger than life, but is still recognisably human.

Another alliterative fragment, of 1247 lines, is variously
known as **Alexander A** ,*The Romance of Alisaunder* or *Alexander
of Macedon*. It is preserved in a school notebook of c1600 (Oxford,

Bodleian Library, MS Greaves 60), but despite the late date of its manuscript, it is often believed to be among the earliest poems of the Alliterative Revival. Skeat, who edited it in 1867 together with *William of Palerne*, which can be dated between 1336 and 1361, originally believed these two poems to be by the same anonymous poet, but later retracted this view. A more recent edition appears in Magoun (1929).

Alexander A deals with Alexander's begetting, his birth and early years, and breaks off in the story of Philip's siege of Byzantium. Its chief source is the I^2 redaction of the *Historia de Preliis*, but its story has been much expanded by additional interpolations from Orosius, mainly dealing with the exploits of Alexander's father Philip. Whereas Orosius is highly critical of both Philip and Alexander, the poet of *Alexander A* presents Philip in a heroic manner, and similarly omits much of Orosius' criticism of Alexander.

In his prologue the poet addresses *"lordes and ooper"* (1.1: 'lords and others') who intend to achieve fame in arms, and promises them the example of *"one pe boldest beurn and best of his deedes"* (1.9: 'the boldest warrior of all and the best in his deeds'). His primary concern seems to be with heroic conduct rather than with morality. After the prologue the poem goes on to tell us about Philip's parentage and birth, and Nectanebus does not appear on the scene until line 453.

Alexander A is not among the most successful Alexander romances. It tells its story with great zest and it successfully combines the story of Philip's wars with that of Alexander's birth and upbringing, but its style and diction tend to be colourless and full of feeble tags; and its description of the beauty of Olympias stands out by its mechanical application of the rhetorical top-to-toe model of *effictio*.

Alexander A is sometimes regarded as a fragment of a lost alliterative Alexander poem of great length of which *Alexander and Dindimus* or *Alexander B* would be a later section. However, in view of the considerable differences in style between the two fragments common authorship seems improbable.

Alexander and Dindimus is a fragment of 1139 lines which is preserved in the sumptuously illustrated MS Bodley 264 of the French *Roman d'Alexandre*, which from the late fourteenth century was in English ownership (Guddat-Figge 1976:253). A fifteenth-century English scribe noted that this romance, however lengthy, did not contain the correspondence of Alexander and the Brahman king. On fol. 67 of MS Bodley 264 he found that one column on the recto and the entire verso were blank; in the vacant second column on the recto he made a note saying that *"here faylep a prossesse of pis rom-mance of Alixander"* ('here an episode of this romance of Alexander is lacking'), referring the reader to the end of the book where the missing passage is *"y-wrete in engelyche ryme"* ('written in English verse'). The text is given on fols. 209-15, which after two blank leaves is followed by a French version of the travels of Marco Polo. *Alexander and Dindimus* is, uniquely among the Middle English Alexander romances, accompanied by a series of nine miniatures.

The fragment opens with the story of Alexander's visit to the Gymnosophists; these naked philosophers strongly resemble the Brahmans, but they do not live on an island. Alexander promises them any gift they may desire, but the Gymnosophists ask for *"Ai-lastynge lif"* (l.70: 'everlasting life'), which Alexander is obliged to admit is not in his power to bestow, since he is a mortal himself. Much of the discussion with the Gymnosophists duplicates the later correspondence with Dindimus. Alexander then comes to mysterious trees whise fruits are guarded by birds that spit deadly fire, after which he reaches the inaccessible island of the Brahmans, and the five letters of the *Collatio* follow. At the end of the fragment Alexander erects a pillar to mark the limit of his conquests.

The source of *Alexander and Dindimus* is again the I^2 recension of the *Historia de Preliis*, which, at this point and elsewhere, orders the episodes differently from the other versions. The Latin source is followed quite closely. The Middle English poem is not a thoroughly successful composition. Its language tends to be wordy and rather flat, and on the whole it does not compare favourably with other English renderings of the same material.

Two brief **fragments**, of eight and six lines, of another allit-erative poem on Alexander are given in a note by Turville-Petre (1979). These two extracts were copied in 1941 by Neil Ker from a fragmentary manuscript belonging to one Mr James Fairhurst. This manuscript is now apparently lost, so that all that we have at present is these fourteen lines. They are a translation of two passages from *Les Voeux du Paon*.

That the Vows of the Peacock were much in demand in late medieval Britain also appears from another fragment, of 566 lines in rhymed eight-line stanzas, preserved in the Findern Manuscript (Cambridge University Library, MS Ff.I.6), which has been edited by Karl Rosskopf (1911). A new edition would be very welcome.

The fragment contains two episodes, one telling of a court of love held in an unnamed city defended by Cassamus, who has enlisted Alexander's help against his opponent, the Indian king Clarus. The other episode is set in the besieging camp, where Clarus is admonished on his proper behaviour towards his knights. Alexander himself is present only as a background figure. Much emphasis is placed on love and courtly etiquette. The *Cassamus Fragment* is not great poetry; neither its versification nor its narrative qualities are able to inspire much enthusiasm.

A much better piece altogether is **The Prose Life of Alexander**, which has come down to us as the first item in the Lincoln Thornton Manuscript (Lincoln Cathedral Library MS 91, formerly MS A.5.2 or A.1.17). Robert Thornton was a Yorkshire country gentleman who c1440 compiled a large miscellany in what are now two manuscripts, one in Lincoln and the other MS Additional 31042 in the British Library. The Lincoln MS opens with a series of romances which includes the unique copy of the *Alliterative Morte Arthure*. The opening leaves of the *Prose Life* are unfortunately lost, and what survives now begins towards the end of the scene where Alexander kills his natural father, the magician Nectanebus (here, as in *The Wars of Alexander*, named Anectanabus). There are two further lacunae in the body of the text, again due to the loss of leaves. Westlake's edition of 1913 gives only the text; Neeson (1971) gives us a better edition with introduction, commentary and glossary, but it is an unpublished doctoral dissertation which is not readily accessible.

The *Prose Life* is a fairly close translation of the *Historia de Preliis* I^3, and the story that it tells is very similar to that of *The Wars of Alexander*. We are given the same profusion of letters and the same emphasis on omens and prophecies; indeed, most of the characteristics of the I^3 version are present in both Middle English derivatives. Yet there are also obvious differences. In some places the *Prose Life* appears to follow the Latin readings characteristic of the I^1 or I^2 redactions rather than of I^3. For instance, in the letter from Aristotle to Alexander that we discussed above, the *Prose Life* does not include Aristotle's observation that his former pupil must have a divine streak in him, but instead follows the I^1/I^2 variant at this point, to return to I^3 for the conclusion of the letter; it thus avoids attributing divine qualities to Alexander. A major difference between the *Prose Life* and *The Wars of Alexander* occurs in their treatment of the Gog and Magog episode. *The Wars* follows the brief I^3 account of Alexander's inclusion of the twenty-two tribes faithfully, although it lists twenty-two kings rather than nations. The *Prose Life*, however, identifies Gog and Magog with the ten lost tribes of Israel, and gives an account which seems to be largely derived from Peter Comestor's *Historia Scholastica*. The ten tribes send a messenger to Alexander asking his permission to leave the country where they are confined; but when Alexander hears that they were imprisoned there because of their unfaithfulness to the God of Israel, and also that it has been prophesied that they shall never return to their native land, he decides to enclose them more securely. When, however, he cannot succeed in this purpose, he prays to God to complete his work. The mountains then move together, making it impossible for the ten tribes to leave the place of their captivity. However, at the end of time they will break out of their prison and cause great bloodshed.[5]

While the *Prose Life* generally offers a close rendering of its Latin source, it does occasionally omit phrases and sentences and makes brief additions elsewhere. Most of these additions make for greater clarity and explicitness. It is an intelligent piece of work, which treats its source material critically, and it is well-written and fluent. It deserves a proper edition.

The last two Alexander romances that we shall discuss both come from Scotland. The *Buik of Alexander*, in more than 11,000 four-stress rhymed couplets, is a close rendering of two French additions to the Alexander material, the *Fuerre de Gadres* and *Les Voeux du Paon*. We have found these texts combined elsewhere, notably in the brief synopsis of Alexander's life in *The Parliament of the Three Ages*. Here, however, the stories are told at a leisurely pace and at considerable length, with much emphasis on love and courtly manners and on individual prowess on the battle field. *Les Voeux du Paon* takes its name from the vows made over the body of a peacock, which various knights attempt to carry out during the siege of Effesoun by Clarus. The poem is also known as *Le Roman de Cassamus* from the hero who defends the city.

The *Buik of Alexander* has come down to us in an edition printed by Alexander Arbuthnet c1580. The date of composition is given as 1438. It has been attributed unconvincingly to John Barbour, the author of the late fourteenth-century historical romance *The Bruce*. Ritchie's edition, in four volumes, also gives the text of the *Buik*'s French sources.

Both the *Fuerre de Gadres* and *Les Voeux du Paon* are also represented in Sir Gilbert Hay's *Buik of King Alexander the Conquerour* (c1460), but here they are told more economically and

---

[5] On the Gog and Magog legend and its ramifications, see Anderson (1932).

integrated into the longest and most comprehensive account of Alexander's career in medieval English that we possess, and one of the most interesting. For many years Hay's poem remained largely unknown. Herrmann (1900) had printed extracts from it, but his partial edition is not easily accessible; Lascelles (1936) had given attention to its story of Alexander's visit to the Earthly Paradise which is all but unique in medieval English literature; but the brief passage that Lumiansky devotes to it in the *Manual* (Severs 1967:111) accurately reflects our defective knowledge until 1986, when John Cartwright published an account of Hay's poem and its sources, and since then the complete text has appeared from the Scottish Text Society.

Before composing the *Buik of King Alexander the Conquerour*, Hay had been active as a translator. His prose manuscript, dated 1456, contains several translations from the French of books dealing with various aspects of knighthood, and includes a version of the *Secretum Secretorum*. According to Cartwright (1986:229) his poem can be viewed as an extended *exemplum*, showing, in the person and actions of Alexander, knighthood in action. To Hay Alexander is indeed an exemplary hero, an ideal knight and ruler, philosopher as well as conqueror.

Cartwright identifies the poem's chief sources as the French *Roman d'Alexandre*, the *Historia de Preliis* I[2] and the *Secretum Secretorum*. In addition, the anecdotal tradition is represented in such episodes as Alexander's meetings with Diogenes and with the Pirate, and of Aristotle's infatuation with Campaspe. This highly diverse source material is combined into a well-integrated story, which gives its poet ample opportunity for commentary and explanation. The early sections of the poem give much attention to Alexander's education by Aristotle, drawing on the *Secretum Secretorum* for their material. Among the arts Aristotle teaches his royal pupil are "*artmagik and necromancie*" (1.421: 'magic and necromancy'), but he also

> Bad him nocht vse, bot keip him fra dessait,
> And all sic thing was devilrie and falset.   (422-3)

> (Bade him not to use it, but to keep aloof from deceit, and all such things that were devilry and falsehood.)

Magic was a fascinating, but sinister art, since it was believed to involve association with demons and worship of the devil.

In Hay, too, Alexander is destined by God, or the gods, to conquer the world. When he is preparing himself to meet King Nicolas in single combat, we read that he

Wist weill þat God haid grantit him fortune,
And thocht he suld throw hevinlie desteny
Conques þis erd, and soueran of it be.   (1828-30)

(Knew well that God had granted him fortune, and thought that
through heavenly destiny he was to conquer this earth and be its
sovereign.)

and his conviction *"That he suld never in feild disconfit be"* (1.1925:
'that he should never be defeated in battle') gives him courage to con-
front all enemies.

Unfortunately, Hay's Alexander poem has not survived in its
entirety. There are two sixteenth-century manuscripts, British Library MS Addit. 40732 and Edinburgh, Scottish Record Office MS
GD 112/71/9, which is probably a copy of MS Addit. 40732; but both
MSS lack the opening sections.

Hay's *Buik of King Alexander* stands last in the line of the English medieval Alexander tradition. Not long after his poem had been
composed many ceased to believe uncritically in the tales of marvels
and monsters which for many centuries had been among the chief
attractions of the Alexander story. Cartwright (1986:229) refers to
two continental biographies of Alexander, dated 1468 and 1521,
which condemn the romances as full of lies, and treat Alexander's
life in a spirit of ridicule. In Hay no such scepticism or ridicule can
be found. In his poem various strands of the medieval Alexander tradition are skilfully interwoven into a poem which, though occasionally verbose and long-winded, and not without some inconsistencies,
forms a fitting conclusion to the long line of medieval romances on
Alexander the Great.

In the romances that have been reviewed here the treatment of Alexander has been seen to vary considerably, mainly because of differences in the sources used. Yet, despite all these variations in treatment, some common features can be discerned. In all romances
Alexander is a great and admirable hero and a magnanimous and
generous leader of men. He may not be immune to the sin of pride,
but generally he is well aware of his human limitations. In this respect the romances differ sharply from the sections on Alexander in
such works as Lydgate's *Fall of Princes* or Higden's *Polychronicon*,
which picture a viciously proud Alexander who is eager for divine
honours and can be wantonly cruel. In the romances we find a vary-
ing emphasis on the philosophical side of Alexander, but in none is

this entirely disregarded. Apart from the derivatives of *Les Voeux du Paon*, love plays only a subordinate role, and the only woman who is able to hold Alexander's devotion is his mother Olympias. Emphases may also vary on omens and prophecies as indicative of a divine destiny which Alexander has to fulfil. Although none of our romances contains an explicit reference to the prophecies of Daniel, Alexander's empire was the third in the succession of dominions outlined there, and his conquest of the world could thus be seen as part of the divine order of history. On the other hand, his sudden death at the climax of his power held a suitable warning to contemporary rulers, that they were similarly subject to the inexorable movement of Fortune's wheel. Alexander stories were never simple entertainment, they held a manifold relevance for their medieval readers.

SELECT BIBLIOGRAPHY

1. Texts

Aethicus Ister—*Die Kosmographie des Istrier Aithikos im lateinischen Auszuge des Hieronymus.* Hrsg. von H. Wuttke. Leipzig: Dyk'sche Buchhandlung. 1853.
Alisaunder, The Romance of. Ed. W.W. Skeat. EETS, ES 1 (1867) (In the same volume as *William of Palerne*, which Skeat then thought to be by the same author. This poem is also known as *Alexander A* or *Alexander of Macedon.* See also Magoun 1929).
Alexander and Dindimus. Ed. W.W. Skeat. EETS, ES 31 (1878) (See also Magoun 1929).
Alliterative Morte Arthure, The. Ed. V. Krishna. New York: Franklin. 1976.
Alphabet of Tales, An. Ed. M.M. Banks. 2 Vols. EETS, OS 126, 127 (1904-5) (contains several anecdotes on Alexander).
Arrian. *The Campaigns of Alexander.* Trans. A. de Selincourt. Harmondsworth: Penguin. 1971.
Buik of Alexander, The. Ed. R.L.G. Ritchie. 4 vols. Scottish Text Society (1921-29).
Cassamus Fragment—Rosskopf, K. (1911). *Editio Princeps des mittelenglischen Cassamus (Alexanders-Fragmentes).* München.
Chaucer, G. *The Riverside Chaucer.* Ed. L.D. Benson. Oxford: Oxford University Press. 1988.
Dictes and Sayings of the Philosophers, The. Ed. C.F. Bühler. EETS, OS 211 (1941).
Diodorus of Sicily: 12 Vols. Tr. C.H. Oldfather. Loeb Classical Library. London: Heinemann. 1933-67.
Epistola Alexandri ad Aristotelem. Ed. W. Walther Boer. Beiträge zur klassischen Philologie 50. Meisenheim am Glan: Anton Hain. 1973 (orig. pub. 1953).

Gower, J. *The English Works*. Ed. G.C. Macaulay. 2 Vols. EETS, ES 81, 82 (1900-2).

Hay, Sir G. *The Forraye of Gadderis, The Vowis, extracts from Sir Gilbert Hay's Buik of King Alexander the Conqueror*. Ed. A. Herrmann. In: *Wissenschaftliche Beilage zum Jahresbericht der II. städtischen Realschule zu Berlin*. Berlin. 1900.

Hay, Sir G. *The Buik of King Alexander the Conquerour*. Ed. J. Cartwright. 3 Vols. Scottish Text Society (1986, 90-). (Vol.1, containing the Introduction, has still to appear.)

Higden, R. *Polychronicon Ranulphi Higden Monachi Cestrensis, together with the English translations of John Trevisa and of an unknown writer of the fifteenth century*. Ed. C. Babington and J. Lumby. 9 Vols. Rolls Series 41. London: H.M. Stationery Office. 1865-1886 (Repr., 1964).

Historia Alexandri Magni (Historia de Preliis) Rezension J^1. Ed. A. Hilka and K. Steffens. Beiträge zur klassischen Philologie 107. Meisenheim am Glan: Anton Hain. 1979.

Historia Alexandri Magni (Historia de Preliis). Rezension J^2 (Orosius-Rezension). Ed. A. Hilka. Vol. 1. Zum Druck besorgt durch H.-J. Bergmeister. Beiträge zur klassischen Philologie 79. Meisenheim am Glan: Anton Hain. 1976.

Historia Alexandri Magni (Historia de Preliis). Rezension J^2 (Orosius-Rezension). Ed A. Hilka. Vol. 2. Zum Druck besorgt durch R. Grossmann. Beiträge zur klassischen Philologie 89. Meisenheim am Glan: Anton Hain. 1977.

Historia de Preliis Alexandri Magni Rezension J^3, Die. Ed. K. Steffens. Beiträge zur klassischen Philologie 73. Meisenheim am Glan: Anton Hain. 1975.

Jacques de Longuyon, *Les Voeux du Paon*. Ed. R.L.G. Ritchie in *The Buik of Alexander*. 4 vols. Scottish Text Society (1921-29).

Josephus, Flavius, *Jewish Antiquities*. Trans. R. Marcus. Loeb Classical Library. London: Heinemann. 1937.

Julii Valerii Epitome. Ed. J. Zacher. Halle: Buchhandlung des Waisenhauses. 1867.

Julius Valerius. *Res gestae Alexandri Magni*. Ed. A. Mai. Milan: Regiis Typis. 1817.

Justinus, M. Julianus, *Epitoma Historiarum Philippicarum Pompei Trogi*. Ed. O. Seel. Stuttgart: Teubner. 1972.

Kyng Alisaunder. Ed. G.V. Smithers. 2 vols. EETS 227, 237 (1952-57).

Lydgate, J. *Fall of Princes*. Ed. H. Bergen. 4 vols. EETS, ES 121-124 (1924-27).

Lydgate, J, and B. Burgh. *Secrees of Old Philisoffres*. Ed. R. Steele. EETS, ES 66 (1894).

Magoun, F. P. (1929). *The Gests of King Alexander of Macedon*. Cambridge, Mass.: Harvard University Press. (Contains an edition of *Alexander A* and *Alexander and Dindimus*).

Mandeville's Travels. Ed. M.C. Seymour. Oxford: Clarendon Press. 1967.

Middle English 'Letter of Alexander to Aristotle', The. Ed. V. DiMarco and L. Perelman. Costerus n.s. 13. Amsterdam: Rodopi. 1978.

Of Arthour and Of Merlin. Ed. O.D. Macrae-Gibson. 2 Vols. EETS 268, 279 (1973-79).

Orosius, Paulus. *Historiarum adversum paganos libri VII*. Ed. C. Zangemeister. Leipzig: Teubner. 1889.

Orosius, The Old English. Ed. J. Bately. EETS, SS 6 (1980).

Parlement of the Thre Ages, The. Ed. M.Y. Offord. EETS 246 (1959).
Petrus Comestor. *Historia Scholastica*. Ed. J.P. Migne. Patrologiae Cursus Completus, Series Latina 198.
Plutarch's *Lives*. 11 vols. Tr. B. Perrin. Loeb Classical Library. London: Heinemann. 1914-26.
Prose Alexander, The: A Critical Edition. Ed. M. Neeson. Unpublished doctoral dissertation, University of California at Los Angeles. DA 72-2872. 1971.
Prose Life of Alexander, The. From the Thornton Manuscript. Ed. J.S. Westlake. The Text. EETS, OS 143 (1913).
Pseudo-Methodius—Trevisa, John. *Dialogus inter Militem and Clericum, Richard FitzRalph's Sermon: 'Defensio Curatorum' and Methodius: 'Þe Bygynnyng of þe World and þe Ende of Worldes'*. Ed. A.J. Perry. EETS, OS 167 (1925).
Pseudo-Methodius—d'Evelyn, C. (1918). The Middle-English Metrical Version of the *Revelations* of Methodius; with a Study of the Influence of Methodius in Middle-English Writings. *PMLA* 33. 135-203.
Quintus Curtius Rufus. *Res gestae Alexandri Magni*. Trans. J.C. Rolfe. Loeb Classical Library. London: Heinemann. 1946.
Roman d'Alexandre, The Medieval French. Ed. E.C. Armstrong, A. Foulet *et al.* 8 Vols. Elliott Monographs 36-43. Princeton: Princeton University Press. 1937- .
Secretum Secretorum. Nine English Versions. Ed. M.A. Manzalaoui. EETS 276 (1977).
Solinus, C. Julius. *Collectanea rerum memorabilium*. Ed. T. Mommsen. 2. Aufl. Berlin: Weidmann. 1895 (Repr., 1958).
Thomas of Kent. *The Anglo-Norman 'Alexander' ('Le roman de toute chevalerie')*. Ed. B. Foster with the assistance of I. Short. 2 Vols. Anglo-Norman Text Society, 29 and 31. London: Westfield College, 1976.
Three Old English Prose Texts. Ed. S. Rypins. EETS, ES 161 (1924) (Contains the Old English Letter of Alexander to Aristotle).
Turville-Petre, T. (1979). A Lost Alliterative Alexander Romance. *Review of English Studies* 30. 306-307.
Walter of Châtillon. *The Alexandreis*. Trans. R.T. Pritchard. Mediaeval Sources in Translation 29. Toronto: Pontifical Institute of Mediaeval Studies. 1986.
Wars of Alexander, The. Ed. W.W. Skeat. EETS, ES 47 (1888).
Wars of Alexander, The. Ed. H.N. Duggan and T. Turville-Petre. EETS, SS 10 (1989).

2. Secondary literature

Aerts, W.J., Jos.M.M. Hermans, E. Visser (eds.) (1978). *Alexander the Great in the Middle Ages. Ten Studies on the Last Days of Alexander in Literary and Historical Writing*. Nijmegen: Alfa.
Aerts, W.J., E.R. Smits and J.B. Voorbij (eds.) (1986). *Vincent of Beauvais and Alexander the Great. Studies on the 'Speculum Maius' and its translations into medieval vernaculars*. Groningen: Egbert Forsten.
Aerts, W.J. and M. Gosman (eds.) (1989). *Exemplum et Similitudo. Alexander the Great and other heroes as points of reference in medieval literature*. Groningen: Egbert Forsten.
Anderson, A.S. (1932). *Alexander's Gate, Gog and Magog, and the Inclosed Nations*. Academy Publications 12. Cambridge, Mass.: The Mediaeval Academy of America.

Bunt, G. H. V. (1978). Alexander's Last Days in the Middle English *Kyng Alis-
aunder*. In: Aerts *et al.* (1978). 202-29.
Cartwright, J. (1986). Sir Gilbert Hay and the *Alexander* Tradition. In: *Scottish
Language and Literature, Medieval and Renaissance*. Ed. D. Strauss, H.W.
Drescher. International Conference 1984 - Proceedings - Scottish Studies:
Publications of the Scottish Studies Centre of the Johannes Gutenberg Uni-
versität Mainz in Germersheim 4. Frankfurt a.M./Bern/New York: Peter
Lang.
Cary, George (1956). *The Medieval Alexander*. Edited by D. J. A. Ross. Cam-
bridge: Cambridge University Press. (Repr., 1967).
Dijk, H. van, and E.R. Smits (eds.) (1990). *Dwergen op de schouders van reu-
zen*. Groningen: Egbert Forsten.
Duggan, H.N. (1976). The Source of the Middle English *The Wars of Alex-
ander*. *Speculum* 51. 624-36.
Duggan, H.N. (1986a). The Shape of the B-Verse in Middle English Alliterative
Poetry. *Speculum* 61. 564-92.
Duggan, H.N. (1986b). Alliterative Patterning as a Basis for Emendation in Mid-
dle English Alliterative Poetry. *Studies in the Age of Chaucer* 8. 73-105.
Fox, R.L. (1973). *Alexander the Great*. London: Allen Lane. (Repr., London:
Futura, 1975).
Green, P. (1974). *Alexander of Macedon. 356-323 B.C. A Historical Biog-
raphy*. Rev. ed. Harmondsworth: Penguin. 1974.
Guddat-Figge, G. (1976). *Catalogue of the Manuscripts Containing Middle En-
glish Romances*. München: Wilhelm Fink.
Hamilton, G. L. (1927a). A New Redaction (I^{3a}) of the *Historia de Preliis* and
the Date of Redaction I^3. *Speculum* 2. 113-46.
Kaluza, M. (1892). Strophische Gliederung in der mittelenglischen rein alliterie-
renden Dichtung. *Englische Studien* 16. 169-80.
Keiser, George R. (1984). The Romances. Chapter 13 of *Middle English Prose:
A Critical Guide to Major Authors and Genres*. New Brunswick, N.J.: Rut-
gers University Press.
Kitchel, L.M. (1973). *A Critical Study of the Middle English Alexander Ro-
mances*. Unpublished doctoral dissertation, Michigan State University. DA
73-29,728.
Lascelles, M. (1936). Alexander and the Earthly Paradise in Mediaeval English
Writings. *Medium Ævum* 5. 31-47, 79-104, 173-88.
Mehl, D. (1968). *The Middle English Romances of the Thirteenth and Fourteenth
Centuries*. London: Routledge and Kegan Paul.
Merkelbach, R. (1977). *Die Quellen des griechischen Alexanderromans*. Zweite,
neubearbeitete Auflage unter Mitwirkung von Jürgen Trumpf. Zetemata 9.
München: C.H. Beck.
Pfister, F. (1976). *Kleine Schriften zum Alexanderroman*. Beiträge zur klas-
sischen Philologie 61. Meisenheim am Glan: Anton Hain. (contains an ap-
pendix with several short texts, including the passage on Jeremiah in Epi-
phanius' *Liber prophetarum*)
Renault, M. (1975). *The Nature of Alexander*. London: Allen Lane.
Ross, D.J.A. (1961). The I^3 *Historia de Preliis* and the *Fuerre de Gadres*.
Classica et Mediaevalia 22. 205-21.
Ross, D.J.A. (1988). *Alexander Historiatus. A Guide to medieval illustrated
Alexander Literature*. 2nd ed. Athenäums Monografien Altertumswissen-
schaft: Beiträge zur klassischen Philologie 186. Frankfurt am Main: Athe-
näum.

Severs, J. B. (1967) (ed.). *A Manual of the Writings in Middle English 1050-1500*. By Members of the Middle English Group of the Modern Language Association of America. Fascicule I: *The Romances*. New Haven, Conn.: The Connecticut Academy of Arts and Sciences.

Turville-Petre, T. (1977). *The Alliterative Revival*. Cambridge and Totowa, N.J.: D.S. Brewer, Rowman & Littlefield.

Turville-Petre, T. (1980). Emendation on Grounds of Alliteration in *The Wars of Alexander*. *English Studies* 61. 302-17.

Turville-Petre, T. (1987). Editing *The Wars of Alexander*. In: *Manuscripts and Texts: Editorial Problems in Middle English Literature*. Ed. D. Pearsall. Cambridge: D.S. Brewer. 144-60.

NARRATIVE MODE AND INTERPRETATION
OF
SIR GAWAIN AND THE GREEN KNIGHT

FRANS DIEKSTRA

Sir Gawain and the Green Knight is a romance with a highly improbable plot that is presented in a very lifelike manner. Broadly speaking, in considering the narrative mode of the poem we may distinguish the supernatural or fabulous mode, and the realistic or mimetic mode. The fabulous is evident in the patent absurdity of the plot when presented in naturalistic terms. We need think only of the preposterous challenge, the shape-shifting, the miraculous recuperative powers of the Green Knight, the farfetched role of Morgan le Fay, or the psychological anomaly of Bertilak risking being cuckolded in the process of testing Gawain. The realistic mode is evident in the recognisable world of fourteenth-century chivalry as presented in the castle scenes, the banquets, the hunts, the hospitality, the fun and games by the fireside, the trappings of the knights, the detailed accounts of courtly behaviour. The combination of these two elements, though familiar in the genre of romance, is rather unique in *Sir Gawain and the Green Knight*. As W.P. Ker (1955:102) said long ago:

> Not much is done by the writer to explain it [i.e. the marvellous]; at the same time nothing is left vague. The author might almost have been a modern novelist with a contempt for romance, trying, by way of experiment, to work out a 'supernatural' plot with the full strength of his reason; merely accepting the fabulous story, and trying how it will go with accessories from real life, and with modern manners and conversation.

Compared with most other verse romances the element of the marvellous is managed with restraint. Nor, for that matter, does the poem reveal the sentiment and pathos that feature so largely in other specimens of the genre, as instanced in the killing of the children in *Amis and Amiloun*, the seven-years cherishing of the embalmed body of the lover in *The Squire of Low Degree*, the extreme devotion of the jilted girl in *Lay le Freine*, or the devotion and trials patiently endured of an Emaré and a Grisildis. In contrast, the realistic element is supported by all the technical and expressive means at the poet's disposal. The result is an effect of shock when the magic and terror of the fabulous imagination encroach on the world of everyday reality. The author succeeds in making his readers accept the supernatural and absurd as worthy of a serious man's life. The test that Gawain is subjected to turns out to be a fascinating series of moral conflicts, in which Gawain needs all his determination, resourcefulness and idealism. Though he does not emerge entirely unscathed, he has acquired a new self-knowledge.

The distinction between the fabulous and the realistic is not an academic one, or one which only presents itself to twentieth-century observers. It must have been evident to a contemporary audience, and must also have set problems to the author in terms of organisation and plot structure. An analogous instance is when an author attempts to turn an anecdote or a joke into a fully-fledged narrative and finds that he has to solve problems that never occurred in the original. It is the problem also of many modern versions of fairy tales: the increase of realism soon reaches a point of diminishing returns when questions are answered that should not be asked. In what follows I should like to examine these two modes separately and see in how far they contribute to the strength of the whole and in how far they give rise to difficulties in terms of organisation and problems of interpretation. As a test-case I will consider the problem of Gawain's confession at ll.1882ff, and the evaluation of Gawain's partial failure.

If we first consider the realistic mode, it becomes at once evident that what I have broadly referred to as "realistic" is only partly so. It is true that we find long descriptions that can be studied as information on contemporary conditions, but it is clear that the type of reality described is one heightened and idealised. The rationale for this is that romances such as *Sir Gawain and the Green Knight* are "mirrors of chivalry". They reflect the ethic code, the ideals and fashions of a courtly class; a considerable part of their appeal and prestige was their exemplary function. What the courtesy books, the treatises of paternal and maternal instruction did at the theoretical level was presented in action by the *mores* depicted in the chivalric romances.[1] They presented to their audience an idealised view of their own life—or that of their betters—reflected in imaginative lit-

[1] See also Nicholls, 1985, esp. pp.112-42.

erature. The romances present pleasing pictures of the splendour of courtly life, in which the mundane problems of everyday drudgery are carefully suppressed. These pictures tend to concentrate on the highlights of social life: the social gatherings at festivals, jousts, banquets, the courtly conversations, the feats of chivalry, the detailed presentation of social etiquette, the receptions, the salutations, the leavetakings with all their ceremony and sentiment. Everything is infused with enthusiastic intensification. Hence the romance style is a superlative style: the heroes are the most noble, valiant and wellmannered; the ladies the most beautiful and '*debonaire*', the enemies the most fierce and ruthless. In *Sir Gawain and the Green Knight* all the courtiers are young and sprightly.

This heightening beyond the actual has the evident function of providing both poet and audience with a shared dream of self-realisation—partly perhaps an escapist dream, as for instance in *Sir Launfal*. But the best romances present a model to live up to, a mirror by which an audience could test and adjust their own standards. It is in this setting that the principal theme of romance develops, i.e. the theme of the lone hero braving it out against uneven odds. Of course this is a 'universal' of literature, but it is the main theme of the romances, which are for the greater part quests or tests in which the hero strives after self-realisation through the exercise of exemplary virtue. It is in this aspect of the emotional heightening of everyday experience that the fabulous and the realistic meet in their most congenial combination. However, what I should like to stress in this context is that the description of manners was to some extent an end in itself, designed to satisfy the never-flagging curiosity of one half of the world as to how the other half lives.

With regard to the exemplary description of manners we should keep in mind that the French examples had gone much further. Poets such as Chrétien de Troyes had put into their work the spirit of polite conversation and the refinements of amatory sentiment. The great handbook of the spirit of fine behaviour, the *Roman de la Rose*, too, had set the tone in this respect. Though in part an ironical account of the falling in love of the hero, the poem is also an 'art of love', as is explicitly announced in the work itself: it is a guide for prospective lovers and was evidently designed to meet the need of an audience that delighted to be instructed in the stylised patterns of courtly flirtation and in the fine-spun paradoxes of love. It is not until the period of Chaucer and the *Gawain*-poet that the English romances reach a comparable level of sophistication.

Much of the description of manners in *Sir Gawain and the Green Knight* can be seen as contributing to this exemplary function. It accommodates questions such as: what is the proper way to behave in certain situations; what is the courtly attitude to such and such a problem? To the already initiated it would provide flattering confirmation of their sense of decorum. The speech of Gawain (ll.341ff) in which he claims the blow for himself shows not only exemplary courage and initiative but is also a model of courtesy. It gives evidence of modesty, consideration for others, but also of expedience, self-assertion and an intelligent appraisal of the situation.[2] When Gawain leaves Camelot in order to search for the Green Chapel, we are offered a view of the knights and ladies of the court. They are grieving since they believe they will never see Gawain among them again. But instead of showing their grief they maintain a bright exterior, evidently in order not to make things heavier for Gawain:

> Kny3tes ful cortays and comlych ladies
> Al for luf of þat lede in longynge þay were,
> Bot neuer þe lece ne þe later þay neuened bot merþe:
> Mony ioylez for þat ientyle iapez þer maden.   (539-42)

> (Knights very courteous and beautiful ladies suffered grief for love of Gawain; but none the less they spoke only of cheerful things. Without joy in their hearts they uttered pleasantries for that noble knight.)[3]

Similar interest in manners is reflected in the timing of the questions as to the background and business of visitors. Arthur invites the Green Knight first to be entertained and afterwards to state his business (ll.254-5). Of similar interest is the delayed and discreet inquiry as to Gawain's court of origin (ll.901ff) and the even longer delayed inquiry as to the purpose of his journey (ll.1046ff). Salutations are generally described in detail since they reflect the interest of the initial stages of social intercourse. We may note Gawain's dialogue with the porter (ll.811ff) and the words of welcome by the lord of the castle (ll.835ff). Gawain's first meeting with the ladies—they do not present themselves till it is time to go to chapel—shows his courteous

---

[2] See the excellent analysis of Gawain's speech in Spearing, 1972:43-7; see also Brewer, 1966:67-78.

[3] All quotations from the poem are from the revised edition by Norman Davis. The translations are my own.

but different treatment of the older and the younger one. The older one he greets respectfully, the lovely one he embraces and kisses, adding a few courtly phrases and offering his service—'*service*' having all the connotations of the courtly love tradition.

Gawain's exemplary virtues are highlighted in the depiction of his shield, and the poet thought the digression important enough to allow it to delay the action of his narrative. The detailed technical description of the hunts, the care with which Gawain's horse is stabled, the set of clothes he is offered, these are only a few points that give evidence of the joy in presenting courtiers with such exemplary good manners. The most explicit reference to the interest in codes of behaviour is at ll.910ff, where the courtiers of Bertilak's castle express their delight at having Gawain as their guest:

> And alle þe men in þat mote haden much joye
> To apere in his presense prestly þat tyme,
> Þat alle prys and prowes and pured þewes
> Apendes to hys persoun, and preysed is euer;
> Byfore alle men vpon molde his mensk is þe most.
> Vch segge ful softly sayde to his fere:
> 'Now schal we semlych se sleȝtes of þewez
> And þe teccheles termes of talkyng noble,
> Wich spede is in speche vnspurd may we lerne,
> Syn we haf fonged þat fyne fader of nurture.
> God hatz geuen vus his grace godly for soþe,
> Þat such a gest as Gawan grauntez vus to haue,
> When burnez blyþe of his burþe schal sitte
> > and synge.
> > In menyng of manerez mere
> > Þis burne now schal vus bryng,
> > I hope þat may hym here
> > Schal lerne of luf-talkyng.'   (910-27)

(And all the men in that castle took delight in the news and quickly sought the company of the knight who had such an excellent reputation for valour and noble virtues. He excelled above all men on earth in courtesy. Every man whispered to his neighbour: 'Now we may watch refined manners and the impeccable phrases of courtly conversation. Without asking we may learn how to profit from his conversation, now that we have among us that paragon of good breeding. God has truly favoured us with his grace that he grants us to have such a guest as Gawain in our midst at this cheerful Christmas gathering. Now this knight will teach us understanding of noble manners. I expect that all who listen to him will learn about the art of lovers' conversation.')

Significantly, Gawain's courtesy is here virtually equated with court-liness in speech, just as its opposite, *vilanye*, tended to be used in the specialised meaning of rudeness in speech.[4] An instance of the art of polite flirtation is provided by the bedroom scenes. The speeches are artfully metaphorical; the imagery is that of the besieged fortress, the captive prisoner bound by the bonds of his lady, the surrender to superior forces, the making of a truce, the captured victim's plea for mercy. The lady stealthily enters Gawain's bedroom, seats herself on the bed and watches him wake up—or rather his imitation of waking up:

> 'God moroun, Sir Gawayn,' sayde þat gay lady,
> 'Ȝe ar a sleper vnslyȝe, þat mon may slyde hider;
> Now ar ȝe tan as-tyt! Bot true vus may schape,
> I schal bynde yow in your bedde, þat be ȝe trayst':
> Al laȝande þe lady, lanced þo bourdez.
> 'Goud moroun, gay,' quoþ Gawayn þe blyþe,
> 'Me schal worþe at your wille, and þat me wel lykez,
> For I ȝelde me ȝederly, and ȝeȝe after grace,
> And þat is þe best, be my dome, for me byhouez nede':
> And þus he bourded aȝayn with mony blyþe laȝter.
>   (1208-17)

('Good morning, Sir Gawain,' said the handsome lady, 'you are a careless sleeper: it is so easy to slip in here. Now you are cap-tured. Unless we can arrange a truce, I shall bind you in your bed, be sure of that.' The lady laughed as she spoke these words. 'Good morning, lovely lady,' said Gawain. 'If that is your desire, I will let it happen with pleasure. For I will yield myself promptly as your prisoner, and cry for mercy; it is the only solution, for it seems to me I have no other choice.' And thus he jested and laughed in return.)

Gawain immediately picks up her manner of speech. In either case the poet emphasises the facetious nature of the conversation, which is accompanied by lighthearted laughter. The lady alternates the allu-sive banter with more direct advances; she says that they are not go-ing to be disturbed; they have the castle to themselves. The statement

---

[4] Cf. in this respect what Chaucer says of the Knight in the *General Prologue* to the *Canterbury Tales*: "*He nevere yet no vileynye ne sayde / In al his lyf unto no maner wight*" (ll.70-1: 'In all his life he had never yet said any rude word to any sort of person').

"*3e ar welcum to my cors*" (1.1237), although it might theoretically be interpreted as 'I am at your disposal' (see the note by Norman Davis) is at least unambiguous in its amorousness. Here the lady employs additional imagery from legal terminology:

> 'Me behouez of fyne force
> Your seruaunt be, and schale.'   (1239-40)
>
> ('Absolute necessity constrains me to be your servant, and so I shall be.')

The conversation is playfully amorous, but it is also a tricky fencing game. It is interesting to compare the interchanges in Andreas Capellanus' *De Arte Honeste Amandi*, in which the lady systematically refutes the carefully wrought arguments of her suitor. But what in Andrew has more than a touch of scholastic debate is here part of a complex set of temptations on the one hand and conflicting obligations and loyalties on the other. The lady takes the offensive, and Gawain is reduced to parrying her thrusts. As it turns out, Gawain's performance in this game is a matter on which his reputation and even his life depend.

That the type of flirtatious talk employed by the lady was seen as a model is evident from comparable scenes which employ the imagery of captivity and surrender in the same playful way. Compare Chaucer's *Troilus and Criseyde*:

> This Troilus in armes gan hir streyne,
> And seyde, "O swete, as evere mot I gon,
> Now be ye kaught, now is ther but we tweyne!
> Now yeldeth yow, for other bote is non!"   (iii.1205-8)
>
> (Troilus held her tight in his arms and said, 'Sweetheart, now you are captured, now there is only the two of us! Now you must surrender, you have no other choice!')

Criseyde's answer adds piquancy to this:

> "Ne hadde I er now, my swete herte deere,
> Ben yold, ywis, I were now nought heere!"   (iii.1210-1)
>
> ('If I had not already surrendered before, sweetheart, I would not now be here!')

This type of conversation gets to the root of the respective roles of
men and women, and in particular of what is socially acceptable in
relations between the sexes. It was forward conversations of this type
that had such a disheartening effect on the amorousness of the hero in
the *Book of the Knight of La Tour-Landry*, who relates that at one
time his father introduced him to a noble lady with the idea that she
might be a suitable marriage partner:

> & my fader sette me in langage with her, that y shulde
> haue knoulech of her speche and langage, and so we fell
> in wordes of prisoners, and y saide, "damsell, it were
> better to fall to be youre prisoner thanne to mani other,
> for y trow youre prison shuld not be so harde to me as it
> shulde be and y were take with Englisshe men." And she
> ansuered, "y haue saie sum not long sethe that y wolde
> were my prisoner." And y asked her yef she wolde putte
> hym in euell prison; and she saide, nay, she wolde kepe
> hym as she wolde her owne body; and y saide he was
> happi that might come into so noble a prison.   (p.18)

> (And my father induced me to have conversation with her so that I
> might become acquainted with her speech and conversation. And
> so we came to talk on the subject of prisoners; and I said, 'Lady,
> it would be better to be your prisoner than anyone else's, for I
> trust you prison would not be so cruel to me as when I were cap-
> tured by the English.' And she answered, 'I have recently seen
> someone whom I would like to be my prisoner.' And I asked her
> if she would treat him harshly in her prison; and she said, no, she
> would watch over him as herself. And I said that whoever he was,
> he would be lucky to have such a noble prison.)

Afterwards his father inquired after his impression of the lady;
whereupon the Knight answered that although the lady was of noble
birth, yet her forward language and flighty manner had so discom-
fited him that he had lost all appetite for her. For which he had reason to be thankful; the lady became involved in a scandal and died
young. The knight concludes by advising his daughters to behave de-
murely, with proper regard for their reputation and marriage pros-
pects.

That the romances should also present a code of an ideal masculine mentality is hardly surprising. In *Sir Gawain and the Green
Knight*, apart from the more explicit virtues of courage, loyalty and
courtesy, the feature that is most evident, though less explicit, is that
of an undercooled toughness that maintains a bright exterior and is

even capable of grim jokes in the most daunting circumstances. We find it in Arthur when the Green Knight has galloped away, his head in his hand, and the hall falls silent. Far from being daunted, the King shows superior coolness by graciously leading his Queen back to the dinner table and brushing off the whole episode as a pleasant pastime, the sort of thing that he prefers a Christmas dinner to begin with:

> Þaȝ Arþer þe hende kyng at hert hade wonder,
> He let no semblaunt be sene, bot sayde ful hyȝe
> To þe comlych quene wyth cortays speche,
> "Dere dame, to-day demay yow neuer;
> Wel bycommes such craft vpon Cristmasse,
> Laykyng of enterludez, to laȝe and to syng,
> Among þise kynde caroles of knyȝtez and ladyez.
> Neuer þe lece to my mete I may me wel dres,
> For I haf sen a selly, I may not forsake."   (467-75)

(Though Arthur the gracious king was amazed in his heart, he did not show it, but raised his voice to address the beautiful queen with courteous speech, 'Dear lady, do not be dismayed. Such things are suitable pastimes for Christmas, interludes, laughter and song, along with courtly dances of knights and ladies. All the same I can now proceed to my dinner, for I have seen a marvel, I cannot deny it.')

Gawain, whom we may picture with a somewhat dazed look in his eyes, still clutching his axe, is told, *"Now sir, heng vp þyn ax, þat hatz innogh hewen"* (l.477: 'Now sir, hang up your axe, for it has hewn enough'). It is slight touches like these that so pleasingly contribute to the depiction of the familiar British virtue of the stiff upper lip. In *Havelok* this characteristic is expressed more simply in two lines:

> Evere he was glad and bliþe;
> His sorwe he couþe wel miþe.   (949-50)

(He was always glad and cheerful; he could conceal his sorrow very well.)

Gawain, who is of course the hero proper, never loses his mental resilience. Even at moments of greatest pressure his thoughts and musings retain a characteristic lilt: *"Hit is þe corsedest kyrk þat euer I com inne!"* (l.2196: 'It is the most cursed church that ever I came into!'). When he hears the blade of the axe being whetted, Gawain realises its implications with a shock, but his language grimly manages to continue the imagery of worship and devotion that befits this 'chapel of the devil':

> ... 'Bi Godde,' quoþ Gawayn, 'þat gere, as I trowe,
> Is ryched at þe reuerence me, renk, to mete
>   bi rote.'   (2205-7)

> ('By God,' said Gawain, 'I believe that gear is prepared in my honour, in order to receive me with due ceremony.')[5]

The actual encounter with the Green Knight in the episode of the return blow is interesting for its treatment of the hero when facing uneven odds. It is also interesting for its treatment of male competition and intimidation. The romances have a long tradition of this. Compared with the epic speeches in *Beowulf* between Beowulf and Unferth, with its unrestrained boasting and hard-hitting aggressiveness, this scene is decidedly playful. Yet the tension is all there, somewhat below the surface. The Green Knight is not watching out for Gawain's arrival; he appears to be unconcerned and is fully occupied in grinding his axe. It is Gawain who has to draw attention to his arrival. Apart from the general eeriness of the scene, this fact subtly emphasises Gawain's disadvantageous position. Indeed, the Green Knight is *literally* in a superior position and looks down on Gawain. When he acknowledges Gawain's arrival, the Green knight does not come down to join Gawain at once but returns to his whetting:

> 'Abyde,' quoþ on on þe bonk abouen ouer his hede,
> 'And þou schal haf al in hast þat I þe hyȝt ones.'
> Ȝet he rusched on þat rurde rapely a þrowe,
> And wyth quettyng awharf, er he wolde lyȝt.   (2217-20)

> ('Wait,' said a voice on the bank above Gawain's head, 'and you shall have without delay what I once promised you.' Yet the speaker went on with that rushing noise, and turned aside to continue with his whetting before he would come down.)

---

[5] The use of high-spirited metaphorical language at moments of heightened emotional intensity is found is a less courtly context in *Gamelyn*, where the hero's exploits in a wrestling match with the local thug in the market place are commented on by the beaten party in terms appropriate to buying and selling (ll.269ff). Similarly, the scene in which the clergy are beaten up shows the two avengers punctuating their blows with ecclesiastical terminology appropriate to the imposition of penance (ll.503ff).

His movements when he does come down to Gawain are described in terms of ebullient vitality:

> When he wan to þe watter, þer he wade nolde,
> He hypped ouer on hys ax, and orpedly strydez,
> Bremly broþe on a bent þat brode watz aboute
> on snawe.   (2231-4)

(When he reached the water, not wanting to wade it, he jumped across using his axe as a jumping-pole, and came striding boldly, fierce and grim onto that broad grassy snow-covered stretch that lay all around.)

The deliberate ease and macho swagger represent familiar intimidating tactics and underline his advantage. Gawain, who is awaiting him, does not deign to greet him with as much as a bow. The Green Knight, unperturbed, engages on a series of bantering remarks. He appears to be genuinely pleased that Gawain has turned up. Gawain is, he says, admirably punctual in keeping his appointments. The site is ideal for keeping trysts; they will have it all to themselves; they can romp about as they please—an interesting echo of the words of the lady in the bedroom scenes. The polite form of address used between Gawain and the lord of the castle has here given way to *thou* and *thee*. While Gawain is going through what is probably the most gruelling experience of his life, the Green Knight keeps up an easy conversation which evokes associations with that of an overeffusive dentist whose flow of words is not checked by the uncomfortable monosyllables of his patient. The series of interruptions has the effect of a deliberate teasing, a cat-and-mouse game in which Gawain's patience is severely taxed.

With the element of the supernatural we plunge into the fabulous world of the folktale imagination. It is the strength of the folktale that its moral conflicts are presented in terms of stark ineluctable dilemmas. The clash of conflicting obligations provides the plots of most traditional tales and lends them their interest and pathos. In the world of the traditional tale nothing is necessarily what it appears to be. This world is ruled by laws that are relentless and unpredictable; it presents threats and uncertainties that seem to be beyond human control. Even the moral assumptions of this imaginative world are in some ways different. The folktale imagination shrewdly recognises that the moral laws agreed upon by society are not an adequate safeguard against the threats of fate; it recognises that good intentions are not necessarily rewarded and do not necessarily lead to the desired results. Thus Perceval, in the versions of Chrétien and Wolfram von Eschenbach, is blamed for failing to inquire after the health of the wounded knight; but he finds it difficult to understand why. The irrational is always lurking around the corner. The hero faced with the trials thus put in his way can do no more than to show his determination. Balyn, the knight with the two swords in Book Two of Malory's *Morte Darthur*, is particularly infelicitous in most of his undertakings. He is victimised by a series of circumstances over which he has little or no control. He is blamed several times for what he finds it difficult to accept blame for. Yet he accepts the consequences of his actions in a spirit of humility and remorse. Although the curse of his magic sword has sealed his fate from the start, yet he stubbornly refuses to allow his bad luck to get him down. His victory is his unbroken spirit.

Gawain is faced with the fact that contrary to all rational calculation the Green Knight picks up his head after it has been chopped off. The challenger has thus altered the rules of the game, or rather he has introduced an entirely new game, in which normal human beings lose their bearings. Gawain's reaction shows that although he has no illusions, his spirit is undaunted:

> Þe knyȝt mad ay god chere,
> And sayde, 'Quat schuld I wonde?
> Of destinés derf and dere
> What may mon do bot fonde?'   (562-5)

> (The knight kept up his spirits and said, 'Why should I be daunted? Against the vicissitudes of fortune, what can one do but show a bold front?')

Characteristically, Gawain is not told where he can find the Green Chapel. In this respect the imagination of the folktale is related to that of dreams (see Erich Fromm, 1952).

The absurdity of the plot of the poem when viewed as naturalistic mimesis is evident: the central episode is an absurd challenge by a complete stranger, which is solemnly taken up by the assembled nobility of the nation.[6] The fact that the ridiculous proposal of the beheading game involves the participants in both murder and poten-

---

[6] The absurdity of the poem at the plot level is well presented by Brewer, 1976: 569-70.

tial suicide is somehow beyond the moral purview of the romance. The poem does not invite us to pursue that type of moral implication. If we are tempted—induced by the strength of the mimetic level—to apply rationalistic and mimetic standards to this type of traditional material, we get into difficulties of interpretation, as the history of *Gawain* criticism shows. Undue assumptions of naturalism—as well as undue emphasis on allegory and symbolism—have turned Morgan le Fay into the central motivating force of the poem, have turned the guide into a disguised Green Knight, have turned the court of Arthur into a sinful and decadent gang, Gawain into a fool.

But—to take up this last point—Gawain is evidently no fool. The mere fact that he is the hero of the romance should make this assumptions implausible on *a priori* grounds. The hero is the image of ourselves with which we want to identify. But also in the poet's actual treatment, which employs all the superlative terms of romance tradition to describe exemplary perfection, we are made to realise that Gawain incorporates superhuman excellence. Even the frequently heard statement that Gawain is so 'human'—with the implication that he has his faults, like all of us—is only part of the truth. Admittedly, Gawain has his weak spot, but his near-perfection still marks him as a model beyond ordinary human achievement. The 'human' quality is effected by the art of the poet, who has presented Gawain not as an abstract aggregate of virtues, but as perfection realised as the result of a dramatically presented series of tests and conflicts.

The point is that certain questions simply should not be asked. Thus it is futile to speculate on the exact motivation of the test further than what we learn from the poet. By the same token it is irrelevant to pursue the machinations of Morgan le Fay beyond what the poet himself tells us—which is precious little. His explanation reads like an afterthought and is aptly described by Speirs as "a bone for the rationalizing mind to play with, and to be kept quiet with" (1957: 218—Friedman, 1966, argues that Morgan le Fay is the weak spot in the poem).

On the other hand the imagination has its own logic. Although the fantasies of the romances are not susceptible to rationalistic or mimetic paraphrase, they can be intuitively grasped. As Brewer has noted, imaginative readers intuitively respond to the laws of romance fantasy. Speaking of the story of the choice of caskets in *The Merchant of Venice* he says, "Every reader of romance knows immediately and without being told that the greatest treasure must be contained within what appears to be the meanest container" (1978: 32). Similarly readers of folktales know that the youngest son will marry the princess and that to recline under a tree at noontide invites the spirit of magic. In reading this type of literature we need as it were a built-in switch that allows us to block out the 'noise' of the world of naturalistic analysis and to concentrate on the 'mythic' content. Reading on these two levels requires a certain flexibility in allowing our imagination to guide us in our responses.

This gap between the logic of ratiocination and the logic of the imagination leads to many difficulties in the interpretation of medieval literature. A case in point is the romance of *Amis and Amiloun*. Loyalty between friends is the dominant theme to which everything else is made subservient, to the extent that it implicates them in deceit and murder. At one point Amis does not hesitate to sacrifice his children when he learns in a vision that it is only by means of their blood that Amiloun can be cured of leprosy. Amis sends his wife to church—it is Christmas night—takes they key of the nursery, and cuts off the heads of his two children, collecting their blood in a vessel. At the realistic level we are shocked, particularly if we allow our minds to dwell on the unnatural, immoral, even pathological aspects of the episode. At the sociological level we may even note that the killings reflect the assumption that children are somehow 'owned' by their parents, and that anyway it is hypocritical to present the killing of one's offspring as a noble sacrifice. However, at the imaginative level there is much to assuage our abhorrence. We retain somehow a basic trust that with this extreme sacrifice all will finally turn out well, with both Amiloun cured and the children miraculously restored to life.[7]

In this context Chaucer is interesting for the way in which he dramatises the pull between the realistic and the mythic/moral levels. In his work the play with this clash tends to become a theme in its own right. Chaucer appears to have a preference for folktale plots that retain something of the starkness and simplicity of the folktale imagination. The simplicity is, however, strained to the limit by the demands of a sophisticated naturalism. Instead of suppressing the incongruities between the two levels, Chaucer tends to create a new tension, which adds a further dimension to the story—ironical, playful, or philosophical, as the case may be.

Thus in rehandling the folktale of Grisildis in *The Clerk's Tale* Chaucer brings out all the pathos of the original story, which stresses

---

[7] Imaginatively the episode may be associated with Abraham's readiness to sacrifice Isaac, or even with the sacrificial death of Christ for mankind: cf. Romans 8:32: He that spared not even His own Son but delivered him up for us all ...

patience and endurance under the most gruelling changes of fortune. At the same time he steps back from his material and subjects it to the enquiry of a sophisticated, free-ranging intelligence. The rationalising mind takes offence at the 'meekness' with which Grisildis undergoes the cruel and senseless testing by her husband; indeed, it questions the very basis of the virtue of patience when we see her giving up her children to death without as much as a grumble. But in the numerous asides, and more explicitly in the sardonic *Envoy*, we are presented with all the alternative echoes that common sense finds congenial and indeed imperative. What Chaucer does here amounts to dangerous brinkmanship, since he compels us to respond to both the mythic level (with its tearful pathos and religious overtones) and to the rationalistic level (with its irreverent mockery). This characteristic of Chaucer's art has given rise to many puzzled comments, such as the one by Block (1953:616), who describes Chaucer's procedure as revealing an "irreconcilable dualism of purpose".

A similar confrontation of common sense ands the moral values of the folktale is found in *The Franklin's Tale*. Here the essence of the moral conflict is that '*trouthe*', loyalty to one's pledged word, should be observed at all costs, whatever the odds. The situation arises that the husband, with tears in his eyes, feels obliged to send his wife to a lover whom she does not want. The wife is struggling with the idea of committing suicide in order to escape the obligation of her rash promise. The conflict is thus reduced to its starkest form: for the wife the dilemma is either death or dishonour; for the husband the dilemma is particularly cynical: either shame or dishonour. At the basic level of the story there is no room for the casuistic approach that would explain to Dorigen that prior obligations override later promises, or that foolish promises need not always be kept. (One might even argue that the very terms of her foolish promise were a confirmation of her love for her husband.) Nor is there room for the husband to consider whether to cuckold himself in order to indulge his wife's indiscretion is a respectable dilemma for a man who is interested in honour. To the mythic imagination casuistry is evidently the corrupting influence of the rationalising mind. It is characteristic of this material that it seems reluctant or unable to stress more than one virtue at a time. Chaucer has, however, introduced the common-sense approach in his narrator's comments (ll. 1493ff) and principally in the structural design of his tale where the conflict of loyalties becomes a test-case for an unusual and idealistic marriage arrangement.

In Chaucer's *Physician's Tale* the shocking scene in which a
loving father kills his daughter to safeguard her from losing her virginity is based on the relentless conviction that losing one's virginity
is a fate worse than death. To criticise the story for not having considered alternative solutions to the dilemma—after all, couldn't she
escape, wear a disguise, appeal to a superior court?—would be to
question the narrative mode in which the story is presented and to
dilute its morality.

Difficulty in welding elements of the plot and of rationalised
motivation are frequently found in the romances. They may in part
be due to the corruption introduced by the scribal process. A striking
case of this is found in *The Squire of Low Degree*, where the
motivation of the tests and even the exact sequence of episodes present something of a puzzle. But I am not concerned with these. In
other instances motivation looks like an afterthought on the poet's
part in an attempt to present the elements of the traditional plot in a
coherent structure of cause and effect, action and motivation. Thus in
Havelok the decision of Godard not to kill Havelok on the spot along
with his two sisters, is accounted for by a momentary qualm of conscience in Godard. But as a motivation this is decidedly weak; neither
his thoughts nor his actions endorse this, and we feel that the exigen-
cies of the plot and the striving for rationalistic motivation are not
fully integrated.

One interpretative crux for which the gap outlined above is, I
think, relevant is the so-called 'false' confession of Gawain. Much
discussion has gone into the problem whether Gawain's confession is
a sacrilege, a minor breach of the courtly code, an instance of Freudian repression on Gawain's part, a regrettable slip on the poet's part,
or none of these things. The fact is of course that in his confession
Gawain is silent about his determination to keep the girdle, in spite of
the exchange-of-winnings agreement with the lord of the castle. Let
us briefly recall the end of the third temptation scene.

Gawain has twice refused the lady's request for the exchange
of a keepsake. The lady has managed to construe as a downright
rejection of her charms Gawain's truthful statement that he has no
amorous attachments, nor for the time being intends to have any. She
tells him she knows when she is put in her place and that he is making
light of her lovesickness. We witness Gawain's refusing a request of
the lady for the third time when he turns down the offer of the green
girdle. The reader feels this virtually amounts to discourtesy—certainly in the eyes of the lady, but also in Gawain's own eyes; we know
how sensitive he is on this point. In this verbal fencing game Ga-

wain's refusal of the ring on the grounds that he could never match her gift with an equally precious one, is turned by the lady to her advantage. She unties the girdle and offers it to Gawain, saying he cannot refuse this time since the girdle is in itself something simple and unworthy. As if it were an afterthought, she adds that it renders the wearer invulnerable. This time Gawain is bound to react in spite of his initial refusal. This gift strikes him as the piece of luck that he badly needs. In accepting the girdle he will be able to kill two birds with one stone. It will put an end to the importunity of the lady with a good grace, and provide him with a talisman to protect his life into the bargain.

Indeed, at this point Gawain has no cause to feel displeased with himself. He has not allowed his problems in the face of impending death to get the better of him. He has never even considered trying to shirk the tryst. The acceptance of the girdle satisfactorily puts an end to the most seductive attack on his chastity, one which had urged him near the limit. It is at this moment of triumph, when he relishes the prospect of further good luck, that the lady uses her final trump card. She adds a perfectly natural request, and one which is certainly in line with her general suggestion of shared intimacy, namely Gawain is not to reveal the gift to her husband. The girdle is clearly a compromising gift.[8] The protection of the lady's reputation is so ingrained in the social consciousness of the male lover that to comply with such a request would be virtually a blind reaction.

It is evident that Gawain has now enmeshed himself in an extricable tangle of conflicting obligations. Even if he had wanted he could not now return the girdle to Bertilak without compromising the lady. But the fact is that he does not want to return the girdle. When the lady has said farewell, he carefully puts the girdle by, where he can pick it up later. Immediately afterwards he goes to confession:

> Syþen cheuely to þe chapel choses he þe waye,
> Preuély aproched to a prest, and prayed hym þere
> Þat he wolde lyste his lyf and lern hym better
> How his sawle schulde be saued when he schuld seye
> > heþen.

---

[8] Its symbolic overtones need not be spelled out. They are imaginatively and traditionally determined, as are those of the more traditional sleeve. The poet himself refers to it as a love-token—*drurye* (1.2033), and a *luf-lace* (1.1874, 2438). One might also think of the implications of the *zona castitatis* of theological literature.

Þere he schrof hym schyrly and schewed his mysdedez,
Of þe more and þe mynne, and merci besechez,
And of absolucioun he on þe segge calles;
And he asoyled hym surely and sette hym so clene
As domezday schulde haf ben diʒt on þe morn. (1876-84)

(Then he promptly made his way to the chapel, discreetly went up
to a priest and prayed him there to hear his confession, and to
counsel him how to save his soul when he should go hence. There
he made a clean breast of things and told all his misdeeds without
exception, and asked forgiveness. Then he requested the priest for
absolution; and the priest absolved him so completely and ren-
dered him so pure as if judgement day were appointed on the day
after.)

The confession concluded, Gawain seeks the company of the ladies
and generally enjoys himself in a lighthearted way. Since we have the
poet's word for it that Gawain's confession is valid, we should perhaps accept this without further comment. Gawain's real failure is
given detailed analysis further on in the poem; false confession is not
mentioned.

Gollancz's view that the author simply did not notice that
Gawain made a sacrilegious confession (in his edition of the poem,
1940:123) is by most critics rejected indignantly as an insult to the
poet's art. Most interpretations have assumed that the episode makes
sense only if it can be demonstrated that either Gawain's offence is
trivial (and hence there is no false confession) or that the poet is
shrewdly ironical about this strange self-deception of Gawain, whose
apparent cheerfulness after confession must hide a bad conscience.
This latter view has been given currency by Burrow (1965:104-10
and 127-33). He argues that the confession is false but is balanced by
Gawain's 'confession' to the Green Knight at the Green Chapel.
Green interprets the false confession as the "irony of muddled conscience" and argues that Gawain is not really guilty, since "there are
moral issues which the rational mind will not face, or face dispas-
sionately, when survival seems to be at stake and when so many miti-
gating circumstances can be invoked to cloud the issue"(1966:192f).
This is a typical 'psychologising' approach. It 'safeguards' Gawain's
conscience at the cost of attributing to him a kind of moral blackout.
One wonders if Gawain's case is helped by this. Foley (1974:77)
attempts to minimise the seriousness of the exchange-of-winnings
agreement and argues that Gawain has merely "broken the rules of a
courtly game." T.D. Hill (1980) argues that according St. Augustine
a joke is not to be accounted a lie. If the agreement was jocose, Ga-

wain's failure is at worst a venial sin. Brewer (1980:77) in reaction to Burrow denies that there is any irony in the poet's remarks about Gawain's confession. I think Brewer is right. His further statement, however, that "a sinful intention is not a sin and cannot be confessed" strikes me as dubious theology and is in any case a bow to the claims of irrelevant naturalism which he has so effectively combatted elsewhere. More to my purpose is his refusal to regard the confession scene as belonging to the imaginative level of the poem. He takes it as "part of the local realism by which the verbal realisation gives as vivid and recognisable a surface as possible to the story" (Brewer, 1980: 80).[9]

It seems to me that no explanation of the confession scene is acceptable that does not take Gawain's offence in keeping the girdle seriously. How much the poet was concerned with the moral bearings of Gawain's behaviour is abundantly clear from the scene at the Green Chapel. The attempts to minimise Gawain's fault militate against the mythic imagination, which would never accept a solution of its moral problems based on the casuistry gleaned from a skilful use of theological manuals. In the moral world of the traditional tale Gawain's obligation to his host is no less serious than his obligation to keep the tryst at the Green Chapel. It is one of the pillars of the plot; it would be a mistake to regard it as a mere parlour game that Gawain can ignore with impunity. The confession scene, on the other hand, is not part of the level of the traditional plot. It is part of the other level of the poem: the interest in manners, conventions, the Christian ceremonies that form the background of life for the characters. At this level the reader is reminded that in dangerous circumstances and before undertaking a journey, a good Christian withdraws into the cubicle of his mind to settle his account with his Maker. The confession scene operates at the same level as the passage at ll.750ff, that tells us that Gawain wanted to interrupt his journey to observe his religious duties at Christmas. It is thus part of the level of the romance that provides a mirror of exemplary behaviour.

Now is not this a confusing procedure in so punctilious a poet? To a certain extent the answer is yes; it illustrates the difficulties of the poet in structuring his narrative. We find here the seams and sutures of the plot structure. The scene presents his readers with an almost Chaucerian problem: the vividness of the surface realism with which the scene of the agreement to exchange winnings is presented

---

[9] For a discussion of 'local realism', see Brewer, 1978:44.

may lead us to take that agreement less seriously than was envisaged in terms of the plot. We might be tempted to view it as a trivial obligation incurred over drinks in a parlour game. Consequently the poem risks the question whether in the last temptation scene the pressure of the solid virtues of chastity and courtesy—along with Gawain's very natural desire for self-preservation—is adequately balanced by this seemingly less solid obligation to the host. It thus risks an interpretation that 'defends' Gawain's fault for the wrong reasons (witness Foley and Hill). The difference with Chaucer is that the *Gawain*-poet never makes us feel that he had any ironical intentions of the type that exploits the values of common sense to undercut the traditional material of his story.[10] Here, at this point of intersection between the folktale morality and the realistic scale of values of the everyday world, the subject of a Christian sacramental confession is ill at ease. However, we should not exaggerate the crux. I am sure that many readers have never been perturbed by the apparent contradiction which in recent years has received so much emphasis. It seems evident to me that the last thing the poet would have wanted was to get involved in a discussion of whether cheating in a parlour game is material for the confessional. It would have been just as alien to his concerns as a discussion of whether it is acceptable Christian morality to chop off someone's head in answer to a challenge at a Christmas party.

There remains the related problem whether Gawain's own assessment of his failure is to be taken at its face value. I think it is. Of course, at the psychological level his embarrassment is an understandable reaction when is suddenly confronted with the deflation of his ego; but there is more to it:

> Þat oþer stif mon in study stod a gret whyle,
> So agreued for greme he gryed withinne;
> Alle þe blode of his brest blende in his face,
> Þat al he schrank for schome þat þe schalk talked.
> Þe forme worde vpon folde þat þe freke meled:

---

[10] What is more in evidence in the poem is the poet's humorous interest in the 'comedy of manners', as for instance in the way Gawain is pictured as cornered by the lady on what might be termed his own ground, or in the way Gawain's predicament is presented as a conflict of opposing virtues: courtesy is at odds with chastity, and with Gawain's obligation to his host. As Brewer has put it, "It is an exquisite problem when virtue is assaulted not by vice, but by another virtue" (1980:76).

'Corsed worth cowarddyse and couetyse boþe!
In yow is vylany and vyse þat vertue disstryez.'
Þenne he kaȝt to þe knot, and þe kest lawsez,
Brayde broþely þe belt to þe burne seluen:
'Lo! þer þe falssyng, foule mot hit falle!
For care of þy knokke cowardyse me taȝt
To acorde me with couetyse, my kynde to forsake,
Þat is larges and lewté þat longez to knyȝtez.
Now am I fawty and falce, and ferde haf ben euer
Of trecherye and vntrawþe; boþe bityde sorȝe
          and care!'   (2369-84)

(Gawain stood lost in thought a long while; he was so mortified
that he was shuddering inwardly. All his heart's blood rose to his
face, and he winced with shame at the words of the knight. The
first thing he said was, 'A curse on cowardice and covetousness;
they spell dishonour and vice which destroy virtue.' Then he pull-
ed at the knot to untie it, and threw it fiercely at the Green Knight:
'Lo, there is the breach of faith, a curse on it! Out of fear for your
blow cowardice taught me to make a pact with covetousness and
to forsake my nature, which is generosity and loyalty that mark
the true knight. Now I am found wanting and false, I who have
always been afraid of treachery and disloyalty: I curse them
both!')

It is not necessary to analyse one by one all the sins of which he
accuses himself. It is evident that they are all offences against the
courtly code which Gawain feels he has violated. Even *couetyse* may
be broadly interpreted as keeping for oneself what one is not entitled
to, i.e. the girdle.

I think one should be reluctant to interpret Gawain's vehement
self-denunciation merely as an impulsive over-reaction produced by
his embarrassment when he realises he has been watched closely all
along. Such a view would emphasise mimetic psychologising effects
at the cost of the moral bearings of the story.[11] Nor should the fact
that the Green Knight reacts to Gawain's outburst with a peal of
laughter be taken as the ultimate indication of how the poet wanted
his audience to evaluate Gawain's performance. The Green Knight's
jovial reaction fits his jovial character. To him Gawain stands out
among other knights as 'a pearl among peas' (1.2364) and there is no

[11] For a different opinion, arguing that Gawain's viewpoint is limited and that his
judgement of the adventure is mistaken, see Benson, 1965:193-4.

reason to disagree with him. Gawain's achievement bespeaks super-human determination. How then can these views be made to tally?

To my mind, both Bertilak's view and Gawain's view are exemplary reactions to Gawain's adventure. They only differ in point of view, and their points of view are strictly determined by the courtly code itself. Having failed in a relatively minor point, Gawain shows due remorse and does not spare himself. He tends to exaggerate rather than to minimise his error. In this respect he is true to the Christian penitential code as well.[12] A strong form of the view that sinners should not try to find excuses for their sins was expressed by St. Gregory:

> Piarum mentium est ibi culpa agnoscere ubi culpa non est.
>
> (It is a mark of pious minds to acknowledge guilt where there is no guilt.)[13]

What characterises Gawain's words is the unconditional avowal of guilt, not the attitude of a grocer counting pence.

Moreover, it seems natural to view Gawain's self-accusation as a counterpart of the ideal of perfection portrayed in the emblem of the pentangle which symbolises Gawain's integrity as a Christian knight. The figure of the 'endless knot' suggests that to fail in one respect is to upset the the unity of the whole. Gawain reacts to the shattering of his integrity with due mortification. Now, the idea that the loss of one link in the chain renders the whole chain worthless is a familiar concept in medieval moral theology. There exists an extensive literature on the subject of the connection of the virtues, with a tradition that goes back to the Fathers of the Church and to classical philosophy.[14] The fundamental questions were: 'Is it true that if one

---

[12] That the two need not be in conflict is shown by H.[?Henry] of Saltrey's legend of St. Patrick's Purgatory (c1185). He gives an account of the knight Owein's decision to undertake a penance commensurate with the immensity of his crimes. Although written by a monk, the work reflects the spirit of chivalry in presenting the visit to Purgatory as 'a novel and unusual act of chivalry', an extraordinary enterprise in which the spirit of *noblesse oblige* is applied to 'a new kind of chivalry' (H. of Saltrey, pp.53-4).

[13] Quoted by Peraldus (Guillaume Peyraut) in his *Summa Vitiorum* (c1236) IX. ii.3, in the section on the foolishness of those who defend their own sins.

[14] See, for instance, the treatments by Lottin, 1949 and 1954, Michel, 1950, and Utz, 1937.

possesses one virtue, one possesses all virtues?' and 'If one lacks one virtue, can one be said to have any virtue at all?' A text frequently quoted in this connection is James 2:10: "And whosoever shall keep the whole law, but offend in one part, is become guilty of all." I do not think we need insist on the relevance of the details of these theological discussions for our Middle English romance, nor am I in favour of a detailed 'penitential' interpretation of the poem. Yet I do think it likely that the poet was familiar with the gist of such discussions and that they influenced his use of the pentangle symbol as well as his attitude to Gawain's Christian ideals.

Bertilak's attitude to Gawain's fault is determined by factors different from those that apply to Gawain. Once his role as a malign testing agent is concluded, Bertilak reacts as the genial host whom we have learned to know in the castle scenes. In the context of the Christian view of morality it is not his role to draw up a check-list of all aspects in which a fellow-Christian has gone astray. The attitude that befits him is that of magnanimity and generosity. Of course he has to steer clear of flattery, which by definition would be to offer a false view. The laughter takes away the edge of any hint of a patronising attitude. Ideally his assessment should be made in a spirit of forgiveness and fellow-feeling, the spirit that in the *Ancrene Wisse* leads a monk who heard that one of his brothers had fallen into sin to comment: "*Ille hodie. ego cras. pet is. he to dei. & ich to marhen*" (p.143: 'he to-day, I to-morrow'). But we do not have to confine our view to the literature of penance. Duke Theseus in Chaucer's *Knight's Tale* presents a similar exemplary view towards the transgressions of Arcite and Palamon, on whom he is to pronounce judgement:

> And although that his ire hir gilt accused,
> Yet in his resoun he hem bothe excused,
> As thus: he thoghte wel that every man
> Wol helpe hymself in love, if that he kan,
> And eek delivere hymself out of prisoun.
> And eek his herte hadde compassioun
> Of wommen, for they wepen evere in oon,
> And in his gentil herte he thoughte anon,
> And softe unto hymself he seyde, "Fy
> Upon a lord that wol have no mercy...   (1765-74)

(And although his anger blamed their guilt, yet allowing his reason to prevail he excused them both: he considered that in matters of love every man will help himself if he can, and that a man will naturally escape from his prison. Moreover his heart had compas-

sion for women, for they weep continually.[15] And in his noble
heart he reached this conclusion at once, and softly said to himself, "Shame on a lord who refuses to show mercy...)

Theseus' attitude reflects the medieval contempt for a plodding sense
of justice and extols the idea that 'justice without mercy is but cruelty' and that 'mercy transcends justice'. Gawain's and Bertilak's reactions, then, are complementary, both reflecting exemplary conduct, Gawain in the unconditional nature of his remorse, Bertilak in
his spirit of jovial magnanimity. The same may be said of the reaction of Arthur's court; it has the same implications as the cheering
remarks of Bertilak. Arthur comforts Gawain, who is still suffering
from the after-pains of his ordeal. The laughter of Arthur and the
court should not be interpreted as insensibility to what Gawain has
gone through, leaving him isolated in his shame. Still less is the
courtiers' adoption of the green baldric to be taken as an ironical reflection on their morals, since they adopt as a sign of triumph what to
Gawain is a sign of shame. There is no indication in the poem that
justifies us in imputing this kind of moral callousness to Arthur's
court. Rather their action reflects that spirit of fellow-feeling that
puts the best possible construction on the endeavours of one's peers.
Their attitude is the perfect courtly and Christian counterpart of the
image that Gawain has of himself as the lost sheep returning to the
fold. It fittingly provides the happy ending that the story calls for.

[15] Or: 'wept continually', since the reference is probably to Theseus' wife and
Emelye specifically.

REFERENCES

Amis and Amiloun. Ed. M. Leach. EETS, OS 203 (1937; repr. 1960).
Ancrene Wisse. Ed. J.R.R. Tolkien. EETS, OS 249 (1962).
Benson, Larry D. (1965). *Art and Tradition in* Sir Gawain and the Green Knight.
    New Brunswick, N.J.: Rutgers University Press.
Blanch, Robert J. (ed.) (1966). Sir Gawain *and* Pearl: *Critical Essays.* Bloom-
    ington, Ind., and London: Indiana University Press.
Block, E.A. (1953). Originality, Controlling Purpose, and Craftsmanship in
    Chaucer's *Man of Law's Tale. PMLA* 68. 572-616.
Book of the Knight of La Tour-Landry, The. Ed. Thomas Wright. Rev. ed.
    EETS, OS 33 (1906; repr. 1973; 1st ed., 1868).
Brewer, D.S. (1966). Courtesy and the Gawain-Poet. In: *Patterns of Love and
    Courtesy. Essays in Memory of C.S. Lewis.* Ed. John Lawlor. London:
    Edward Arnold. 54-85.
Brewer, Derek (1976). The Interpretation of Dream, Folktale and Romance with
    Special Reference to *Sir Gawain and the Green Knight. Neuphilologische
    Mitteilungen* 77. 569-85.
Brewer, Derek (1978). The Nature of Romance. *Poetica* 9. 9-48.
Brewer, Derek (1980). *Symbolic Stories: Traditional Narratives of the Family
    Drama in English Literature.* Woodbridge, Suff.: D.S. Brewer and Rowman
    & Littlefield.
Burrow, J.A. (1965). *A Reading of* Sir Gawain and the Green Knight. London:
    Routledge and Kegan Paul.
Chaucer, Geoffrey. *The Riverside Chaucer.* Ed. L.D. Benson. Boston: Hough-
    ton Mifflin. 1987.
Emaré. In: French and Hale, 1964:i.423-55.
Foley, Michael M. (1974). Gawain's Two Confessions Reconsidered. *Chaucer
    Review* 9. 73-9.
French, W.H. and C.B. Hale (eds.) (1964). *Middle English Metrical Romances.*
    2 Vols. New York: Russell and Russell (1st publ., 1930).
Friedman, Albert B. (1966). Morgan le Fay in *Sir Gawain and the Green Knight.*
    In: Blanch, 1966:135-58. (Repr. from *Speculum* 35 [1960]. 260-74.)
Fromm, Erich (1952). *The Forgotten Language: An Introduction to the Under-
    standing of Dreams, Fairy Tales and Myths.* London: Victor Gollancz.
Gamelyn. In: Sands, 1966:154-81.
Green, Richard Hamilton (1966). Gawain's Shield and the Quest for Perfection.
    In: Blanch, 1966:176-94. (Repr. from *Journal of English Literary History*
    29 [1962]. 121-39.)
Havelok. In: *Medieval English Romances.* Ed. A.V.C. Schmidt and N. Jacobs. 2
    Vols. London: Hodder and Stoughton. 1980. i.37-121.
Hill, Thomas D. (1980). Gawain's Jesting Lie: Towards an Interpretation of the
    Confessional Scene in *Gawain and the Green Knight. Studia Neophilologica*
    52. 279-86.
Ker, W.P. (1955). *Medieval English Literature.* London: Oxford University
    Press (1st ed., 1912).
Lay le Freine. In: Sands, 1966:233-45.
Lottin, Odon (1942-60). *Psychologie et morale aux XIIe et XIIIe siècles.* 6 Vols.
    Louvain: Abbaye du Mont César, and Gembloux: J. Duculot.
Lottin, Odon (1949). *La connexion des vertus chez saint Thomas d'Aquin et ses
    prédécesseurs.* In: Lottin, 1942-60: Vol.III, part 2, ch.xiii. 197-252.

Lottin, Odon (1954). *La connexion des vertus morales acquises de saint Thomas d'Aquin à Jean Duns Scot*. In: Lottin, 1942-60: Vol.IV, part 3.ii, ch.xxv. 551-663.

Malory, Sir Thomas. *The Works of Sir Thomas Malory*. Ed. Eugène Vinaver. London: Oxford University Press. 1954.

Michel, A. (1950). *Vertu*. In: *Dictionnaire de Théologie Catholique*. Paris. Vol. xv. 2784-91.

Nicholls, Jonathan (1985). *The Matter of Courtesy: Medieval Courtesy Books and the Gawain-Poet*. Woodbridge, Suff.: D.S. Brewer.

Peraldus, Gulielmus. *Summa Vitiorum*. Antwerp: Apud Martinum Nutium.1587.

Saltrey, H. [?Henry] of. *Saint Patrick's Purgatory: A Twelfth Century Tale of a Journey to the Other World*. Trans. Jean-Michel Picard. Intro. Yolande de Pontfarcy. Dublin: Four Courts Press. 1985.

Sands, Donald B. (ed.) (1966). *Middle English Verse Romances*. New York and London: Holt, Rinehart and Winston.

Sir Gawain and the Green Knight. Ed. I. Gollancz. EETS, OS 210 (1940; repr. 1966).

Sir Gawain and the Green Knight. Ed. J.R.R. Tolkien and E.V. Gordon. 2nd ed. rev. N. Davis. Oxford: Oxford University Press. 1967 (1st ed., 1925).

Spearing, A.C. (1972). *Criticism and Medieval Poetry*. 2nd ed. London: Edward Arnold (1st ed., 1964).

Speirs, John (1957). *Medieval English Poetry. The Non-Chaucerian Tradition*. London: Faber and Faber.

Squire of Low Degree, The. In: French and Hale, 1964:ii.721-55.

Utz, F.M. (1937). *De connexione virtutum moralium inter se secundum doctrinam St. Thomae Aquinatis*. Vechta in Oldenburg: Albertus Magnus-Verlag der Dominikaner.

GAME AND EARNEST
IN
SIR GAWAIN AND THE GREEN KNIGHT *

HENK AERTSEN

"Medieval life was brimful of play." The Dutch historian Johan Huizinga makes this claim in *Homo Ludens*, a 'study of the play element
in culture', as the subtitle puts it. In this analysis of the various aspects of culture *sub specie ludi* Huizinga comes to the conclusion that
there is a "play factor" in all of the major civilising activities, from
ritual to poetry to warfare, though not in modern warfare, which he
says "has on the face of it, lost all contact with play" (1970:237). In
an earlier study, *The Waning of the Middle Ages*, he had briefly
pointed to elements of play in medieval society; these lay in the idea
of chivalry, which, according to the chroniclers, reduced in the fifteenth century the motives and course of history to "a spectacle of the
honour of princes and the virtues of knights, to a noble game with
edifying and heroic rules" (1955:68); with regard to "the noble
sports, tourneys and jousts" he observes (1955:80):

> Sportive struggles always and everywhere contain a
> strong dramatic element and an erotic element. In the
> medieval tournament these two elements had so much
> got the upper hand, that its character of a contest of
> force and courage had been almost obliterated by its
> romantic purport. With its bizarre accoutrements and
> pompous staging, its poetical illusion and pathos, it fill-
> ed the place of the drama of a later stage.

Hence he concludes (1955:80):

> The life of the aristocracies when they are still strong,
> though of small utility, tends to become an all-round
> game. In order to forget the painful imperfection of re-

* The research for this paper was carried out within the framework of the Free
University of Amsterdam research project "Exposition of Texts from Older
Tongues" (LETT 88/11), financed by the Dutch Ministry of Education.

ality, the nobles turn to the continual illusion of a high
and heroic life. They wear the mask of Lancelot and of
Tristram.

In *Homo Ludens* Huizinga specifically deals with the play element in
culture throughout history, and the medieval period is one of the
civilisations examined (1970:205):

> Medieval life was brimful of play: the joyous and unbut-
> toned play of the people, full of pagan elements that had
> lost their sacred significance and been transformed into
> jesting and buffoonery, or the solemn and pompous play
> of chivalry, the sophisticated play of courtly love, etc.
> ... The initiation and dubbing of knights, the enfeoffing
> of a tenure, tournaments, heraldry, chivalric orders,
> vows—all these things hark beyond the classical to a
> purely archaic past [i.e. a Celto-Romanic rather than a
> Graeco-Roman past], and in all of them the play-factor
> is powerfully operative and a really creative force. ...
> In fine, the influence of the play-spirit was extrava-
> gantly great in the Middle Ages, not on the inward
> structure of its institutions, which was largely classical
> in origin, but on the ceremonial with which that struc-
> ture was expressed and embellished.

Although it is true that Huizinga was so obsessed with play that he
saw instances and elements of play almost everywhere, his statement
that "medieval life was brimful of play" is scarcely an exaggeration.
This does not mean that medieval life was not serious, harsh or cruel:
the consequences of the Black Death, of the long wars dragging on
endlessly, of the feudal system, affected life in the Middle Ages enor-
mously, but one could say that people in the Middle Ages armed
themselves against these hardships by inventing games and by looking on life itself as a game so as to soften the dire consequences of
these hardships.

When confronted with the opinion that medieval life is brimful of play, the medievalist-philologist will instinctively turn to his
domain to see how the play concept is expressed in it: thus he will
consider the language and literature of the period, and with regard to
Middle English literature there are a number of features that will
strike him at once. First, the best-known literary work produced in
this period, Chaucer's *Canterbury Tales*, is a framework story in

which the framework is a game in two respects: the pilgrimage to Canterbury is, at least for some of the pilgrims, a kind of medieval holiday (cf. Robinson's note to 1.465 of the *General Prologue*: "the pilgrimage in Chaucer's day was a favorite form of traveling for pleasure" [1957:663][1]), and at the end of the General Prologue the Host devises the plan of the story-telling contest with a referee, a prize to be won, penalties for those not abiding by the referee's decisions, etc. Secondly, the best example of courtly romance in Middle English, *Sir Gawain and the Green Knight* (henceforth *SGGK*), is in fact a long series of games, each played according to the rules appropriate to the game in question. In the analysis below we shall examine how Huizinga's theory of play relates to this romance.

In the course of his study of the play element in culture Huizinga defines the "play concept" three times (1970:32, 47, 154); these three definitions are basically the same, although in the later definitions Huizinga adds a few important subsidiary features. His first definition runs as follows:

> Summing up the formal characteristics of play, we might call it a free activity standing quite consciously outside 'ordinary' life as being 'not serious', but at the same time absorbing the player intensely and utterly. It is an activity connected with no material interest, and no profit can be gained by it. It proceeds within its own proper boundaries of time and space according to fixed rules and in an orderly manner. It promotes the formation of social groupings which tend to surround themselves with secrecy and to stress their difference from the common world by disguise or other means.

In this definition, Caillois says (1961:4), "all the words are important and meaningful." For reasons of space we cannot quote the other definitions here, but conflating all three definitions, we arrive at the following seven characteristics of play:

---

[1] Unfortunately, this note has not been retained in the *Riverside Chaucer*, where we now read instead: "A love of pilgrimages, for illicit purposes, is typical of women in estates satire ... In her Prologue (III.551-62), the Wife [of Bath] makes clear that her pilgrimages were not for devotional purposes" (Benson, 1987:818).

1. it is a voluntary activity or occupation;
2. it is executed within fixed limits of time and space;
3. it is subject to rules freely accepted but absolutely binding;
4. it has its aim in itself: it is outside the sphere of necessity or material utility;
5. it is accompanied by a feeling of tension and joy;
6. it is different from ordinary life;
7. it is followed by mirth and relaxation.

It is significant that in the later definitions Huizinga no longer says that play is different from ordinary life in that it is not serious, because on one of the pages leading up to the first definition he had argued in fact (1970:24) that "some play can be very serious indeed. ... Children's games, football, and chess are played in profound seriousness; the players have not the slightest inclination to laugh." Play cannot be equated with non-seriousness, because play, like laughter and the comic, is only a category coming under the heading 'non-seriousness': "laughter ... is in a sense the opposite of serious-ness without being absolutely bound up with play", and similarly the comic "has certain affinities with laughter—it provokes laughter. But its relation to play is subsidiary." And Huizinga goes on to argue (1970:24):

> Play is not foolish. It lies outside the antithesis of wis-dom and folly. The later Middle Ages tended to express the two cardinal moods of life—play and seriousness—somewhat imperfectly by opposing *folie* to *sense*, until Erasmus in his *Laus Stultitiae* showed the inadequacy of the contrast.

"Play and seriousness" as "the two cardinal moods of life"—in Mid-dle English these concepts are found in a single idiomatic expression, *in ernest or in game*, which was very frequent and may even have been a common medieval type of idiom, as it is also found, for in-stance, in Middle High German (*mit erneste und mit spiel*; see Aert-sen, 1987:74). The high frequency of occurrence of this particular phrase in Middle English, together with the occurrence of similar phrases in the other medieval vernaculars, may indeed support our claim made above that Huizinga's observation that "medieval life was brimful of play" does not imply that medieval life was not serious.

Huizinga himself comments on the relation between play and seriousness, when he says (1970:64):

The conceptual value of a word is always conditioned by
the word which expresses its opposite. For us, the opposite of play is *earnest*, also used in the more special sense
of *work*; while the opposite of earnest can either be play
or jesting, joking. However, the complementary pair of
opposites *play-earnest* is the more important.

After discussing the various words which different languages have to
express the notion 'earnest', he reaches the following conclusion
(1970:65):

observing the play-earnest antithesis somewhat more
closely, we find that the two terms are not of equal value: play is positive, earnest negative. The significance of
'earnest' is defined by and exhausted in the negation of
'play' – earnest is simply 'not playing' and nothing
more. The significance of 'play', on the other hand, is
by no means defined or exhausted by calling it 'not earnest', or 'not serious'. Play is a thing by itself. The play-
concept as such is of a higher order than is seriousness.
For seriousness seeks to exclude play, whereas play can
very well include seriousness.

The "play-earnest antithesis" is one of the underlying themes of
SGGK, as we will show in the reading of the romance given below.
This does not in any way deny other interpretations of the poem: that
it can be read in several ways simply attests to the great skill and
versatility of the poet.

As Davis (1968:324) points out in his review of the *Concordance* by
Kottler and Markman, *SGGK* is the only one of the poems written by
or attributed to the *Gawain* poet "in which there is any *game* or
gomen (which together appear 13 times[2])." The reason for its absence in *Cleanness, Patience, Pearl* and *St.Erkenwald* can only be
guessed at; it may have to do with the didactic-moralistic subject
matter of these poems, but, if so, the presence in these poems of *plei*
and *leik*, the meaning of both of which is similar to that of *game*,
would be equally difficult to explain. It is perhaps easier to explain

---

[2] This number only refers to the instances of the noun in the singular; in addition
there are in *SGGK* five occurrences of the plural *gamnez* or *gomnez*.

why *game* is so frequent in *SGGK*: Cook (1963) and Stevens (1972) have shown that the play concept figures prominently in this romance, with regard to its subject matter as well as with regard to its structure and stanza form. Stevens, for instance, quotes Huizinga's description of the function of play "as a contest *for* something or a representation *of* something" (Huizinga, 1970:32; Huizinga's emphasis), and both aspects of play are clearly present in the poem, Stevens says (1972:69):

> play as contest ... forms the basic narrative substance of *Sir Gawain* ... Clearly play as representation inheres in the holiday atmosphere. The song, the jest, the feast are part of the poem's landscape of play. But it inheres also in the poetic texture with its multitude of verbal tricks and decorations. The very stanza, with its long lines of explosive alliteration, its one-stressed bob, and its tail section of rhyme, combines the range of options in Middle English versification. Irregular in length, embroidered by every device known to mediaeval rhetoric, alliterating now by two's and now by four's, the stanzas move forward in an unruly sort of order. Behind it all is a playful poet, who, only once, peeks out from behind its fabric to announce that he will tell the whole outrageous adventure as he heard men tell it "with lel letteres loken" [(l.35: 'embodied in truthful words', *SGGK*, p.72, note to ll.35-6)] ... The poem is a sheer tour de force, full of artful play and delight.

As a matter of fact, this playful poet peeks out more than once from behind its fabric: especially in the rhyming sections rounding off the stanzas, he can be said to intervene in the narrative on a number of occasions. When he does so, he brings, as it were, the action to a brief standstill for a summary of events or for a personal comment, thereby relieving the tension momentarily, and frequently he addresses the audience directly. For instance, at the end of the third fitt, on the eve of the hero's decisive encounter with the Green Knight, the poet inserts this bob and wheel[3]:

---

[3] All quotations from the poem are from the Tolkien and Gordon edition as revised by Norman Davis. The translations are my own, unless stated otherwise.

> Let hym liȝe þere stille,
> He hatz nere þat he soȝt;
> And ȝe wyl a whyle be stylle
> I schal telle yow how þay wroȝt.   (1994-7)

> (Let him there undisturbed; he has close at hand what he was looking for; if you will be silent for a while, I shall tell you how they acted.)

Nothing substantial is added to the plot, the action or events of the poem by these lines; they merely act as a kind of punctuation in the narrative. Similarly, at the end of the first fitt, the poet steps in and has some practical advice for Gawain:

> Now þenk wel, Sir Gawan,
> For woþe þat þou ne wonde
> Þis auenture for to frayn
> Þat þou hatz tan on honde.   (487-90)

> (Now because of the danger take good heed, Sir Gawain, that you do not neglect for fear to make a trial of this adventure that you have taken on your hands.)

Here again the function of the bob and wheel is to provide a break in the narrative, not to add anything to it. If we think of the oral tradition and the actual recitation of this romance, it may well be that the long alliterative lines were said or perhaps chanted to a rhythm provided by a minstrel on a harp or similar instrument and that the concluding sections of the bob and wheel were actually sung. In this way the presentation would allow an additional contrast between the long alliterative lines which contain the basic narrative substance, and the rhyming lines of the bob and wheel which generally contain some kind of subjective statement by the poet.

Stevens sees the poet's playful mood also reflected in the vocabulary of the poem which makes "pervasive reference to game, laughter and festival" (1972:68), as can be deduced from the number of occurrences of words denoting these concepts, and, after making an observation similar to the one by Davis quoted above, he notes (1972:67):

> Everything from the duel, to story telling, love making, deer and fox hunting, polite conversation, even the pentangle, is at one time or other called "game". The Green Knight's challenge is twice explicitly named a "Cryste-

mas gomen" (283, 683), and the Christmas season itself
on one occasion is referred to as a 'layk", meaning
"game, fun, sport", ... a full synonym of *game*.[4]

This word *layk* occurs nine times in all (noun and verb together),
play five times (noun and verb), *jape* 'joke' twice, *bourde* (noun and
verb) '(to) jest' five times; in addition, there are fourteen instances of

---

[4] Stevens does not provide line references for these instances of *game*. The examples relating to "story telling" and "polite conversation"are hard to pin down with
certainty, but the other instances he mentions can be identified as:
  - duel, 1.365: *Ryche togeder con roun, / And sypen þay redden alle same / To
ryd þe kyng wyth croun, / And gif Gawan þe game.* (ll.362-5: 'The nobles took
whispered counsel together, after which they unanimously advised to relieve the
crowned king of the duel and to give it to Gawain.');
  - love making, 1.1532: *I com hider sengel, and sitte / To lerne at yow sum
game; / Dos, techez me of your wytte, / Whil my lorde is fro hame.* (ll.1531-4: 'I
have come here all alone, and I am sitting here to learn from you some love-mak-
ing; come, teach me from your cleverness, while my lord is away from home.');
  - deer hunting, 1.1319: *And ay þe lorde of þe londe is lent on his gamnez, /
To hunt in holtez and heþe at hyndez barayne.* (ll.1319-20: 'And all the time the
lord of the land is occupied in his sports, hunting barren hinds in woods and
heaths.');
  - fox hunting, 1.1894: *3et is þe lorde on þe launde ledande his gomnes. / He
hatz forfaren þis fox þat he fol3ed longe.* (ll.1894-5: 'Still the lord is pursuing his
sports in the field; he has headed off the fox that he pursued for a long time.');
  - pentangle, 1.661: *Now alle þese fyue sypez, for soþe, were fetled on þis
kny3t, / And vchone halched in oþer, þat non ende hade, / And fyched vpon fyue
poyntez, þat fayld neuer, / Ne samned neuer in no syde, ne sundred nouþer, /
Withouten ende at any noke I oquere fynde, / Whereeuer þe gomen bygan, or
glod to an ende.* (ll.656-61: 'Now all these five groups, in truth, were fastened
upon this knight, and each one joined to another so that none had an end; and
were fixed upon five points that were never wanting; nor did they come together
on any side, or come apart either, without end at any corner that I find anywhere,
wherever the tracing [i.e. the process of drawing] began or came to an end.'
[*SGGK*, p.96, note to 1.656]);
  - the Christmas game, 1.283: *Forþy I craue in þis court as Crystemas gomen,
/ For hit is 3ol and Nwe 3er, and here ar 3ep mony* (ll.283-4: 'Therefore I ask in
this court for a Chrsitmas game, for it is the season of Christmas and the New
Year, and there are many valiant knights here.'); and 1.683: *Who knew euer any
kyng such counsel to take / As kny3tez in cauelaciounz on Crystmasse gomnez!*
(ll.682-3: 'Who ever knew any king to take such advice, as knights were engaged
in trifling disputes during their Christmas diversions!').
  - the Christmas season, 1.1023: *Much dut watz þer dryuen þat day and þat
oþer, / And þe þryd as þro þronge in þerafter; / Þe ioye of sayn Jonez day watz
gentyle to here, / And watz þe last of þe layk, leudez þer þo3ten* (ll.1020-3:
'Great merriment was made there that day and the next, and the third day equally
crowded with delight came immediately after; the joy of St. John's Day was delightful to hear and was the last of the festivity, so knights there remembered').

mirthe in its various spellings, eleven of *ioye*, seven of *fest* 'feast, festival', two of *mynstralcie* 'music', and two of *haliday* 'festival'.[5] Laughter is also frequent in the poem, as there are twenty-one instances of *laȝe* (verb) and *laȝter* (noun) combined: "everybody in the poem seems to laugh at one time or another and even in the most difficult moments" (Stevens, 1972:67). The ladies at Arthur's court laugh (1.69: *Ladies laȝed ful loude, þoȝ þay lost haden* 'Ladies laughed very loudly, even if they had lost'); the Green Knight laughs when no one dares to accept his challenge (1.316: *Wyth þis he laȝes so loude þat þe lorde greued* 'Thereupon he laughs so loudly that the lord is dismayed'); Arthur and Gawain laugh when they see the Green Knight ride off (1.464: *Þe kyng and Gawan þare / At þat grene þay laȝe and grenne* 'There the king and Gawain laugh and grin at that green one'); Bertilak laughs when he learns that Gawain has arrived at his castle (1.909: *Loude laȝed he þerat* 'Loudly he laughed at it'); Gawain laughs when he has "learnt of the whereabouts of the Green Chapel" (Burrow, 1965:84-85; 1.1079: *Þenne watz Gawan ful glad, and gomenly he laȝed* 'Then Gawain was very glad, and merrily he laughed'); the lady laughs on each of her three visits to Gawain (1.1212: *Al laȝande þe lady lanced þo bourdez* 'The lady laughed as she uttered these playful words'; 1.1479: *And ho ... settez hir softly by his syde, and swyþely ho laȝez* 'And she ... sits down softly by his side and quickly she smiles'; 1.1757: *Þe lady luflych com laȝande swete* 'The lovely lady came, laughing sweetly'); and the entire court at Camelot laughs when Gawain returns (1.2514: *Þe kyng comfortez þe knyȝt, and alle þe court als / Laȝen loude þerat* 'The king comforts the knight, and the entire court too laugh loudly at this').

In this context it is therefore noteworthy (a point not made by Stevens) that on the third day of the Exchange of Winnings neither the lord of the castle nor Gawain laughs, whereas they both laughed when they first made their agreement:

'Who bryngez vus þis beuerage, þis bargayn is maked':
So sayde þe lorde of þat lede; þay laȝed vchone. (1112-3)

('If anyone will bring us the drink (with which to seal this agreement), this agreement is made', so spoke the lord of that company; they laughed each of them.)

---

[5] Stevens' figures are slightly different, because he sometimes disregards plural forms and does not always combine the instances of verb and noun.

Likewise they both laugh after they had completed the first exchange of winnings:

> Þay laȝed, and made hem blyþe
> Wyth lotez þat were to lowe.   (1398-9)

(They laughed, and made merry with words full of praise.)

However, on the second day it is only the lord who laughs: he does so when he catches sight of Gawain, i.e. before the actual exchange takes place:

> Þe lorde ful lowde with lote and laȝter myry,
> When he seȝe Sir Gawayn, with solace he spekez.
> (1623-4)

(Very loudly, with merry speech and laughter, the lord speaks joyfully, when he sees Sir Gawain.)

but on the third day neither of them laughs before, during or after the exchange, and although the exchange is followed by the usual merrymaking in the castle hall[6] (ll.1952-3), Gawain and his host are merely glad (1.1955) and it is the ladies in the hall who laugh (1.1954):

> With merþe and mynstralsye, wyth metez at hor wylle,
> Þay maden as mery as any men moȝten—
> With laȝyng of ladies, with lotez of bordes
> Gawayn and þe godemon so glad were þay boþe. (1952-5)

(With entertainment and music, with dishes to their pleasure, they enjoyed themselves as much as any men might—with laughing of ladies, with words of jests, so glad were Gawain and the master of the house.)

Could it be that there is no laughter in Gawain or his host on the third day, because Gawain, on the one hand, is too preoccupied with whatever is going to take place at the Green Chapel the next day, and per-

---

[6] Burrow believes that the function of these scenes of dining and drinking is "to establish this fact in the reader's imagination — host and guest becoming 'fellows' as they feast together over Christmas" (1965:95). The Exchange of Winnings is from this point of view "a gesture of fellowship". It will be remembered that felaȝschyp (1.652) is one of Gawain's virtues.

haps also with his impending breach of the agreement by keeping back the girdle, while his host, on the other hand, senses the tension of the situation: will Gawain live up to his word as a knight or not? After all, as we are told later, the lord of the castle himself has devised Gawain's temptation by his wife (l.2361). When the third exchange is made—though not really completed, because Gawain does not hand over the girdle—neither Gawain nor Bertilak has reason to laugh during the merrymaking that follows, Gawain feeling guilty and Bertilak being disappointed at Gawain's deceit. It might be argued that Gawain does not really feel guilty, since he went to confession immediately after the lady's third visit and before the exchange is made, and he was completely absolved by the priest. Elsewhere in this volume Diekstra comments on this confession and on how it may, and perhaps should, be interpreted. Whether Gawain feels guilty or not, it is a fact that Gawain's thoughts are more on his encounter with the Green Knight the next day than on merrymaking at dinner, because we are told in the same stanza that Gawain asks Bertilak again for directions how to get to the Green Chapel, reminding Bertilak of his promise to help him find it (ll.1069-70). Bertilak replies, *"In god faype, ... wyth a goud wylle / Al þat euer I yow hy3t halde schal I redé"* (ll.1969-70: 'In truth, ... all that I have ever promised you I shall gladly hold ready'), and then assigns a servant to Gawain to act as his guide. In other words, in this stanza, the last but one of Fitt Three, the emphasis seems to be very much on Gawain's preoccupation with the events of the next day. Stevens rightly observes that from the moment the Green Knight rushes into the hall at Camelot, "game and earnest are inextricably entwined" (1972: 68), and the exchange of winnings on the third day illustrates this very well.

Interesting parallels to this observation by Stevens are provided by Bergner and Burrow. Bergner (1986:404) calls attention to the symbols carried by the Green Knight as he enters Arthur's court:

> These are 'a holyn bobbe' (line 206) and 'an ax' (line 208), which clearly stand for peace *and* war, jest *and* earnest, two extremes which are obviously reflected in the Green Knight's appearance, two extremes between which the narrative consistently and constantly moves.

That the narrative indeed moves between these extremes is seen not only in the third exchange of winnings discussed above, but also in the fact that the Green knight explains the significance of the first of his two symbols only:

> 3e may be seker bi þis braunch þat I bere here
> Þat I passe as in pes, and no ply3t seche.   (265-6)
>
> (By the branch that I carry you may be assured that I proceed in peace and seek no hositility.)

By making the Green Knight at this stage explicitly interpret the meaning of the holly branch but not of the axe (that comes later, when he discloses the terms of the Christmas game that he is looking for), the poet aims at, and succeeds in, creating the lighter, more playful and less serious atmosphere that he needs as the setting for the Christmas game. Burrow speaks of the "complicated game-earnest ambivalence of the Green Knight in the first fitt" (1965:24), and this statement will be discussed below in its proper context.

If the testing of Gawain's "constancy, courtesy and chastity" (cf. Berry, 1959:152) is one of the underlying themes of the poem, play as contest—the other function of play according to Huizinga (see above)—might be called the plot, and is represented in the poem as two distinct games: the Beheading Game, referred to by the Green Knight as "*a Crystemas gomen*" (1.283; quoted in note 4 above), and the Exchange of Winnings, referred to by Gawain as something that the lord of the castle is pleased to *layke*, i.e. play or amuse himself with (1.1111: *And þat yow lyst for to layke, lef hit me þynkes.* 'it seems to be delightful that it pleases you to play').

The Beheading Game results from the Green Knight's challenging King Arthur to a duel. To accept this challenge is to accept the rules of the duel (cf. Huizinga's second definition of play as "a *voluntary* activity ... executed ... according to *rules freely accepted* ..." [1970:47; my emphasis]), and it is precisely the terms of the duel dictated by the challenger, rather than the fear of death, that are the cause of Arthur's hesitation to accept the challenge (this also goes for all the others at Arthur's court, including Gawain). As Stevens assumes (1972:69f), the duel by alternation, by which the knight accepting the challenge is allowed to strike one blow at the Green Knight but will have to take a return blow in a year's time, puts the champion in an awkward position, since the code of chivalry demands that the knight do his utmost, i.e. deal a fatal blow, while to do so would at the same time prevent the completion of the game as provided by the rules, the opponent having been killed and therefore unable to deal the return blow. In other words, the knight accepting the challenge and thereby accepting the terms of the duel will, by performing in the way that chivalry requires of him as a knight, become a spoilsport, since the second leg of the game—to use a modern sports idiom—cannot be played. If Stevens' assumption is correct, the dilemma that Gawain is faced with—to deal a fatal blow and be a spoilsport, or to fail as a knight and play the full game according to the agreed terms—is the first test of Gawain's constancy and honour as a knight, and illustrates the interplay of game and earnest in the poem.

However, the narrative takes a different turn, as we know. The Green Knight, as a supernatural being (one of the implications of the colour green), is not subject to the ordinary laws of nature: he is able to pick up his severed head and deliver a long speech, exhorting Gawain to show up for the return blow according to the agreed terms of the duel. Stevens claims that the Green Knight "exacted a binding agreement under false pretenses" (1972:70), because he knew in advance that no harm could come to him, so that the risk involved in the game was not the same for the two contestants, and as a result Gawain, the sure winner at the outset, is now destined to lose. The weak point in Stevens' argument is that a contract obtained with false pretences is, normally speaking, null and void in any court of law, but no one at Arthur's court raises his voice in protest, once it is clear that Gawain's opponent is no ordinary mortal; the counterargument could be, it is true, that a knight of the Round Table would not resort to legal technicalities and would stand by his word as a knight.

Moreover, when the Green Knight announces the terms of the duel—the rules of the game—for the first time, he does so in "grave, formal and rather legalistic language", as Burrow puts it (1965:22):

If any so harde in þis hous holdez hymseluen,
Be so bolde in his blod, brayn in hys hede,
Þat dar stifly strike a strok for an oþer,
I schal gif hym of my gyft þys giserne ryche,
Þis ax, þat is heué innogh, to hondele as hym lykes,
And I schal bide þe fyrst bur as bare as I sitte.
If any freke be so felle to fonde þat I telle,
Lepe ly3tly me to, and lach þis weppen,
I quit-clayme hit for euer, kepe hit as his auen,
And I schal stonde hym a strok, stif on þis flet,
Ellez *þou wyl di3t me þe dom* to dele hym an oþer
    barlay,

> And 3et *gif hym respite,*
> *A twelmonyth and a day*;
> Now hy3e, and lct se tite
> Dar any herinne o3t say. _____(285-300)

(If there is anyone in this house who considers himself to be so
brave, so bold in his blood and so mad in his head, that he fear-
lessly dares to strike a blow in return for another, I shall give to
him as a gift this noble battle-axe, this axe which is exceedingly
heavy, to take hold of as he pleases, and I shall withstand the first
blow, not wearing any armour, just as I sit here. If there is any
man bold enough to try what I am speaking of, let him run to me
quickly and let him take hold of this weapon—I renounce it for
ever, he may keep it as his own. And, unflinching in this hall, I
shall stand and take a blow from him, provided that you will ad-
judge me the right to deal him another blow in my turn, and yet I
shall give a respite of a year and a day; now hasten and let see
quickly if there is anyone here who dares to say anything.)

The italicised phrases in this passage make Burrow (1965:22) conclude that

> this is more like the language of a legal contract than of
> a Christmas game. The Green Knight is inviting some
> one of Arthur's knights to bind himself 'bi statut', as
> Gawain later puts it [l.1060: 'by solemn legal agree-
> ment'; HA], to fulfil the conditions which he proposes.
> *Clearly this is 'earnest' rather than 'game'* [emphasis
> added; HA]—a vein of legal earnest which can be traced
> later in the scene.

The "vein of legal earnest" is seen again when the Green Knight
makes Gawain repeat the terms of the agreement, just before the latter delivers the first blow (ll.382-5), and here again the terminology
used is that of the law. The consequence of the use of this kind of
language is that "the complicated game-earnest ambivalence of the
Green Knight in the first fitt makes it *possible* for the hero to treat
his obligations lightly, but it does not make it *right* for him to do so"
(Burrow, 1965:24). It is therefore very clear that, as soon as the
Green Knight appears on the scene, game and earnest are indeed the
two extremes between which the narrative moves from then on.

Between the home and away games in the Beheading Game,
there is the other contest in the poem, the Exchange of Winnings or
Gifts, which is intended as a further test of Gawain's constancy,

courtesy and chastity. As Stevens points out, Huizinga (1970:83) has described the play quality of the 'gift ritual':

> its purpose is the mutual exchange ... of certain articles having no economic value[7] either as necessities or useful implements ... The whole proceeding is accompanied by all kinds of formalities interspersed with *feasting* and magic, in an atmosphere of *mutual obligation and trust*. *Hospitality* [emphasis added; HA] abounds, and at the end of the ceremony everybody feels he has had his full share of honour and glory.

"Feasting", "mutual obligation and trust", "hospitality", they are all important aspects of Gawain's stay at Bertilak's castle. This second type of contest is not "agonistic" in the sense that it can be won or lost, it is a contest for honour and glory which the contestants can win by matching each other's gifts. Such a competition for honour, Huizinga says, "may also take ... an inverted form by turning into a contest in politeness", and such a "courtesy-match" might be called "an inverted boasting-match, since the reason for this display of civility to others lies in an intense regard for one's own honour" (1970:87). Two other games are part of, or rather lead up to, the "courtesy-match" of the Exchange of Winnings: the hunt and the temptation. The temptation is in fact also a kind of hunt: the equation of hunting and wooing in courtly literature is found in Andreas Capellanus, who speaks of the service of Venus as a kind of hunting (Burrow, 1965:86, n.20). The contrast between these two games has often been noted (cf. Burrow, 1965:87): the hunt is an outdoor activity, the temptation an indoor activity. There is, however, another contrast which is perhaps more relevant: the Beheading Game starts off as a test of Gawain's physical strength, whereas the Exchange of Winnings is a test of his moral strength, since it tests his basic virtue as a knight, his *trawþe*, his fidelity or constancy, and in the final fitt of the poem the second part of the Beheading Game develops into a test of Gawain's moral strength as well. Gawain really is victorious only in the first part of the Beheading Game, and fails in the two tests of his moral strength; there instead of honour he only wins shame— having kept the girdle in the first test, and in the second flinching

---

[7] Huizinga's third definition of play explicitly mentions this aspect: "... outside the sphere of necessity or material utility." Cf. the seven characteristics of play given earlier in this chapter.

from the Green Knight's first attempt at a return blow, losing his temper after the second feigned attempt, and having his deceit revealed to him after being hit on the shoulder in the third attempt. Despite this, upon his return to Camelot the shame he has won is turned into honour, because no one there ever thought to see Gawain come back alive from the Green Chapel, and his return is interpreted as his success. Here again there is the contrast between the outer Gawain and the inner Gawain: the outer Gawain is successful, having survived the Beheading Game, which he was expected to lose, and that is what the Knights at Arthur's court see; the inner Gawain, however, has lost the tests of moral strength, but no one can see the shame that he feels within him, and even the symbol of his shame, the girdle, becomes to the others a symbol of honour.

With regard to the two games that are part of the Exchange of Winnings, Stevens notes that they were "elaborately codified in the Middle Ages, each with its own manuals of instruction" (1972:72); the rules and conventions governing the hunt are to be found in William Twiti's *Art de Venerie* and in the Duke of York's *Master of Game*, while the rules of courtship were laid down by Andreas Capellanus in his treatise *De Arte Honeste Amandi*. But whereas the hunt is played according to the rules, the close season, for instance, being strictly observed (ll.1156-7; cf. the note to these lines on p.107), Stevens claims that the courtship is not, since there is "an exact reversal of roles", as the lady is the seducer, not the man, and the lady plays the active part while Gawain remains passive and inert, quite in contrast with his character. Although this interpretation seems to be supported by Gollancz's reading of l.1237, *ȝe ar welcum to my cors* 'You are welcome to my body', where the lady's "bluntness in coming to the point testifies to her inexperience in such a role" (note in Gollancz's edition, p.113), I feel that Stevens' claim is not fully convincing. The line just quoted can readily be given a different explanation, 'You are welcome to me', as is done by Burrow (1965:81) and by Davis in a note to this line, pp.108-9. Moreover, Burrow's remark (1965:79) that "in *Troilus*, as in *SGGK*, it is the woman who dominates (emprisons, commands) the man" suggests that the situation in *SGGK* is by no means exceptional, and in the poems of Charles d'Orleans the lady plays a similar role of dominance. Gawain's inertness is, contrary to what Stevens claims, quite in keeping with his character, as it stems from his virtues of *clannes* and *cortaysye* (l.653): as a knight he should on no account displease or offend the lady, but at the same time he should preserve his *clannes*, his purity, his freedom from sin, in this case his chastity, and this dilemma forces him into a passive role. Kissing her was simply a matter of obeying her order, and was not necessarily adulterous in itself (Burrow, 1965:85). If the lady's seduction of Gawain had taken the two of them beyond the kissing stage, Stevens' point would have been valid, but it is unlikely that the *Gawain* poet had such intentions with the narrative, because adulterous courtly love "seems to play little or no part in fourteenth-century English ideals of courtesy" (Burrow, 1965:84).

The play element in *Gawain* cannot be mistaken: it is realized in the plot in various ways, in the stanza form and in the vocabulary. Yet one is conscious all the time of the tension which, as Huizinga says in his second and third definitions of play (cf. the fifth characteristic of play on p.86 above), accompanies play; this, indeed, is one of the dramatic effects in the poem. The *Gawain*-poet thus combines game and earnest but never forgets to include laughter, sometimes reduced to a nervous smile, to relieve the tension (as, for instance, when Gawain returns to Camelot, uncertain of how he will be received after the disclosure of his shame at the Green Chapel). It is hardly surprising, therefore, that there should be so many references to *game* (and laughter) in the poem.

REFERENCES

Aertsen, H. (1987). *Play in Middle English. A Contribution to Word Field Theory*. Amsterdam: Free University Press.
Bergner, H. (1986). The Two Courts. Two Modes of Existence in 'Sir Gawain and the Green Knight'. *English Studies* 67. 401-16.
Berry, F. (1959). *Sir Gawayne and the Grene Knight*. In: *The Pelican Guide to English Literature*. Ed. B. Ford. Vol.I: *The Age of Chaucer*. Harmondsworth: Penguin. 148-58.
Burrow, J.A. (1965). *A Reading of* Sir Gawain and the Green Knight. London: Routledge and Kegan Paul.
Caillois, R. (1961). *Man, Play, and Games*. Trans. M. Barash. New York: Free Press of Glencoe. (Translation of *Les jeux et les hommes*. Paris: Gallimard. 1958).
Chaucer, Geoffrey. *The Complete Works of Geoffrey Chaucer*. Ed. F.N. Robinson. 2nd ed. Boston: Houghton Mifflin. 1957 (1st ed., 1933).
Chaucer, Geoffrey. *The Riverside Chaucer*. Ed. L.D. Benson. Boston: Houghton Mifflin. 1987.
Cook, R.G. (1963). The Play-Element in *Sir Gawain and the Green Knight*. *Tulane Studies in English* 13. 5-31.

Davis, N. (1968). Review of *A Concordance to Five Middle English Poems: Cleanness, St. Erkenwald, Sir Gawain and the Green Knight, Patience, Pearl* by B. Kottler and A.M. Markman. *Medium Ævum* 37. 324-8.

Huizinga, J. (1955). *The Waning of the Middle Ages*. Harmondsworth: Penguin. (First publ., 1924). (Translation of *Herfsttij der Middeleeuwen*. First publ., 1919).

Huizinga, J. (1970). *Homo Ludens*. London: Granada (Paladin). (First publ., 1949. London: Routledge and Kegan Paul.). (Translation of *Homo Ludens*. Haarlem: Tjeenk Willink. 1938; repr. 1952).

Sir Gawain and the Green Knight. Ed. I. Gollancz. EETS, OS 210 (1940).

Sir Gawain and the Green Knight. Ed. J.R.R. Tolkien and E.V. Gordon. 2nd ed. rev. N. Davis. Oxford: Oxford University Press. 1967 (1st ed., 1925).

Stevens, M. (1972). Laughter and Game in *Sir Gawain and the Green Knight*. *Speculum* 47. 65-78.

PSYCHOLOGY AND THE MIDDLE ENGLISH ROMANCES

Preliminaries to Readings of *Sir Gawain and the Green Knight*, *Sir Orfeo*, and *Sir Launfal*

BART VELDHOEN

When, in *Sir Gawain and the Green Knight*, the Green Knight suggests a beheading-match, we, the audience, sit back in approval. We recognise the kind of story, we recognise the world which we are invited to enter. Or, as Derek Brewer (1978:20) puts it much more emphatically:

> In *Sir Gawain and the Green Knight* a large man at Christmas time, happening to be bright green, proposes the ridiculous and suicidal exchange of the beheading-game—you cut off mine and I'll cut off yours—which is solemnly taken up.... The marvellous is inherent in most romances, involving the improbable, impossible and supernatural. The true reader of romance does not merely take these in his stride; they are what constitute one of his chief pleasures.[1]

The logic of this story, then, is different from the rules that govern our everyday reality and from the rules that govern our moral conduct. Yet the deviant logic does not alienate us from the world of this story—in fact it does that far less than modern science fiction tends to do. We appear to accept it as natural, with the same ease with which children accept fairy-tales: they may find them deeply disturbing, as dreams can be, and they may have to reassure themselves that witches and giants "do not exist", but, paradoxically, they feel at

---

[1] Rather than clutter my argument with a large number of references, I refer the interested reader to two excellent survey-descriptions of the genre: Derek Brewer (1978) and F.N.M. Diekstra (1975) and the bibliographies and references contained in those. Among further specific debts I owe, I should refer in particular to John Stevens (1973), and to the later studies by Derek Brewer (1980), Piero Boitani (1982) and those in Derek Brewer (1988).

home in them and derive a particular enjoyment from them. Similarly the "true reader of romance" feels at home in the romance-world and is equally deeply disturbcd by its products. Fascinated we are not, or rarely—to create fascination a narrative would have to operate on a different level of characterisation—but, for the audience, the combination of being disturbed and feeling at home, and the particular pleasure derived from that combination, can be safely claimed for the genre.

The romances have in common with many other modes of story-telling a narrative world which is in our terms non-naturalistic. Among these stories—which do *not* require the "willing suspension of disbelief", as Derek Brewer (1978:42) has noted, because they do not create illusions of reality—it is not to my purpose to establish the finer distinctions, as between fairy-tales, folk-tales, legends, saints' lives, myths and romances, because they all show, in their various ways, that psychological quality that I should like to argue is the hallmark of the romances. However, simply to say that the romance-world does not operate on the level of actual material reality would be too inclusive: that would be true for the fable, allegory, satire, history and chronicles, and the moralisation of myths as well—in short, for practically all medieval literature, with the possible exception of the *fabliaux*. The symbolic mode of the romances and related genres will have to be distinguished from the exemplary and allegorical modes, because the first requires a different logic of interpretation.

In practice we are rarely in doubt as to where we are. When the Knight of the Red Crosse enters the "shadie grove" in Book I, Canto One of Edmund Spenser's *The Faerie Queene*, we recognise, by the pride of the trees, the light being shut out, the birds singing in scorn of the sky, the labyrinthine paths leading ever deeper in, that this is an allegory of a man moving towards or in Error. When properly translated the scene teaches us something of the nature and dangers of error, in the manner of metaphor. Similarly the Garden of Mirth in the *Roman de la Rose*, or the Gardens of Love in Chaucer's *Booke of the Duchesse* and *Parlement of Foules* or in *The Floure and the Leafe*, all teach us about the nature and dangers of love. Likewise, the field and valley of Langland's *Piers Plowman* hint at the nature and dangers of society and the human position. However, when we come to the passing of the seasons or the winter landscape in *Sir Gawain and the Green Knight* (*SGGK*), or the wilderness in *Sir Orfeo*, or the forest and water of *Sir Launfal*, these landscapes tell us about the men; they do not represent or analyse abstract notions in a metaphorical way, but rather reflect, symbolically, psychological states or stages of development on the part of the respective protagonists. The distinction between the allegorical and exemplary modes on the one hand and romance and related genres on the other hinges on the difference between teaching moral lessons and providing psychological insights. It is not my purpose to claim this as a reductive distinction, as if the one excludes the other, but simply as a working differentiation, because it makes a difference in one's interpretation of the narratives. The Knight of the Red Crosse's killing of the monster Errour is a moral lesson: it reaches us how to behave and what to be prepared for. The beheading game in *SGGK*, whatever it may mean, certainly does not teach a moral lesson. A beheading could conceivably be used allegorically, but it would never be a game in an allegory.

In basic narrative technique the romances resemble the dream allegories and morality plays: both kinds dramatise inner conflicts, a *bellum intestinum* between various aspects or facets of the mind or soul; an inner conflict, not a conflict between people, and within which the conflict functions as a trigger for a learning-process. Both kinds start from an ideal, and introduce characters to illustrate or analyse that ideal dramatically, something which gives to those characters their typical flatness. The complex tensions are dramatised *between* the "characters", not *in* them. In that respect romance and allegory differ from comedy and tragedy, which start from human characters, rather than from a preconceived ideal, virtue or folly, and then proceed to illustrate what actions and interactions proceed typically out of such characters. Compared with these more typically humanist modes, romance and allegory seem to be distinctly medieval, products of the age of nominalists and realists, of scholastic dissections and of rhetorical debates between various facets of complex phenomena.

Just as comedy differs from tragedy in its vision and its structure, so also do romance and allegory differ in categories, purpose and action. Even though both dramatise interaction between aspects of the mind, allegory presents abstract virtues and vices and types of social roles whereas romance puts aspects of ideal man on the stage. The technique may be similar, but the materials are different. A figure such as Sir Orfeo—lover, king and musician in one—is typically romance material. In allegory he would require three characters, or three different levels of operation. Allegory tends to dissect, romance to make connections, which are then explored in such a way that one idea enriches, complicates and explains the other. Furthermore, the wilderness and the fairyland in *Sir Orfeo* are not so much successive, but connected stages. More so than in allegory, romance shows character-in-action, an action determined by, and therefore to be read as, the psychology of the protagonist's character. In other words, romance presents an "individual" process, as opposed to the doctrinal, generalised ideals personified in allegories (and satires of the type of *Piers Plowman*). *SGGK* may be doctrinal in its celebration of the chivalric virtue of "*trawpe*" (fidelity), but, by showing the conflicts of fidelity and the insufficiency of the abstract ideal, it is explorative rather than moral. Its purpose is not to provide moral teaching, as allegories and related genres do, but to explore insights into motives and growth.

It follows that the difference in the kinds of action between the two modes can be rather telling. The encounters in allegory are successive, as has been suggested above, the succession being determined by a doctrinal logic. We learn from them by "following"—by observing more or less as outsiders, or else through a guide who is also observing. A romance-encounter, on the other hand, usually involves the assertion of the protagonist against an opponent, the protagonist pitting himself against an obstacle, a threat or a misgiving; we, the audience, are invited to share the hero's experience and—hopefully—to approve his actions. A good, beautifully condensed, example is Sir Gawain's first encounter with the Green Chapel (ll. 2189-216): what we get is not an *exemplum* or allegory of what the antagonist is—by romance logic that explanation must follow in the form of action, as it does in ll.2217-38 and the ensuing scene—but an expression of how it feels to Gawain, in all his successive psychological reactions:

> "Now iwysse," quoþ Wowayn, "wysty is here:
> Þis oritore is vgly, with erbez ouergrowen;
> Wel bisemez þe wyȝe wruxled in grene
> Dele here his deuocioun on þe deuelez wyse.
> Now I fele hit is þe fende, in my fyue wyttez,
> Þat hatz stoken me þis steuen to strye me here.
> Þis is a chapel of meschaunce, þat chekke hit bytyde!
> Hit is þe corsedest kyrk þat euer I com inne!"   (2189-96)

("To be sure," said Gawain, "it is desolate here; this chapel, overgrown with herbs, is forbidding; it suits the man clad in green, indeed, to perform his pious practices here in the devil's fashion. Now I feel, in my five senses, that it is the devil who has imposed this appointed meeting on me to destroy me here. This is a chapel

of disaster; may it be struck by evil! It is the most accursed church
that I have ever come to!")

The Green Chapel is not described in terms that suggest what it is or
what it signifies, but as a projection of Gawain's fears and misgiv-
ings; and in this it serves to define the hero and the nature of the experience. Gawain's fear of the coming encounter is given free reign
for a moment, via a process of associations: because the chapel is desolate and forbidding, worship there must be the opposite of that of a
common chapel, and therefore must be satanic. The challenger must
be the devil himself, if this is his home, and consequently the danger
to Gawain mortal: he hasn't a chance. But in cursing the occasion,
Gawain also rises to it. As a true hero he proceeds to assert himself
against the forces of evil; we see him picking himself up in the next
lines:

> With heȝe helme on his hede, his launce in his honde,
> He romez vp to þe roffe of þe roȝ wonez.   (2197-8)

(With his high helmet on his head, his lance in his hand, he makes
his way up to the roof of the rude dwelling)

He has, literally, got himself back on top of the situation, at his most
peacock-proud. Despite this, his newly-regained character is not
allowed to establish itself, and a noise reduces him to fear again for a
moment:

> Þene herde he of þat hyȝe hil, in a harde roche
> Biȝonde þe broke, in a bonk, a wonder breme noyse,
> Quat! hit clatered in þe clyff, as hit cleue schulde,
> As one vpon a gryndelston hade grounden a syþe.
> What! hit wharred and whette, as water at a mulne;
> What! his rusched and ronge, rawþe to here.   (2199-204)

(Then he heard, from that high hill, coming from a hard rock beyond the brook, on a hillside, a marvellously violent noise. Lo, it
re-echoed on the rock, as if it should split, as if someone was
sharpening a scythe on a grindstone. Lo, it whirred and made a
grinding noise, like water at a mill; lo, it rushed and rang,
grievous to hear.)

That this is fear again, not just fright, is shown by Gawain's imme-
diate association of the grinding noise with a scythe. He had no way
of telling what was the cause of the noise, and he should, logically,

have expected an axe. But the sound "from beyond" immediately
brings back his fear of the grim reaper, of the inevitability of his
death. It was indeed "*rawþe to here*" (1.2204) and the pain is Gawain's. This time he recovers with somewhat more difficulty, but
reaches his full heroic stature again in the end:

> Þenne 'Bi Godde,' quoþ Gawayn, 'þat gere, as I trowe,
> Is ryched at þe reuerence me, renk, to mete
>   bi rote.
>   Let God worche! "We loo"—
>   Hit helppez me not a mote.
>   My lif þaȝ I forgoo,
>   Drede dotz me not lote.'

> Thenne þe knyȝt con calle ful hyȝe:
> 'Who stiȝtlez in þis sted me steuen to holde?
> For now is gode Gawayn goande ryȝt here.
> If any wyȝe oȝt wyl, wynne hider fast,
> Oþer now oþer neuer, his nedez to spede.'   (2205-16)

(Then "By God!" said Gawain, "that contrivance, I believe, is intended out of respect to meet me, a knight, with due ceremony.
Let God work His will! Saying 'alas' will not help me at all.
Though I must lose my life, a noise shall not make me afraid."
Then the knight called quite loudly: "Who is master in this place,
to keep an appointed meeting with me? For good Gawain is now
walking right here. If any man wants anything, let him come hith-
er quickly to get his business done, now or never.")

Gawain first picks himself up in the old heroic manner of laconic
irony, but the accompanying oath "*Bi Godde*" (1.2205) produces,
again by association, the equally heroic resignation shown in the
stanza's "wheel". Having so far recovered himself, he can perform
the proper ceremony of announcing himself and his purpose: his true
self, loyal to his promise. And that is precisely what the Green
Knight acknowledges when he finally appears: "*Of steuen mon may
þe trowe*" (1.2238: 'One can trust you to keep an appointment').
There is, of course, a further challenge to Gawain's regained selfhood, in the form of the Green Knight's insulting and insolent approach; as a result of this the action unfolds that will show Gawain's
true character.
    This example also illustrates that the pattern of action in ro-
mances tends to be cyclic, as opposed to the more typically linear action of allegory and the exemplifying modes. A circle or a wheel in

allegory is almost invariably connected with Fortune, whereas cir-
cles or cycles in romances reflect regeneration, a symbolic death-
and-rebirth. As I have argued elsewhere (Veldhoen, 1981 and 1988),
the logic of the plot is so contrived that the various contrasts and conflicts which indicate the stages of progress are presented in a psychological order of rising and falling and picking up again, until the
selfhood aimed at is reached in a symbolic place or action or situation
of achievement—for example, Orfeo in the fairy-king's palace in *Sir
Orfeo*, the moment when Tryamour confronts Guinevere in *Sir
Launfal*, the final meeting between Sir Gawain and the Green
Knight, are such moments. In none of these cases is the incident the
end of the story: in each case another cycle is added to celebrate or
"clinch" the achievement and to put it in its proper perspective.

In the final distinction allegory is, I believe, essentially a pre-
scriptive mode, and romances are much more tentative. That is why
we feel so at home in the romances, in spite of their disturbing insights.

The first suggestion of the cyclic nature of the experience presented by *SGGK* is its very opening. The opening reference to Troy
and Brutus gives status to the world of this tale, implying a noble an-
cestry and a purpose. A similar construction is used in *Sir Orfeo*, as
also in *Havelok the Dane*. The fact that the story is concluded with
another reference to Brutus and Troy makes the line a circle. We do
not have a string of events, but a circumscribed world within which
we see certain ideals being tested. As with the double start of *Sir
Launfal*, with the Round Table and then Arthur's wedding, or the
triple opening of *Sir Orfeo*, complete with Breton lays, noble descent
and the court and minstrelsy, so in *SGGK* do we also find a double
opening, in the lengthy description of Arthur's court feasting to
celebrate both Christmas and the New Year. So within the framework of the nobility of this world—the apparently linear framework
of history—the story begins with celebration; not, as in *Sir Launfal*,
with a celebration of "the best knights ever were", or as in *Havelok*
with "good kings", but with the celebration of the New Year—a
clearly cyclic phenomenon. It is a celebration of a harmony between
man (the court), ideals (Christmas) and nature (New Year). This
harmony is celebrated with its proper ceremony of the distribution
of "ȝeres-ȝiftes" (l.66: New Year's gifts) and with a readiness, if not
eagerness, to test out the new cycle.

That testing out is, naturally, Arthur's adventure, since he is
the king, the personification of that ideal and noble kingdom. Arthur's restlessness and his promise not to eat until he has heard or

seen an adventure (ll.85-106) dramatise his readiness to have a taste
of the new cycle first. So, naturally, he accepts the Green Knight's
challenge, although Gawain takes over, because it would be improp-
er for the king to continue. This taking over is neither a paradox nor
a reflection on Gawain's pride. It is a technique commonly used in
romances and in folk and fairytales, wherein the protagonist is
"split" (for an explanation of the Jungian use of this term, see below).
One remembers the many tales in which two or three brothers or
sons each contribute component parts to the action, which gains in
complexity through its being structured along the lines of these complementary or alternative approaches. From all the complex potential of the human character one principal figure is split off, who becomes the *persona* specially equipped for the particular encounter.
This particular *persona* and his specific encounter bring out the significance of the experience by their highlighted specificity. In other
words, if the Green Knight's challenge is naturally King Arthur's
adventure, Gawain *is* Arthur for the present purposes. He is one of a
number of aspects of Arthur as he goes into action, while Arthur is
the collective good king. His different "sides" can be dramatised by
other characters—often Sir Gawain, Sir Kay the Seneschal, or Sir
Launcelot du Lake. Thus different, alternative, or even conflicting
sides of a personality can be dramatised in this kind of story. For the
logic of the story it is immaterial whether Arthur or Gawain undertake the adventure, but since the adventure requires the young and
courteous and *bachelor* sides of Arthur, it is Gawain who is the
obvious replacement. That Gawain is a "split" of Arthur is borne out
by the story when "*gode Gawan watz grayped Gwenore bisyde*"
(l.109: 'good Gawain was seated beside Guinevere') when the restless
and eager king is standing "*stif ... hisseluen*" (l.106: 'himself erect'),
and by Gawain's reception at Bertilak's castle with full royal pomp as
"*prynce withouten pere*" (l.873: 'prince without peer") in ll.850-74.

The test to which Gawain is subjected seems a trick in bad
taste, a fairy-trick in which superhuman magic makes the odds uneven. The reader might ask, indeed, why odds should be even; yet he
would probably like to think that Gawain had a chance, at least. The
question is even asked whether one is in honour bound to keep an
agreement with a supernatural opponent:

> To quat kyth he becom knwe non þere,
> Neuer more þen þay wyste from queþen he watz wonnen.
>   What þenne?
> Þe kyng and Gawen þare

> At þat grene þay laȝe and grenne,
> ȝet breued watz hit ful bare
> A meruayl among þo menne.
>
> Þaȝ Arþer þe hende kyng at hert hade wonder,
> He let no semblaunt be sene, ...   (460-8)

(Nobody there knew to what land he went, any more than they knew where he had come from. What then? The King and Gawain laughed and grinned there at that green one, nevertheless it was declared a marvel quite plainly among the men. Though the gracious King Arthur was amazed in his heart, he did not show any sign of his feelings, ...)

The answer is, unquestioningly, in the affirmative, and if the question is raised again by the bystanders at Gawain's departure in ll.672-86, it is only to remind us of the odds. For their part Arthur and Gawain stick to the bargain, because what is being tested is their "*trawþe*", their reliability whatever the odds. That is what—ideally—a community must be able to expect from their leaders and protectors.

The test takes on the form of a quest, as Gawain himself points out:

> Þe knyȝt mad ay god chere,
> And sayde, 'Quat schuld I wonde?
> Of destiné derf and dere
> What may mon do bot fonde?'   (562-65)

(The Knight remained cheerful, and said, "Why should I shrink back? With grievous and gentle destinies, what can one do but try them?")

We see the knight alone, riding to his destiny through a landscape. In the symbolic patterning of this genre the landscape has, of course, absolute symbolic significance—for instance, the fields and town and water in *Sir Launfal* or in *Havelok the Dane*, the wasteland and the Otherworld in *Sir Orfeo*. The second Fitt of *SGGK* starts with an emphasis on winter battling with spring:

> Forþi þis ȝol ouerȝede, and þe ȝere after,
> An vche sesoun serlepes sued after oþer:
> After Crystenmasse com þe crabbed lentoun,

Þat fraystez flesch wyth þe fysche and fode more symple;
Bot þenne þe weder of þe worlde wyth wynter hit þrepez,
Colde clengez adoun, cloudez vplyften,
Schyre schedez þe rayn in schowrez ful warme,
Fallez vpon fayre flat, flowrez ful warme,
Boþe groundez and þe greuez grene ar her wedez,
Bryddez busken to bylde, and bremlych syngen
For solace of þe softe somer þat sues þerafter
          bi bonk;
     And blossumez bolne to blowe
     Bi rawez rych and ronk,
     Þen notez noble innoȝe
     Ar herde in wod so wlonk.

After þe sesoun of somer wyth þe soft wyndez
Quen Zeferus syflez hymself on sedez and erbez,
Wela wynne is þe wort þat waxes þeroute,
When þe donkande dewe dropez of þe leuez,
To bide a blysful blusch of þe bryȝt sunne.
Bot þen hyȝes heruest, and hardenes hym sone,
Warnez hym for þe wynter to wax ful rype;
He dryues wyth droȝt þe dust for to ryse,
Fro þe face of þe folde to flyȝe ful hyȝe;
Wroþe wynde of þe welkyn wrastelez with þe sunne,
Þe leuez lancen fro þe lynde and lyȝten on þe grounde,
And al grayes þe gres œat grene watz ere;
Þenne al rypez and rotez þat ros vpon fyrst.
And þus ȝirnez þe ȝere in ȝisterdayez mony,
And wynter wyndez aȝayn, as þe worlde askez,
          no fage,
     Til Meȝelmas mone
     Watz cumen wyth wynter wage;
     Þen þenkkez Gawan ful sone
     Of his anious uyage.   (500-35)

(And so this Yule passed by, and the following year, and each
season in turn followed after the other: after Christmas came the
unconvivial Lent, which tests the body with fish and simpler food;
but then the weather in the world struggles with winter, the cold
shrinks down, the clouds lift, the rain falls shining in warm show-
ers, it falls upon fair fields, flowers appear there, both of fields
and of the woods their garments are green, birds make haste to
build nests, and sing loudly on the hill-sides for joy of the gentle

summer that follows behind; and the blossoms swell to bloom along the flourishing and luxuriant hedgerows, then many glorious notes are heard in the wood that is so fair. Next the season of summer with the gentle winds when Zephyrus himself blows gently on seeds and green plants; very lovely is the plant that grows out of them, when the moistening dew drops from the leaves, to await a delightful gleam of the bright sun. But then harvest-time comes hurrying, and encourages the plant quickly, warns it to grow fully ripe because of the approaching winter; through drought the autumn drives the dust up into the air, flying quite high from the surface of the land; in the sky a fierce wind wrestles with the sun, the leaves are snatched from the lime-tree and land on the earth, and the grass withers completely that had been green before; then all ripens and decays that had grown at first, and thus the year runs by in a succession of days, and winter returns again, as the world requires, in truth, till the Michaelmas moon had come with the pledge of winter; then Gawain remembers at once his troublesome journey.)

What stands out clearly in this passage is the sense of struggle and of violence. One also notices that spring is dressed in green ("*grene ar her wedez*", 1.508: 'their garments are green'). A connection, perhaps even a close relationship, could be surmised between the Green Knight and the new spring or new year. Like the new year the Green Knight may have come to show that "the green" will lift up its head after it has been mown down in harvest, something which man himself is not able to do. The pattern seems to suggest a testing of nature as against the ideals of man. If that is the case, Gawain does not really fail in the end: he did the next best that man can do against nature, and that always involves some extra protection. The Green Knight appears to admit as much when he says in his final summing up:

> ... sothly me þynkkez
> On þe fautlest freke þat euer on fote ȝede.   (2362-3)

(...truly you seem to me the most faultless man who ever paced the earth.)

Here one must remember that "faultless" is a merely negative qualification. In this light Gawain's confession before setting out for the Green Chapel (ll.1876-84) can be accepted as not unduly worrying. Yet he is sad in the end, because the Green Knight is more generous in his assessment of Gawain's guilt, and also because man and his ideals cannot compete against the strength of nature.

The linear is once again matched against the cyclic, the ability to renew oneself as opposed to going through the motions of acting

out the ideal. The picture in ll.500-35, quoted above, seems to suggest something like that, in the tension between the second stanza and
the final "bob and wheel". Because the test has become a quest, the
arming of the hero follows naturally. Equally naturally, or yet more
so, there follows the symbolic (although apparently allegorical) arming with the shield. In a sense the virtues "given" to Gawain in this
way provide the pattern for what follows. These are the virtues he
will show in action, on the outside; they are his emblem, the distin-
guishing mark he carries, his protection, what he holds on to and
demonstrates to the outside world, Gawain's adventure will reveal
how inextricably those virtues are connected with one another. Yet it
may be the special point of this romance to show that they are "carried": that it is a reputation that is being tested, which is not quite the
same as testing the man who flaunts that reputation.

When regarded from the basic pattern of the Green Knight's
parallelling the new year, Gawain's quest for the Green Knight does
not succeed directly *because* he has gone in search of him too late—
after harvest-time: he will not be able to find his adversary again
until the New Year. In the meantime, as it will appear, the Green
Knight lies buried in Hautdesert. So this idea is followed again by an
emphasis on the solitariness of Gawain's experience:

> Þe kny3t tok gates straunge
> In mony a bonk vnbene,
> His cher ful oft con chaunge
> Þat chapel er he my3t sene.
>
> Mony klyf he ouerclambe in contrayez straunge,
> Fer floten fro his frendez fremedly he rydez.   (709-14)

(The knight took strange paths along many inhospitable hill-sides,
very often he turned his way, before he could find that chapel. He
climbed over many a cliff in unfamiliar regions, he rode as a
stranger having wandered far from his friends.)

Instead of finding the Green Chapel, therefore, Gawain must simply
do his usual thing, as the stanza proceeds to narrate. But the knightly
routine receives very little emphasis, because that is not the real
quest.

What the latter is becomes clear from the construction of the
narrative as a whole. Like all literary narratives, romances have
structures characteristic of their genre. The simplest reason for that
is that details of experience, whether in real life or in narrative art,

may be funny or sad or exciting, but never become comic or tragic or romantic unless a pattern is imposed on them. The comic, tragic, or romantic (or any other) view sets the details in order, after rigorous selection, so that the significance of the experience can be handled, both by the author and by the audience. These patterns, by then, often contain "supernatural" elements, because the full complexity of the experience does not allow total dramatisation in naturalistic terms. Abstractions and symbols enter the pattern in the same way as in our dreams symbols appear to help us get a grip on what the experience is about. As has been argued above, in romances and related genres the condensations tend to be symbolic rather than abstractions. Antagonists with supernatural powers—not protagonists, for obvious reasons—and settings in a world of magic are part of this symbolic mode. And with such antagonists and such settings the action is of a ritual kind. The whole is transported on to a plane of heightened significance, as we know it from rituals and dreams. Two qualifications need to be made here. First: the "marvellous" quality of story-telling is by no means exclusive to romances. In fact, even comedy and satire are essentially "marvellous", in spite of their pride in realism, simply because they, too, impose a pattern on the material of experience. The difference is gradual: romances only take the heightening one step further, in a particular direction. Furthermore, the characteristic repetitions and parallels in romance-narratives not only serve a ritual function, but at the same time also build suspense, denote the passing of time, or indicate the relative weight or proportion of certain elements. Fundamentally, the pattern serves to determine the way in which we view the story. It puts us "in the mood". In *SGGK* and in *Sir Orfeo* the quest-structures prepare us for romance first of all; subsequently, the emphasis in *Sir Orfeo* on return and equilibrium places our mood rather on the comic or festive side of romance, whereas in *SGGK* the emphasis on the hero's epiphany or moment of recognition takes us to a more tragic view within the genre.

The typical pattern of *SGGK*, therefore, as of the other romances, is that of the quest. It is an action-based narrative, in which the action arises out of the testing of an ideal in a series of assertions against obstacles. It is a pattern of self-discovery with, usually, a happy ending and poetic justice. In those respects romances differ from the older epic genre, where the hero, typically defending a narrow place, proves himself rather than asserts himself in a process of self-discovery. Happy endings and poetic justice, moreover, are not characteristic of the epic. A comparison between *SGGK* and *Beowulf* may make this clear—not so much between Gawain and Beowulf, but between the Green Knight and Grendel (and the other monsters). Grendel and his peers pose a material threat to the society of which Beowulf is the protector. The challenge is not a test of any virtue that Beowulf represents, but a threat to society on the material level (including life and death as real phenomena). Beowulf's society is, of course, as much better off for his proving himself as Gawain's society is better off for the latter's asserting his *"trawþe"*, but the whole concern, and therefore the patterns, are different, as Beowulf's tragic end indicates. There is in *Beowulf* much concern with society, though little with psychology; the protagonist's heroic virtue is rare and can be lost, to the great detriment of society. Romances, by contrast, are more concerned with psychological explorations of the nature and power and function of various virtues. In that sense their patterns are patterns of self-discovery, in subjective and objective form.

What the real quests in *SGGK* is, is suggested by its pattern, with its frame, in Fitts I and IV, containing Troy and Christmas and the New Year and the Beheading Game, and its centre, in Fitts II and III, containing the passing of the seasons and the Exchange of Winnings. It is in itself significant that the green and gold girdle connecting the two is closely associated with love, in its most physical aspects. In romance-patterning no hero, no virtue, can assert itself without being inspired by love. In Freud's and Jung's psychoanalysis, love takes up a similarly central role, however subdued its manifestations may be. Gawain's selfhood is explored between Guinevere, at whose side Gawain is first found, and Bertilak's wife —along with possibly Morgan le Fay, and, of course, the lady depicted on the inside of the other connecting object, his shield:

> ...þe hende heuen-quene ...;
> At þis cause þe knyȝt comlyche hade
> in þe inore half of his schelde hir ymage depaynted,
> Þat quen he blusched þerto his belde neuer payred.
>   (647-50)

(... the gracious Queen of Heaven ...; for this reason fittingly the knight had her image depicted on the inside of his shield, so that when he looked at it his courage never failed.).

The structure of *SGGK*, with its many parallels and contrasts, repetitions and interlinkings, has been amply discussed and analysed by others, and will no doubt continue to attract attention. My purpose has only been to suggest and illustrate a basic framework within which the finer analyses are to be understood. That *SGGK* is not a rambling series of adventures, but a careful and significant construction, needs no further comment; nor does the fact that, in the final analysis, the poem has something very complex and ambiguous to say.

This is where one sees the greatest difference from *Sir Orfeo*. Both romances contain a rash promise followed by a quest in the wilderness, and share a similar construction, in which the quest through the wasteland restores fertility in the end after an initiation into another world. Both poems start from a disruption of the established harmony of the kingdom, after which the hero departs, removes the disruption and returns. Both use a pattern of parallels and contrasts between two courts, and also a contrast between both the latter and the wilderness. The dominant characteristics of the protagonists hold the poems together. This is seen via the motifs of Gawain's shield and Orfeo's harp; both play their part in asserting the heroes' "truth" (i.e. loyalty), and both men keep their promises. In *Sir Orfeo* the harping achieves an ideal of harmony in the end, in love and in government, whereas in *SGGK* the hero is only "split" further, and this indicates where the difference between the two lies. In *Sir Orfeo* love and government are being tested *within* the conventions, whereas in *SGGK* we see the conventions themselves being tested: we see how the demands of the conventions, especially those of courtesy and loyalty, are shown to be in conflict with one another. In *Sir Orfeo* the conventions become arguments with which the final harmony is achieved, and, in contrast to *SGGK*, *Sir Orfeo* celebrates the conventions, purely.

In view of this, the discussion of psychology and the Middle English romances may be continued with *Sir Orfeo*. This work shows the nature of romance-action as essentially ritual action in its clearest form. For its part, *Sir Launfal* will be discussed later, as an attempt to analyse the nature of the characters in romances and their relationships.

In the same way that a comparison between *SGGK* and *Beowulf* helps to clarify a point about the psychological patterning of romance, a comparison between *Sir Orfeo* and the story of Orpheus as told by Ovid in his *Metamorphoses* may tell us more about some of the demands made by romances on their source-material. Perhaps the most striking difference is that of the proportions of the various elements: Ovid's emphases lie clearly in other places than those in *Sir Orfeo*, thus one may conclude that his story creates effects very

different from those of the Middle English romance—or rather the
other way round. The two versions serve different moods. Even the
gods introduced in the openings of the two poems to create a frame
of reference are different: Ovid begins by referring to Hymen,
stressing the importance of the love between man and wife for the
story, and only refers to Bacchus and Apollo in connection with
Orpheus's music near the end; *Sir Orfeo*, however, briefly claims
descent from Pluto and Juno for its protagonist—a telling combination of death and marital bliss or fidelity, which is embedded between a prologue concerning the Breton lays (ll.1-24) and the first
large-scale detail:

> Orpheo most of ony þing
> Louede þe gle of harpyng   (33-4)
>
> (Most of all Orfeo loved the playing of the harp)

This difference runs through both stories: *Sir Orfeo* insists on Orfeo's powerful skill as a harper time and again, whereas Ovid makes
use of Orpheus's reputation on the lyre, but rather stresses love.
Even at the moment of the winning over of the King of the Underworld it is Orpheus's arguments about love that achieve the desired
effect (and possibly entail the condition of not looking back, which is
so conspicuously absent from *Sir Orfeo*). Ovid's narrative pattern
continues with a number of motifs that *Sir Orfeo* also shares, such as
Orpheus's grief after he has lost his wife a second time, his turning
away from women and retiring to the wilderness, where his musical
power is shown in action again. Ultimately, however, Orpheus fails
to triumph over wild nature His final reunion with his wife in the
Underworld is a wry joke in the mood of Ovid's story, a point driven
home by the detail that sometimes he "looks back, as he can do safely
now, at his Eurydice" (p.247). Those same motifs all recur in *Sir Orfeo*, albeit in different places in the pattern. Orfeo promises never to
look on women again, and retires to the wilderness after he loses his
wife. What in Ovid's story was a manifestation of grief, in *Sir Orfeo*
becomes the quest. By a rearranging of the details a tragic story
about the impotence of art against the processes of nature becomes a
celebration of the powers of harmony over the unregenerate forces
that threaten society.

    The question why it should be plots and motifs mainly, and
rarely patterns with an inherent significance, that are handed down
in the history of story-telling, remains an intriguing one. But in this

continual act of reinterpreting archetypal situations we see in *Sir Orfeo* a more explorative approach to the role of music. The art of music becomes a symbol for an attitude which creates harmony in love and in society, and a comparison with an earlier step in the history of reinterpretation of this story may serve to demonstrate that *Sir Orfeo* has a "psychological" quality. In *The Consolation of Philosophy* (III, xii) Boethius retells the story of Orpheus still in tragic terms: the power of Orpheus's music is given a much more prominent role than his love, but it does not work on the man himself (pp.109-15); the power is still conditional. Yet the story is presented by Boethius as part of his argument about unifying diversity. In brief the argument posits that all things in God's creation are inclined to the good, which is God's unifying goodness, and suggests that nothing can preserve its own nature if it goes against that harmony. The basis for the logic underlying *Sir Orfeo* seems to be there: if we accept Orfeo's harping as a symbol of Boethius's harmony, we see why it is so powerful and why the fairy kingdom must lose against it, unconditionally. Boethius draws a moral conclusion from the story of Orpheus: it exemplifies for him how love between people can get in the way of our proper inclination towards heaven. This allegorical approach to the story is replaced in *Sir Orfeo* by an exploration of that harmony, not as a quality of creation as a whole, but as a creative potential of the individual mind. We see a man gifted with the power of musical harmony asserting that power also in love and in government. Experience proves him right on both scores in the end.

One could argue, therefore, that *Sir Orfeo* only exemplifies an underlying doctrine that harmony unifies all human relationships into an ideal community. But the fact remains that the narrative presents this in a psychological rather than a moral form. The harmony is to be achieved in a quest for personal recognition, as the final scene shows, and against obstacles of a psychological and social, rather than of a moral, kind. In its long string of contrasts between Orfeo's life at court and his life in exile, the wilderness represents symbolically the hero's living with a great loss and his gradual initiation into a purer state of selfhood that can assert itself again, when he, as it were, rediscovers his music and the power it has over the creatures of the wilderness. The logic of how this prepares him for his victory over the fairy king is that of an achievement of selfhood, not of the gaining of some doctrinaire moral insight. The fairy kingdom that he overcomes represents a social threat rather than a threat to the soul; in the narrative it gradually becomes penetrable as Orfeo becomes more and more himself again, and his grip on it becomes gradually

firmer, as we see him getting closer after first only perceiving the
general rout:

> Ac o best þai no nome,
> No neuer he nist whider þai become.   (287-88)
>
> (But they did not catch any animals, nor did he know at all where
> they went to.)

The two worlds are not in contact yet. But the following visions become more and more tangible and specific: numbers, faces, banners,
arms, attire, until finally *"on a day"* (1.303) he sees a specified
number of ladies who do make contact between the two worlds by
hawking at specified prey. *"Þat seiȝe Orfeo, and louȝ"* (1.314: 'Orfeo
saw that, and laughed'). Even without reference to Freud on laughter
one recognises that the crucial point of the recovery of selfhood has
been reached in the form of a renewed zest for life. When this allows
the hero to reach the fairy-king's castle, that place is presented with
the typical symbolic paraphernalia of the *mandala*: it is high and
shining, with gold and precious stones, enclosed, and associated with
Paradise. The symbolism suggests that this is the place of achievement for him.
    Further analysis of Orfeo's initiation into the mysteries or na-
ture of the place, represented by his passing through the gallery of
horrors[2], as also of the elements of Celtic folklore and *Tír na n-Oc*
(Land of the Ever-Young) and of classical sun-god fertility implications could be given, but the point I should like to make here is that
the logic of the description only works in a psychological reading: it
would otherwise be inconsistent to ascribe to the enemy camp or
place of evil such life and paradisal splendour. The place is presented
clearly as reflection of the protagonist's state or stage of development; it does not define a moral threat, but the nature of the hero's
experience.
    Even Diekstra, who, on the whole, seems to be suspicious of
symbolic claims about romances, admits (1975:81) about *Sir Orfeo*:

> The trial through adventure of Sir Orfeo is enhanced by
> his dealing with the perils of the inimical world. Orfeo
> penetrates into a Celtic type of magic land and conquers
> its magic powers by his own special brand of magic.

---

[2] A useful suggestion about their origin is given by Dorena Allen (1964).

> Such things, if used in skilful hands, go beyond the
> merely fashionable, and impinge on areas of experience
> which in modern fiction have to be explored by psycho-
> logical analysis or symbolism.

I should wish to argue that Orfeo's special brand of magic is his selfhood. Within the festive structure of an initial equilibrium being first
threatened, then lost, and finally regained by its own strength, Orfeo's quest shows the hero going out alone and regaining and asserting his self against his enemies and friends. As in all romances, it is a
journey of discovery, even though the outcome is known in advance
—as it is in most romances. The happy endings and poetic justice are
typical of the genre; it can hardly be otherwise in a genre that
celebrates the social validity of certain ideals. The absence of such a
pattern would make romances satirical, or at least critical of the
ideal, as *SGGK* shows. The central interest in the regaining and asserting of selfhood, even though the outcome remain predictable,
accounts for the romances' predilection for describing the ceremonies of court life and chivalry as indicative of the social relevance of
proper conduct: the social significance of the ideals that are being
explored derives its authority from the fact that things are done in
the proper manner. Ideals have only authority, no real power, and
therefore have to be enforced by ceremonies.

That same central interest also accounts for the ritual nature of
romance action. Abandoning one's kingdom after the loss of one's
wife, going after a group of ladies after ten years of voluntary exile
in solitariness, returning to one's kingdom in disguise, all these decisions do not make sense in terms of naturalistic fiction, if they are
made, as here, without apparent motivation. They have a dreamlike
lack of premeditation and yet a sensation of underlying meaningful-
ness. They are a non-rational approach to the truth, gaining insight
by repeating traditional actions. Like the rituals of religions and
brotherhoods they simultaneously assert, test and explore the ideal
upheld by the community of the initiated. Like all rituals they are
tests by which one gains the authority of the ideal, by participating
unquestioningly. The validity of the ideal is asserted by the successful
outcome of the action. For the hero the repeating of the traditional
actions brings regeneration with it, a regeneration of selfhood.

Much of the action of *Sir Orfeo* can be understood in terms of
this sense of ritual. The conversation between Orfeo and his wife
immediately after the dream has a highly ritual logic:

'Allas! mi lord, Sir Orfeo,
Seþþen we first togider were,
One wroþ neuer we nere,
Bot euer ich haue yloued þe
As mi liif, and so þou me.
Ac now we mot delen ato;
Do þi best, for y mot go.'
'Allas!', quaþ he, 'forlorn icham.
Whider wiltow go, and to wham?
Whider þou gost, ichil wiþ þe,
And whider y go, þou schalt wiþ me.'   (120-30)

("Alas! My lord, Sir Orfeo, for as long as we have been together,
we have never once been angry with each other, but I have always
loved you as my life, and you me. But now we must part; get on
as best you can, for I must go." "Alas!" said he, "I am forsaken.
Where will you go, and to whom? Where you go, I will go with
you, and where I go, you shall go with me.")

The actual cause of Heurodis's distress is narrated by her only after
this confirmation of their love. The cause of the separation is not
questioned, but the perfect harmony of their love is asserted against
it—on the queen's part as non-comprehension, on Orfeo's part as un-
questioning resolution. He derives his force for, and his insight into,
his future actions from his ritual confirmation. After his failed attempt to defend Heurodis by force, his so-called rash promise has an
equally ritual logic. He announces his leaving by appointing a regent:

For, now ichaue mi quen ylore,
Þe fairest leuedi þat euer was bore,
Neuer eft y nil no woman se.
Into wilderness ichil to,
And liue þer euermore
Wiþ wilde bestes in holtes hore.   (209-14)

(For, since I have lost my queen, the fairest lady who was ever
born, I will never again look at a woman. I shall go into the
wilderness, and live there from now on among wild animals in the
grey woods.)

Again no reason is given, however questionable the decisions as such
are. The course of action is dictated by the connection shown in Orfeo between love and government, which, as has been suggested
above, are linked together in the ideal of harmony that Orfeo repre-

sents. By losing his wife he has lost his self, and therefore his people have lost him, too. The wilderness to which he goes is his own psychological state of loss and vulnerability. After this has been fully developed (ll.234-66), Orfeo's situation of deprivation turns rather into the setting of his quest, again in a purely ritual way. When he starts performing the traditional action of his ideal again, the playing of music not as a symbol of love and government but as a action, he is beginning his quest, with his characteristic weapon. His assertion announced in ll. 120-30, quoted above, is beginning, in stages, to overcome his opponent, who is his own shadow, as I shall demonstrate below. But the unique power of *Sir Orfeo* as a romance is that it does not merely make use of ritualistic unpremeditated action, but makes that rituality thematic. We have seen that in Orfeo's taking up the harp again in the wilderness, and we see it again:

> 'Allas!' quaþ he, 'now me is wo.
> Whi nil deþ now me slo?
> Allas! wreche, þat y no miȝt
> Dye now after þis siȝt!
> Allas! to long last mi liif,
> When y no dar nouȝt wiþ mi wiif,
> No hye to me, o word speke.
> Allas! whi nil min hert breke?
> Parfay!' quaþ he, 'tide wat bitide, .
> Whider so þis leuedis ride,
> Þe selue way ichil streche;
> Of liif no deþ me no reche.'   (331-42)

("Alas!" said he, "Now I am unhappy. Why will death not slay me now? Alas! Miserable am I that I could not die after seeing this just now! Alas! My life lasts too long when I dare not speak a single word with my wife, nor she with me. Alas! Why will my heart not break? By my faith," said he, "come what may, wherever these ladies are riding to, I will go the same way; for life or death I take no care.")

Here the ceremony of courtly love, with its complaints and unwavering duties, becomes the ritual that grants him the boldness to ride straight into a rock without hesitation. When Orfeo is questioned about his foolhardiness in coming into that new world, the ceremony by which wandering minstrels are made welcome at any court is sufficient to give him access. Once there, in what I have already described as Orfeo's place of achievement, the final struggle turns out to be entirely a battle of rituals. The fairy king reacts to Orfeo's

harping with the proper ceremony of granting him anything he likes:
"Now aske of me what it be" (1.450: 'Now ask of me anything whatsoever'). Having just asserted his selfhood, Orfeo now claims it to the
full in asking to be reunited with his wife. Unaware of the bond
between Orfeo and Heurodis, because he does not recognise Orfeo
(in all senses of the word), the fairy king objects to this request, with
what is in itself a proper ceremony; this would be a socially unaccep-
table match:

> 'Nay,' quaþ þe king,'þat nouȝt nere!
> A sori couple of ȝou it were,
> For þou art lene, rowe, and blac,
> And sche is louesum, wiþouten lac;
> A loþlich þing it were forþi
> To sen hir in þi compayni.'   (457-62)

> ("No," said the king, "that would be no good! You two would be
> an ill-matched pair, for you are lean, with shaggy black hair, and
> she is beautiful, without a blemish; it would therefore be an un-
> pleasing thing to see her in your company.")

However, this non-recognition, based precisely on the fact that Orfeo
has come out of his initiation rather dishevelled, enables the hero to
deal the finishing stroke. In the assurance of his full selfhood Orfeo
can put the fairy king in his place, by countering the latter's ceremonial blow with a weightier ceremony:

> 'O sir,' he seyd, 'gentil king,
> ȝete were it a wele fouler þing
> To here a lesing of þi mouþe.   (463-65)

> ("Oh your majesty," he said, "noble king, it would be yet a much
> fouler thing to hear a lie from your mouth.")

It may be thought ironic that the opponent is silenced with a reference to his "truth" (loyalty) which he never had but merely pre-
tended to have by playing the part of a king, but the pattern probably
rather suggests that Orfeo's regaining of full selfhood as the man of
harmony is the thing which establishes the rules of proper conduct.
The fairy king, at least, replies with perfect ceremony: *"Of hir ichil
þatow be bliþe"* (1.471: 'I wish that you have joy of her'). Orfeo
thereupon kneels down with due ceremony, thanks the king and takes
his wife by the hand. The final line of the scene: *"Riȝt as he come þe
way he ȝede"* (1.476: 'He went back exactly the same way as he had

come') emphasises that the thing which enables him to come away with his wife is the very regained selfhood which had also enabled him to reach the abode of the fairy king.

In asserting himself against the latter, Orfeo has overcome his own shadow. This brings me to my final topic: after structure, setting, patterns and action, it remains to look at the characters. It will come as no surprise, given the frequent use of terms such as "selfhood", "persona" and "shadow", if the suggestion is advanced that the logic of the narrative patterns in romances resembles that of patterns also found in psycho-analysis, patterns operating *within* the individual mind, and that, therefore, it may be helpful to enquire whether the analytical distinctions made in psychology have anything to add to our understanding of the romances. For this purpose, *Sir Launfal* has been chosen.

A simple Freudian pattern suggests itself straightaway: the *ego* loses against the *super-ego*, but is restored by the *id*. Launfal loses his libido twice before Guinevere, and his impotence is restored twice by Tryamour. Tryamour's promises and conditions support such a reading, and her gifts to Launfal are rather typical Freudian symbols:

> I wyll the yeve an alner
> Imad of sylk and of gold cler,
> > Wyth fayre ymages thre;
> As of thou puttest the hond therinne,
> A mark of gold thous chalt wynne,
> > In wat place that thou be.
>
> 'Also,' sche syede, 'Syr Launfal,
> I yeve the Blaunchard, my stede lel,
> > And Gyfre, my owen knave;
> And of my armes oo pensel
> Wyth three ermyns, ypeynted well,
> > Also thou schalt have.'   (319-30)

("I shall give you a purse made of silk and pure gold, with three beautiful pictures; every time you put your hand in it, you will gain a gold mark, in whatever place you are. Also," she said, "Sir Launfal, I give you my faithful horse Blanchard, and my own servant-boy Gifre; and a banner with my coat of arms with three ermines depicted well you shall have also.")

The pattern of relationships between the three main characters can be analysed in this way, but it tends to reduce the story to a simple wish-fulfilment dream, with which especially the ending, and possibly more elements, are not consistent.

One way of determining what the story is about, what kind of experience is being explored, is to analyse the various confrontations between the protagonist and the other characters. The other characters "bring out" the specific ideal of the protagonist. In the broad pattern we see an initial situation in which Arthur and his knights keep the land in order and Launfal is practising *"largesse"* (1.31: 'generosity'). When Guinevere arrives, it is not her promiscuity that drives Launfal away. Possibly the queen's promiscuity is to be understood in reference to the fact that in the conventions of Courtly Love the lady of the castle was "lady" to many of the young knights, so that when the convention is transplanted from the lyrical to a narrative mode, a reputation for promiscuity becomes part of the game, which is now a different game. This will play a part later on. Launfal leaves the court, however, because the queen's first action against him is a refusal to practise towards him that same virtue of generosity that he himself represents as a "split" of Arthur's court. Arthur is generous to Launfal, even when the latter takes his leave: he gives him money and companions; the queen, however, gives him nothing, and that is the point, especially since she shows generosity to all the others. Launfal, the paragon of generosity, leaves the court because that virtue no longer rules there. The queen's generosity is of the wrong kind. Similarly, the next confrontation, with the mayor, shows an antagonist refusing to practise generosity. The evil begun by the queen appears to be contagious: it spreads to Launfal's companions, when they refuse to stick with him, and it undermines the order of the land.

The mayor's daughter provides the turning-point: generosity can still be generated by Launfal, but it takes a fairy-mistress to infuse it with new power. That Tryamour is an image of generosity is beyond doubt. If nothing else, the first view of her establishes at least that. The recovery of generosity is ceremoniously dramatised with feasts and acts of generosity, a local tournament to show that the upholder of that virtue can assert himself again, and with more feasts and nightly bliss with Tryamour.

The role of Sir Valentine of Lombardy is intriguing. That Lombardy and the knight's gigantic stature should suggest that "big money" is challenging private generosity is an attractive thought: capitalism would have enough cause for *"greet envye"* (1.506: 'great resentment'). However, the terms of the challenge specify more than once that it is issued for the honour of the lady. Apparently Launfal is to assert his new integrity, not with his lady at his beck and call, but out on his own (in this story this tends to be associated symbolically with crossing water). The episode prefigures Launfal's later trial at Arthur's court, where he also has to assert whether he has fully integrated the generosity that Tryamour represents into his selfhood. Like Gawain, he does not really quite succeed in either test, even if he comes out victorious in both. In the fight with Valentine it is Gifre's repeated invisible assistance that saves Launfal in moments of great need. Against *"alle the lordes of Atalye"* (l. 601: 'all the lords of Ataly'—a city in Lombardy) he does not need that help, but against the original challenger he cannot assert himself alone. His selfhood is not complete without Tryamour's "split-off". At the court not even invisible help in the form of his lady's maids arriving one after the other in her stead is good enough, and Tryamour must join her lover in person and visibly before Launfal can escape triumphantly. The point seems to be made, on the one hand, that a full selfhood of generosity cannot be obtained, while on the other hand, that selfhood is shown to be powerful enough as long as it shows itself clearly connected with love (as Guinevere clearly is not). The emphasis lies apparently on integration itself, not on a festive assertion of its effect. The different endings of *Sir Orfeo* and *Sir Launfal* make that clear.

By adding Tryamour to his *persona* Launfal gains recognition. After his first tournament he is recognised by Valentine as a socially acceptable party, as the full ceremony of the messenger signifies. Yet he is recognised only to be tested further. Arthur's recognition, after Launfal has successfully asserted his newly found self, turns out only to be a new test, in which the king's "better half" is his opponent. And the very end of the story, with Launfal returning annually to issue his challenge, only repeats the pattern. The end is too gloriously victorious to justify the conclusion that Launfal has failed to achieve social acceptance, since he and his lady are living now on an island outside the kingdom. The selfhood gained in conjunction with his lady has asserted itself successfully, and this fact is recognised in the happy ending. Somehow the socially successful steward of Arthur's Midsummer feast, who leads the court in a merry dance, and the challenger of Arthur's knights at the water's edge are the same man. He shows the way. But the well-ordered kingdom of the opening lines is gone. It has been internally divided since the arrival of Guinvere, as the trial-scenes show; at the very least Arthur has separated

himself—the kingdom—from his knights by marrying Guinevere.
By way of contrast, Launfal has found perfect and effective union
with Tryamour. The two women appear to be the opposites between
whom generosity must assert itself. Tryamour may have the power
to overcome Guinevere by what she is, but Guinevere's power of
division, shown at its dramatic height when she puts before Launfal
the tragic choice between the two virtues of loyalty to his lord and
loyalty to his lady, and thereby divides him against himself, weakens
society a great deal.

The pattern, then, is clear enough in what it suggests, though
its coherence depends on our recognising the relationship between
the characters. In themselves they are hollow. We need a key to
understand why, for instance, Guinevere should hate Launfal so
much, as the story repeatedly makes a point of showing, and which is
crucial for an understanding of the whole if it is to mean anything at
all. And since romances convey a social class-ideal, a collective experience, the analytical model devised by Carl G. Jung to analyse the
collective unconscious would seem the most promising for the purpose. His categories for the process of individuation, described in
full by Jung (1959) and usefully summarised by von Franz (1974),
provide a set of relationships very similar to what we must assume is
the underlying basis of romance characterisation and action. Jung's
postulated need for a man to integrate his feminine side in order to
achieve a socially acceptable selfhood runs remarkably parallel to the
conventions of Courtly Love. A love that is not a romantic infatuation, but a source of civilised social behaviour because it comple-
ments the *ego*, that would seem to be what Tryamour is to Launfal.
She could be his *anima*, the feminine complement to the man's *ego*.
Jung describes the *anima*-projections in dreams as looking young,
but suggesting great experience; as wise, but not formidably so,
rather as possessing secret knowledge; as connected with earth and
water; as endowed with great power; and as two-sided: pure, good
and noble in her light aspect, and prostitute, seductress, witch in her
dark aspect. Most of this applies well enough to Tryamour, and begins to bring Guinevere into the picture. Jung postulates further that
if a man has repressed his feminine nature or treats women with
contempt, the dark aspect of his *anima* is most likely to project itself.
That might make sense of Tryamour's first appearance as a
seductress for Launfal, as a result of his contempt for, and spurning
of, Guinevere. Guinevere's own appearance as a prostitute and seductress for Launfal can then also be recognised as a projection of a
repression inherent in his original *persona* as the generous man. The

purely male conviviality of the Round Table of King Arthur's bachelor days celebrated in the first two stanzas of the poem appears to have projected a very dark *anima* in the person of Arthur's new queen, Guinevere. She can be seen as technically Arthur's *anima*, indeed not integrated by him, or as Tryamour's shadow. But since all the characters are only seen in relation to the *persona*—which is itself an insight borrowed from Jung's technique—the pattern is more likely to be that Guinevere is Launfal's *anima* as a kind of mother-figure, and Arthur a father-figure, from both of whom the *persona* must free himself to make development towards selfhood possible.

Images of achieved selfhood (*mandalas*) are not really to be found in this story, in contrast to *Sir Orfeo*, for instance. The closest that *Sir Launfal* comes to one is the description of Tryamour's pavilion. On the other hand, Launfal himself fits the description of the *persona* naturally. Like all romance-protagonists, he is not a particular individual, but a mask (Latin *persona*), a compromise between individual demands and the demands of society. For the conscious *ego* he is a projection like the other categories, but he is the projection of the asserting and acquiring aspect developing into selfhood. Launfal's mask would be his generosity. The projections of a man's fears and doubts and obstacles in his development towards selfhood are the shadows, which for a man are always personified as men. They are the perennial threats. Valentine could be seen as a shadow of fear or of doubt about whether the new Launfal is really himself or merely his lady's puppet. Arthur, too, could be understood as a shadow in his relation to Guinevere and as Launfal's judge towards the end. The mayor, too, is clearly a typical shadow of Launfal's generosity. The *anima*-projections are the feminine complement to the shadows, which in this story could be applied literally to the mayor's daughter and to Arthur's wife.

The technique does not explain everything, certainly not when applied rigidly. It is itself, after all, a model deduced from a variety of experiences, and from experiences in an essentially different area, although that area may have connections with our imaginative faculties. But it may provide a tentative basis for analysis of the logic with which motifs are strung together in romance narratives.

I have tried to approach the subject inductively, to find what underlies the particular form of narrative we call the romances in Middle English; the logic of the argument, however, perhaps works the other way round.

REFERENCES

Allen, Dorena (1964). Orpheus and Orfeo: The Dead and the *Taken*. *Medium Ævum* 33. 102-11.
Boethius. *The Consolation of Philosophy*. Trans. V.E. Watts. Harmondsworth: Penguin. 1969.
Boitani, Piero (1982). *English Medieval Narrative in the 13th and 14th Centuries*. Trans. Joan Krakover Hall. Cambridge: Cambridge University Press. 36-70.
Brewer, Derek (1978). The Nature of Romance. *Poetica* 9. 9-48.
Brewer, Derek (1980). *Symbolic Stories*. Cambridge: D.S. Brewer.
Brewer, Derek (ed.) (1988). *Studies in Medieval Literature: Some New Approaches*. Cambridge: D.S. Brewer.
Chestre, Thomas. *Sir Launfal*. In: *The New Pelican Guide to English Literature*. Ed. Boris Ford. Vol. I: *Medieval Literature*. Part One: *Chaucer and the Alliterative Tradition*, Harmondworth: Penguin. 1982. 440-72.
Diekstra, F.N.M. (1975) Le Roman en Moyen Anglais. (written in English). Part II of J.Ch. Payen and F.N.M. Diekstra. *Le Roman*. Turnhout: Brepols. 71-127.
Franz, M.L. von (1974). The Process of Individuation. In: Carl G. Jung, *Man and his Symbols*. London: Aldus. 158-229.
Jung, Carl G. (1959). *Collected Works*. Vol. 9, Part I: *The Archetypes and the Collective Unconsciousness* and Vol. 9, Part II: *Aion: Researches into the Phenomenology of the Self*. Trans. R.F.C. Hull. Ed. Gerhard Adler, Michael Fordham, and Herbert Read. London: Routledge and Kegan Paul.
Ovid. *Metamorphoses*. Trans. Mary M. Innes. Harmondsworth: Penguin. 1955. (Repr., 1968).
Sir Gawain and the Green Knight. Ed. J.R.R. Tolkien en E.V. Godron. 2nd ed. rev. N. Davis. Oxford: Oxford University Press. 1967 (1st ed. 1925).
Sir Orfeo. In: *Fourteenth Century Verse & Prose* Ed. Kenneth Sisam. Oxford: Oxford University Press. 1921 (Repr. 1967). 13-31.
Stevens, John (1973). *Medieval Romance: Themes and Approaches*. London: Hutchinson.
Veldhoen, N.H.G.E. (1981). I Haffe Spedde Better þan I Wend: Some Notes on the Structure of the ME *Sir Parceval of Galles*. *Dutch Quarterly Review* 11. 279-86
Veldhoen, N.H.G.E. (1988). *Floris and Blauncheflour*: To Indulge the Fancy and to Hear of Love. In: *Companion to Early Middle English Literature*. Ed. N.H.G.E. Veldhoen and H. Aertsen. Amsterdam: Free University Press. 53-67.

ROMANCE AND PARODY

WIM TIGGES

I

Not more than a handful of texts have been marked as in one way or another parodying the metrical romances, some eighty of which survive in Middle English and Middle Scots. Without pretending to be exhaustive, it is the intent of this essay to present a concise account of eleven texts, dating from the late fourteenth to the early seventeenth century, and which have been related in some specific way to the metrical romance, in particular by their meta-textual (usually humorous) comment upon one or more romance characteristics. It will appear that few of these texts are parodic in a strictly generic sense, and that this can be accounted for by the constant adaptation of the romance genre to the expectations of a changing audience, and by the absence of a sophisticated critical attitude towards romances in the period during which they were produced and enjoyed.

Preliminary to my survey a few terminological problems will have to be cleared up. The term "romance" has been defined so often, and, albeit with different emphases, generally with such a satisfactory consensus as to the essential features of this popular genre of medieval literature, that I will not even begin to provide yet another summary of the various definitions and typologies. Few readers, I suppose, will greatly quarrel with me in defining the medieval (Middle English) romance as a narrative genre, which can be succinctly characterised as the story of a single hero of aristocratic birth or aspiration and chivalric nurture (usually a knight), who undertakes an adventure (in the form of one or more tests and/or quests), the successful achievement of which leads to the favour of the hero's feudal lord, his lady, and/or his God.[1]

---

[1] The most concise as well as completely detailed definition is in my opinion still that presented by Helaine Newstead in the first paragraph of her brief introduction to Severs (1967:11), which also contains a list of titles of Middle English romances. For brief summaries and discussions of any of the romance texts referred to in this paper, I refer the reader to this Manual. For a recent, extensive general bibliography on romance, see Barron (1987:243-83). For a more specific annotated bibliography, see Rice (1987).

It is more difficult to give a satisfactory definition of parody, and especially of a medieval notion of this type of meta-text, and the reasons for this problem will soon become apparent. The term "parody" is often mentioned in one breath along with "burlesque", both of which terms are frequently bracketed with the modal notions of satire, humour, irony, and travesty. M.H. Abrams defines burlesque as "an incongruous imitation" of the matter or manner of a serious literary work or genre in such a way that amusement arises from "a ridiculous disparity between its form and style and its subject matter", usually a form of satire. Parody is that variety of "high" burlesque which "imitates the serious materials and manner of a particular work, or the characteristic style of a particular author, and applies it to a lowly or grossly discordant subject" (Abrams, 1981:17-18).

N.F. Blake (1977:116) makes a different distinction between burlesque and parody:

> Parody is the ridiculing of a particular turn of expression, work or genre by imitating its characteristic linguistic features and either modifying them slightly or applying them to ridiculous ends. Burlesque, on the other hand, makes use of current literary conventions and genres to poke fun at social aspirations and ideals without necessarily intending any mockery to fall on the literary forms so exploited. Burlesque looks beyond literature to society, whereas the goal of parody does not go beyond the belittling of a particular literary work or type. Burlesque is general and parody is particular. Finally ... burlesque is more concerned with attitudes than with language, whereas the very heart of parody is the exploitation and echoing of linguistic features .

Quite recently, Joseph A. Dane has come up with yet another relationship between the two concepts, reversing that of Abrams. Having ("preliminarily") defined parody as "the imitative reference of one literary text to another, often with an implied critique of the object text", he then, almost in passing, classifies burlesque as a certain form of parody (1988:4, 6).

In addition to this terminological confusion there is a further complication in that it is rather unclear to what extent medieval romances can be considered to be "literary" texts in the modern sense of the word. The argument in Dane's monograph largely hinges on the point that terms like "parody" and "burlesque" were given their modern status only in the course of the seventeenth and eighteenth centuries, so that it must be questioned whether these terms can be sensibly applied to medieval texts. Blake, on the other hand, points out (1977:127) that in the Middle Ages "it was difficult, if not impossible, to write parody in the way we know it today." The reason for this is that most if not all medieval writing, certainly before Chaucer's time, was highly formulaic and imitative. Individual authorial styles cannot therefore be easily distinguished. Hence, medieval parody, if it exists at all, can be at most of parody generic aspects (Blake, 1977:117). Carol Fewster, in a recent monograph on traditionality and genre in Middle English romance, attributes the reason for the scarcity of romance parody to "romance's self-consciousness in quoting and re-quoting itself ... Romance constantly discusses its own techniques of literary creation. Romance is continually self-parodic in a loose sense, and over-emphasises literary convention" (1987:148). Medieval texts, lacking the modern requirement of "originality", thereby show a degree of intertextuality which precludes a good deal of the possibilities that are offered by parodic imitation.

The major distinction between the "self-parodic" nature of romance and what happens to one or more aspects of the genre in a parody (or burlesque) proper, is the addition of a "conscious and recognisable humor."[2] In what follows I will concentrate on this element of humour. Whether a text containing this meta-literary reaction upon another text should be called strictly a parody, a satire, a travesty, a pastiche or a cento will not be taken into consideration, but from now on I will use the term "parody" in a wide sense for a meta-textual romance comment which is mainly humorously critical of a target text or text type. To make myself quite clear: the main question of this essay will not be whether Chaucer's *Tale of Sir Thopas*, for instance, is a parody or a burlesque, but rather: how can we tell that *Sir Thopas* is a parody, in the sense of a humorous meta-text, whereas *The Squire's Tale* and *The Squire of Low Degree* are not? And what precisely is being parodied in *Sir Thopas*?

---

2 The phrase between quotation marks is from Dane's translation of Paul Lehmann's definition of parody (Dane, 1988:4; for the original text, see Lehmann, 1963:3). Since Lehmann's famous monograph concentrates on the so-called "sacred parody" of religious Latin texts, I have not made further use of it for this essay.

Middle English parody before the appearance of Chaucer
seems in any case to be as conspicuous by its absence as is the Middle
English fabliau outside Chaucer's works. Keith Busby attributes the
scarcity of the fabliau, which he thinks often parodies or burlesques
the romance (1982:33, 39), to the peculiar nature of most Middle
English romances, in which, as he puts it (1982:40), "all analyses of
the finer points of chivalric or courtly behaviour are either excised
... or reduced to a perfunctory minimum." He concludes (1982:41):

> A good number of Old French fabliaux parody or iron-
> ically evoke certain aspects of chivalric or courteous be-
> haviour as found in the Old French romances. If this is
> one of the functions of the fabliau, then it follows that
> Middle English romances, which excise or play down
> these very elements, do not provide conditions condu-
> cive to the creation or development of this genre. An
> audience which has little or no interest in the amorous
> or moral problems of an Yvain or a Perceval is unlikely
> to appreciate fully certain fabliaux, however comic they
> may be in other respects, which use these very problems
> as a basis for their point. On the other hand, it is clear
> that an audience like Chaucer's, which did take delight
> in meditating on these aspects of literature, also appre-
> ciated fabliaux which alluded in this manner to the ro-
> mances.

Busby, elaborating on the theory of Per Nykrog (1973:72-104), may
have a point here, but he fails to explain why these pared-down Middle English texts, which frequently appear to misunderstand the issues and complexities of their Old French sources and analogues, do
not in themselves offer a suitable butt for refined parody. As Busby
himself puts it in a later publication, "parody is ineffective unless the
audience appreciates, what is being parodied" (1988:71-2). Surely an
English-speaking audience (of whatever social status) that appreciated the romances in their native dialect, must also have been aware
of the stylistic weaknesses of some of these romances, and of the
questions evoked by the idealisation of chivalric virtues (such as bravery, loyalty and generosity) that are characteristic of them. Elsewhere I have argued that the early Middle English comic tales of *The
Fox and the Wolf* and *The Land of Cokaygne*, neither of which are
romance parodies in a generic sense, incorporate elements that seem
to ironise or to parody aspects of the contemporary romance, such as

the boasting of the hero in the former, and the play upon catalogues in the latter (Tigges, 1988b and 1988c). There is no apparent reason why such and similar formulaic elements or motifs should not have been subject to more coherent parody in the Middle English period.

Let us proceed then by making a brief inventory of romance features that one might very well expect to be commented on in parody form. As has been said before, the essential elements of a romance are the *knightly* hero on *adventure*, the *test* or *quest*, and the *reward* of the virtues that the hero embodies and idealises. Secondary elements are: a *love* theme, which is bound to be in terms of *fin amours* or courtly love, and the occurrence of the *marvellous* as an obstacle to be overcome, or as a support of the hero. Romances are written in a conventional *high* style, in *formulaic* octosyllabic couplets, tail-rhyme stanzas, or, less frequently, alliterative lines or stanzas. Conventional, too, are the *descriptions* of the hero, of the lady, of the villain or main opponent, of battles and tournaments, of castles, of the romantic pleasance or garden, of food, jewels and armour.

All these elements lend themselves easily to parody or ridicule. An important point here, already alluded to before, is that in a parody the convention, of whatever kind, should be *noticeably* ridiculed. "Without some clear indication by the author," as Blake phrases it (1977:120), "parody must be discounted." It has been rightly pointed out that mere exaggeration does not work as a clear parody-marker for medieval texts, since hyperbole is a conventional aspect of romance style.[3] What then might be expected to create a sense of parody in the recipient of the text? To start with the hero: instead of being a knight or an aspiring knight (such as a squire or a "Childe"), the protagonist might be presented as a churl or another kind of anti-hero.[4] As to the adventure, the quests or tests, these might be made bathetic or from the very start an inversion of chivalric convention. The aim or reward of the test might be made trivial, pointless or absurd. The love theme might be made earthly or ob-

[3] See Blake, 1977:116ff. Derek Brewer adduces a satisfactory psychological explanation of the use of hyperbole in "traditional" cultures, by quoting from Paul Theroux's *The Old Patagonian Express*; the argument centres on the idea that intensity furthers belief (Brewer, 1986:6-8).

[4] Of course, there are romances in which the hero *begins* as a lowly character, e.g. *Havelok* and *Sir Perceval of Galles*, but the recipient knows from the start that he really has to do with a prince or knight whose "adventure" it is to show his true worth and to come into his own.

scene instead of refined and euphemised. The marvellous might be
ridiculed, the style lowered, formulae made to misapply (rather, as
Blake convincingly argued, than overdoing them), descriptions be
made to apply to the wrong kind of object.

In order to be appreciated by an intelligent and critical audience, a parody must not be just debunking, but must in fact possess an
aesthetic of its own. As D.H. Green states in his conclusion concerning irony in medieval romance (1979:392-3):

> With regard to the themes of chivalry and love, irony is
> employed to indicate more the deficiencies of one who
> failed to live up to the ideal than the shortcomings of
> that ideal. When a courtly ideal is apparently called into
> question by irony this takes the form of parodying a
> rival's version of that ideal, so that what comes under
> critical fire is a poetic colleague's imperfect under-
> standing of the ideal, which is thus preserved and
> strengthened in the parodist's own positive view of its
> potentialities. Even when a contemporary ideal is iron-
> ised and not allowed any redeeming features at all ...,
> this serves the constructive purpose of defending anoth-
> er idea felt to be superior and more essential ....
>   In all these cases medieval irony, unlike the admitted-
> ly often nihilistic corrosiveness of modern irony, still
> has a positive function in strengthening the ideal, rather
> than necessarily weakening it, just as any irony, partic-
> ularly if employed at the narrator's expense, can be a
> device to protect and not destroy the illusion created in
> the story. The same point has been made by Lewis who
> suggests that the romance, by allowing laughter and
> cynicism their place inside the poem, is able to protect
> itself against the laughter of the vulgar. The closely
> allied feature of realistic details (considered like irony
> as modifications of an idealised presentation) has been
> suggested as an attempt to render this ideal world more
> meaningful and to communicate it more forcibly, in-
> tending to enrich the ideal and not to criticise it.

Theoretically speaking, it seems hardly likely that the medieval par-
odist would primarily be questioning the ideals, chivalric, bourgeois
or otherwise, embodied by the hero and his activities. What is more
likely is that he would ridicule pretentious behaviour on the part of

contemporaries in terms of romance themes and motifs. On the other hand, a similar, basically didactic intention might serve to upgrade the chivalric behaviour of flesh-and-blood characters by clothing them in the garb of chivalric romance. Loyalty and gratitude may be chivalric qualities, but they can be practised by a simple charcoal-burner as well as, if not better than, by a contemporary knight. What is more, "bourgeois" virtues such as hospitality, thrift and industry, in the later Middle Ages begin to be seen as on a par with the more aristocratic virtues of loyalty, generosity and bravery.

These considerations are quite different from those of the poet trained in rhetoric, who desires to show up the aesthetic failures of an existent text or type of text. The parody "proper" concentrates on the object text's rhetorical failures. A general audience (again, no matter of what social status) would not be greatly bothered by the precise form and structure of the text, which in any case would be mostly received aurally rather than in written form; as long as the story contained a recognisable plot and a pleasing combination of motifs, the formulaic tags and facile rhyming would not be a major obstacle to enjoyment of the story—in this respect the reception of medieval romance is presumably very similar to that of such highly formulaic modern productions as soap-operas, penny novelettes, and detective and science fiction novels of the simpler kind by an average audience. It takes a sophisticated reader, alert to details and in partic-ular desirous of originality of expression and freshness of thought *within* a recognisable tradition, to appreciate both the faults of an in-ferior production and the cleverness of a parody of it—and this may be the main reason for the scarcity of medieval romance parody.

II

Before coming to a final conclusion about the nature of medieval romance parody in English and Scots, I will now proceed to give an account of the texts to which this label may be applicable. The eleven texts I will discuss are not equally parodic, indeed, some of them are hardly so; I divide them into five sub-categories. The first "group", that of parody "proper", consists of only one text, Chaucer's *Tale of Sir Thopas*, to which much attention has already been paid, and which I will mainly discuss here in order to elaborate some of the points made in the previous section. Secondly, there is the group which I would label "comic-didactic romance". To this category be-long *Sir Cleges* and *The Taill of Rauf Coilyear*, and, more tenta-tively as to the comic nature of these texts, *The Wedding of Sir Gawain and Dame Ragnell* and *The Squire of Low Degree*. Next

comes a small group of texts which describe a lower-class brawl in
terms of a chivalric tournament: *The Tournament of Tottenham* and
Alexander Scott's *The Justing and the Debait up at the Drum*. A
fourth group, exemplified by William Dunbar's "Schir Thomas
Norny" and the anonymous "Sir Penny", combines the motif of the
mock-hero with stylistic parody of the tail-rhyme romance. In connection with this group I will also discuss Francis Beaumont's play
The Knight of the Burning Pestle. Finally, there is the single text
Squire Meldrum by Sir David Lindsay, which treats a historical
character in terms of a romance hero.

The most striking things about this collection of texts are:
apart from *Sir Thopas*, they are nearly all of northern derivation;
most of them are of Scottish origin; and they date from around 1400
or later. The reasons or this state of affairs are various: these texts
make an evident appeal to familiarity with a well-established genre;
they are all written in a time when the phenomenon of the individ-
ually recognisable and thus responsible author had appeared on the
stage; and soon after the deaths of Chaucer, Gower, and Lydgate, the
weight of courtly poetry shifted to Scotland.

The possible background to Chaucer's *Tale of Sir Thopas*
(henceforth *Thopas*) is well-documented.[5] Anyone who is at all familiar with the conventional themes, motifs, form and style of Middle English romance will have a shrewd idea that there is something
odd about this Flemish knight-errant with his girdle-length beard but
otherwise somewhat effeminate appearance, pricking like mad
through the buck-and-hare-infested forest that smells of licorice and
nutmeg, and who goes out to find an elf-queen—blissfully ignorant
of the fact that elf-queens, by convention, cannot be searched for but
come and search one out if one is lucky—and bravely informs a
three-headed giant that he will come back and fight when better
armed on the next day, only to forget all about this self-imposed
agreement when he rides out again after a sumptuous feast of ginger-
bread soaked in wine. Lee C. Ramsey offers the commonsensical
comment (1983:211) that "the humor of the tale depends primarily
on inappropriateness and contradictions" and proceeds briefly to
summarise the incongruities, many of which are also noted in the
text editions (1983:211-3).

---

[5] See notes in Robinson, 1968:736ff, now largely superseded by Benson, 1988:
917ff. The textual parallels to *Thopas* have been listed by Loomis (1958:486-
559).

For this tale, put into his own mouth, and shamelessly interrupted by the impatient Host, Chaucer makes use of a form and style
that are not used elsewhere in his works; the curtailed six-line tail-
rhyme stanza, later modified into a stanza-form containing a di-
syllabic "bob" rather resembling the device used in the humdrum romance of *Sir Tristrem*, full of well-known tags and forced rhymes,
is obviously not the kind of fare Chaucer felt it ordinarily suitable to
put before his audience. But does this necessarily mean that Chaucer
was ridiculing contemporary popular romance? Blake rightly suggests (1977:125-6):

> The crucial question remains what features of the lan-
> guage are there in *Sir Thopas* which indicate that a par-
> ody is present? The answer would seem to be that the
> words and constructions used are in themselves unex-
> ceptional and would not cause any comment in a straight
> romance, ... It is difficult to escape the conclusion that
> there is nothing in the language of *Sir Thopas* to indicate
> that it is unusual as a tail-rhyme romance—and this may
> well have been Chaucer's message.

His conclusion is that *Thopas* can only be seen to be parodic because
of the text-external comments (in particular the interruption by the
Host).
     In an interesting paper (1982:311-29) Alan T. Gaylord argues
that in *Thopas* Chaucer indirectly alerted his audience to the changes
he was introducing into the language and style of contemporary literature. Gaylord attacks what he calls Laura Hibbard Loomis' "literary value-judgments which are incorrectly passed off as self-evident"
(1982:314), and proceeds to demonstrate the potential aesthetic appropriateness of conventional stylistic romance features, as in *Guy
of Warwick* and *Lybeaus Desconus* (1982:315-18).[6] It should be noted that in *Thopas* Chaucer refers to these and other popular texts as
"*romances of prys*" (1.897; all textual references are to the Riverside
Chaucer). It is difficult if not impossible to certify whether this qualification would not have been heartily agreed with rather than taken
ironically by Chaucer's courtly audience, unless we are to assume

[6] I have recently argued on similar lines with respect to *Sir Eglamour of Artois*
(Tigges, 1988a:107-15, esp. 108, 113-4).

that these romances had already begun to be regarded as stuff for the lower strata of society, but no longer fit for the court.

However this may be, it seems evident that all of Chaucer's own "romances" (if they may be given that label)[7] are greatly modified adaptations of the original, i.e. conventional genre. To limit ourselves to *The Canterbury Tales*, *The Knight's Tale* is a philosophical discourse clothed in the garb of chivalry, rather than an adventure story; it is notable that the Miller's fabliau reacts to the semantic contents of *The Knight's Tale* rather than to its form or style. *The Man of Law's Tale*, a version of the Constance-*topos* quite popular in many traditional romances,[8] ironically, in view of the teller's disclaimer, highlights the rhetorical trickery of the telling of a tale of suffering, which is here presented from the point of view of the feminine victim to a much larger extent than is usual in the romance versions. *The Wife of Bath's Tale*, too, is a didactic romance that shifts the point of view from the knight's conventional activity to his unchivalric conduct and the consequences his behaviour has for the victim of his exploits (in this respect it is interesting to compare this tale to the later version of the story in *The Wedding of Sir Gawain and Dame Ragnell*, to be discussed below). In *The Squire's Tale*, it is in particular the conventions of the supernatural that come under attack, but the magic horse, mirror, ring and sword are not so much ridiculed as reasoned away by the bystanders, and once the theme of "*gentilesse*", that pervades many of these tales as a *Leitmotiv*, has been touched upon from yet another ("romantic") point of view, the traditional interlacing that must result from the set-up of the plot is abandoned, and the tale remains unfinished. The theme, however, is further enlarged upon in *The Franklin's Tale*, which makes use of the framework of a sub-type of romance, the Breton *lai*, thereby enabling its teller to relate the themes of gentility and generosity to those prime characteristics of the lay, love and the supernatural. When we finally come to *Thopas*, it is as if Chaucer was trying to convey to his audience the notion that without semantic substance, a "sentence" of general human, in particular social, interest, "meaning is reduced to illustrating the vanity of a style that becomes its own

[7] Ramsey refers to them as "intellectualized romances" (1983:215), together with, for instance, *Sir Gawain and the Green Knight*.
[8] See Severs, 1967:120-32; Ramsey, 1983:157-88.

subject" (Gaylord, 1982:326). In *The Tale of Melibee*, on the other hand, the message is all, and poetry quite disappears.[9]

It will be clear that the long-assumed self-evidence of the parodic or burlesque nature of *Thopas* has become subject to serious scrutiny. A very recent example of this is the challenge posed to this position by Joseph A. Dane (1988:185-203). Dane's argument is built upon the literary-historical fact that the first descriptions of *Thopas* as a burlesque or parody date from respectively the middle of the eighteenth and the early nineteenth century. Moreover, whereas twentieth-century critics tend to agree on the parodic or at least humorous reading of *Thopas*, they heavily disagree on the nature of both *The Squire's Tale* and *The Tale of Melibee*. Since many early writers (from John Skelton onwards) provide evidence that they consider *Thopas* to be a "silly" tale, but take *The Squire's Tale* seriously, the question that is evoked is: how can we know that *Thopas* is a parody whereas *The Squire's Tale* is not? The answer to this question appears already to have been provided by Blake (1979) and Gaylord (1982) in combination, neither of which Dane seems to have consulted.[10]

In order to see where we are both with *Thopas* (and Chaucer's other chivalric tales), and with the texts to be considered below, the following addition may be expedient. The ideals of chivalry and of love relationships, both of which feature in romances, may be satirised or lauded, but not parodied. The very notion of idealisation precludes this. On the other hand, parody may only refer to literary aspects of the target work or genre—that is to say, subject-matter (knighthood, love, tournaments and battles, the supernatural and so on) as a literary *topos*, and such formal elements as structure (interlacing), style and diction (formulae and archaisms), and rhyme (tags). The principal parody-marker has been said to be a conscious and recognisable use of humour, directed against one or more of the above elements.[11] It is a curious fact that Harry Bailey apparently fails to see any such humour in *Thopas*—all he notes is that the tale is

---

[9] Cf. Kooper (1984:152), who notes a similar contrast between *Thopas* and *Melibee*.

[10] They do not appear in his extensive bibliography, although other articles by Gaylord on *Thopas* do.

[11] Needless to say, a romance may well contain humour without being parody. To mind comes the giant Ascopart in *Bevis of Hampton*, who protests that he is too big to be baptised. See also the discussion of the "comic-didactic" romance type in the following section.

full of *"verray lewednesse"* (l.921: 'veritable ignorance'), *"drasty speche"* (l.923: 'filthy language'), and *"rym dogerel"* (l.925: 'rough verse'). This is all the more remarkable as the Host is the self-styled arbitrator and judge in the tale-telling contest which *The Canterbury Tales* after all purports to be. To what extent can we depend on this character for our judgment of the tale? Most readers, I suppose, feel that the Host's failure to recognise this tale for what it is, namely a parody on poor romance, is exactly the point that Chaucer was making. On the other hand, by introducing the Tellers, the Host, and Chaucer the Pilgrim in between the poet's authentic voice and our understanding, Chaucer is able to manipulate the context of any single tale, including that of *Thopas*, so that we cannot even be quite certain as to the position we are in to judge the tale from, a point Blake omits to make. All we ultimately have to go by to break the hermeneutic circle is the difference of the metre of *Thopas* from that of any other tale in the collection (Blake, 1977:124), and the curious fact of the "poet" contriving to have himself interrupted in the rudest fashion while reciting *"the beste rym [he] kan"* (l.928; the best verse he is capable of).

III

In the other texts, which will now be discussed more succinctly, we do not even have anything resembling an external context, but, as the above argument will have demonstrated, even the benefit of such a context can be highly dubious. *Sir Cleges*, a late fourteenth-century North Midland text in twelve-line tail-rhyme, has been noted for its combination of fabliauesque elements with those of the *exemplum* or moral tale.[12] Apart from the unusual appearance of a comic plot, there is nothing in this romance that points to its being at all intended as a parody or burlesque. The theme of the indigent knight is common (cf. e.g. *Sir Amadace* and *Sir Launfal*), and the episode of the cherry-tree miracle is presented seriously. The knight has become a more true-to-life character than is usual in romance, being married and possessing tangible estates, and there seems to be some ambiguity

[12] See, for instance, the introductory note to the text as in French and Hale, 1964: 877. All references to the text are to this edition. The tale has been described extensively in the Introduction to the text as edited by George H. McKnight (1913: lxi-lxxv). I wish to emphasize here that in providing bibliographical data of secondary sources related to this and other texts discussed in this paper, no attempt has been made to be exhaustive. The reader is referred to the bibliographies in note 1.

about his motives in l.96, where it is suggested that the charity which
has led to his indigence at the beginning of the poem has been due to
pride. What is more curious, perhaps, is that he is presented as a
knight not of the Round Table but of the retinue of Arthur's father,
Uther (ll.4ff), but this is hardly an indication of parody. The main
joke in *Sir Cleges* is that the hero tricks the greedy court-officials,
and we may well wonder why this fabliau theme of deceit and its
punishment, the central pivot of the plot, is told in what is to all in-
tents and purposes the romance form. A tentative answer to this
question would be that the main theme of the poem, liberality *versus*
greed, is a traditionally chivalric issue. The tale hinges on the question of true gentility, and in this respect it may well be compared to
Chaucer's *Wife of Bath's Tale*, which likewise presents a moral lesson in the form of romance, Arthurian or otherwise, but, like *Sir
Cleges*, draws the issue into the world of a more "modern" aristocratic as well as bourgeois society.

Even closer to *The Wife of Bath's Tale*, because of its plot, is
the mid-fifteenth-century East Midland *The Wedding of Sir Gawain
and Dame Ragnell*. This text reminds one even less of the parody or
burlesque than *Sir Cleges*, although it has been treated as such.[13] The
plot is by no means as comical as the Wife of Bath is allowed to make
it in *The Canterbury Tales*, and in fact it shows up yet another way in
which I think many Middle English romances may be aptly defined,
namely as folktales dressed in the garb of chivalry. Its main theme,
authority, is yet another of those issues which, originating in the
chivalric code (related no doubt to feudal loyalty), lent itself very
properly to discussion in a more "bourgeoisified" context.

Both *Sir Cleges* and *The Wedding* are structured according to
the simple binary device in which an initial problem is posed in Part
One and (more or less comically) solved in Part Two. Something
similar occurs in the late fifteenth-century tail-rhymed Scottish *Taill
of Rauf Coilyear*. The difference is that the hero is not a knight, to
begin with at least, but a "simple" churl, a collier or charcoal-burner. His hospitality and his straightforward and outspoken behaviour
appeal to the "disguised" king Charlemagne, and Rauf is suitably
rewarded when he demonstrates that he can also take the initiative in
coming to the court and defeating a monstrous Saracen, at least as
well as that best of *Douzepers*, Roland, might. Far from being a par-

---

[13] Notably by its editor, Donald B. Sands (1966), who classifies it under "Burlesque and Grotesquerie".

ody of knightly romance, this poem celebrates the innate chivalric qualities in a common citizen. Here, in a manner comparable to that used by Lindsay in *Squire Meldrum*, romance trappings and features provide a literary means of raising the banner of the faithful and well-behaved subject, and Smyser's labelling of this tale (1932:149) as a "burlesque romance" (rather than as a comic or comic-didactic one) on the grounds that such a term "obviates the necessity of passing hazardous judgments as to whether the makar was imitating the *chanson de geste* with malice aforethought, or whether he made the *chanson de geste* appear ridiculous only accidentally, as it were, by drawing upon it for some of the stuff of a ridiculous poem" unnecessarily blurs the issue. Similarly, I think it is under mistaken assumptions that Ramsey categorises *Rauf Coilyear* under the heading of "Upstarts" (1983:196f). In *Rauf Coilyear*, as in *Sir Cleges* and *The Wedding*, there is a rightness about the events described, as well as an appropriateness between contents and style, that makes it difficult for any audience to suspect anything like a debunking of conventional romance. Rather, these texts show romance adapting itself to a changed world-view.

With the last text in my category of comic-didactic romances the matter is more complex altogether. This is the late fifteenth-century East Midland *The Squire of Low Degree* (henceforth *Squire*), written in octosyllabic couplets. Some critics of this poem adhere fervently to the idea that it is a parody—notably K.S. Kiernan, who argues (1973:345) that this romance, known in the sixteenth century under its alternative title of *Undo Your Door*, "is purposefully structured to serve the poet's humorous intentions."[14] In this view "there is scarcely a line in *Undo Your Door* that does not demonstrate the humorous intentions of its poet" (1973:347), but the

---

[14] Cf. Ramsey, who remarks that its "standard quest plot" is "filled with improbabilities" (1983:197), but explains this and other oddities in the text by its being, like *Rauf Coilyear*, a "middle-class" romance. Both Sands (1966) and French and Hale (1964) read it fairly straightforwardly, the former categorizing it under the heading "Chivalry and Sentiment", the latter noting its "well-known medieval motives and devices" (1964:721). As appears from a quotation in Beer (1970: 33), Thomas Nashe considered it to be of equal "Absurditee" with any "acts of Arthur of the rounde table, Arthur of little Brittaine, Sir Tristram, Hewon of Burdeaux" and "the foure sons of Ammon", whereas his contemporary Robert Laneham delighted in it to an equal extent with those works as well as *Sir Eglamour* and *Sir Triamour* (*ibid.*). It was apparently very popular in the late sixteenth century and copied out as late as the seventeenth. The main point is that at this stage it was not generally distinguished from conventional romance, whether liked or disliked.

analysis which is presented in order to prove this categorical statement fails to convince me, most particularly as to the intentionality
of the various crudities which indeed pervade this remarkable text.
Thus, there is indeed a good deal of exaggeration and abundance (especially in the long catalogues), but in contrast to *Thopas*, in *Squire*
they are not incompatible, and so not obviously humorous. In fact,
Fewster convincingly argues (1987:136) that if anything, *Squire* is
less formulaic than most romances.[15] It may well have been the case
that a fifteenth or sixteenth-century audience was struck by some
"funny" effects in this poem, such as the frequent mixing up of piled-
up detail, and the misunderstandings in the plot. Even early on in the
story it appears that the king of Hungary is quite willing to marry his
daughter to the indigent but industrious squire (ll.275-6; text as in
French and Hale, 1964). The squire's "forgetting" to take formal
leave of his lady (l.498) is somewhat remarkable, as is the apparently
complete lack of communication between father and daughter, so
that the former does not know what arrangements the latter has made
with the squire (ll.666-8). Another oddity is the princess's stark-
naked appearance at the door in the middle of the night, after her
initial reluctance to open it for her harrassed lover (ll.673-4).

The crucial question is whether these are incongruities, which
would no doubt be recognised as such by the connoisseur of Middle
English romance in the *fourteenth* as well as in the *twentieth* century,
albeit perhaps for different reasons and with different reactions; or
whether they are intentional "slapstick" to amuse a *fifteenth*-century
audience, or the result of bungling, i.e. inadequate composition, or
simply contributions to the changed expectations of a fifteenth and
sixteenth-century romance audience. I think the last suggestion provides the answer, and my proposition is that *The Squire of Low Degree* is (as romances go) a well-written text, catering for the fifteenth-century high bourgeois preoccupation with the grandilo-
quent, the gruesome and the grotesque. The *Squire*, in other words,
is neither a romance in the traditional sense, nor is it a parody or a
burlesque of one.

Kiernan (1973:352, 363, 365) points to the oddity of the inor-
dinately long speeches that occur in this poem (e.g. those by the
princess which cover ll.151-278 and ll.571-636, and the king's
speech in ll.739-852). As has also been noted by Fewster (1983:139),

---

[15] Fewster devotes a full, eminently sensible chapter to *Squire* (1987:129-49), in
which she deals *in extenso* with the aspects in which the poem cross-refers to
romance conventions.

much of *Squire*, including the so-called "mock-investiture" of the squire by the princess, occurs not in actual narrated fact, but in speeches; the text is extremely "wordy" in this sense, and this, I think, reflects the verbally idealised nature of chivalry in the late Middle Ages and early Renaissance, as well as an increasing sense of the artificiality of romance as a literary genre. To summarise in the words of Carol Fewster:

> The *Squyr* evokes a sense of narrative convention and of genre in its allusion to other romances, and in its use of romance formulae. However, the *Squyr* alters this evoked style, using it partially rather than as a complete narrative style. (1987:132)
>
> The *Squyr* evokes romance style without necessarily being wholly within or defined by that style. ... In fact the *Squyr* expands and moves away from romance formulaic style as a distinctive generic marker. (1987:136)
>
> As a late text, the *Squyr* displays an ability to look back over romance tradition, and to quote from romance at selected points. (1987:137)
>
> The *Squyr* world is a world of artifice and artificiality, and one in which description always does supersede action: the role of narrators and of narratorial language in the poem is primary. It seems to me that the *Squyr* works as meta-narrative—it is about narrativity, on a broader scale than its use of romance. ... It uses the devices of humour, quotation, allusion (the devices of parody, though not necessarily with the broadly reductive intention defined by some writers on parody) to create a work about narration (1987:147).

The Squire of Low Degree, then, verges on parody, but not more so than can be allowed for in the largely self-parodic nature of romance in general. But in addition to this, as a late sample of a genre that had had three centuries in which to develop, it has apparently incorporated elements that are reminiscent of the Italian *novella*—the motif of the preserved corpse, including its mistaken identity, strikes me as distinctly "Boccaccian" decadence rather than as laughable debunking of a long-established type of entertaining narrative.

A poem often mentioned in one breath with *Thopas* as a burlesque is the early fifteenth-century Northern *The Tournament of Tottenham* (henceforth *Tournament*). According to French and Hale (1964:989) this text "shows the same familiarity with the machinery of chivalry and the same unwillingness to take it seriously" (cf. Ramsey, 1983:213-4). In a nine-line stanza which is more common in some Northern mystery plays than in romance, this relatively short text (it has 234 lines) describes a village brawl in terms of a tournament, complete with a "lady" as the prize to be won, together with a brood-hen and a brown cow, presumably thrown in to make the prize more attractive. The reference to a village only slightly to the north of medieval London in a Northern text, which puzzled French and Hale, may point to the possibility of the poem being partly a skit against the presumed pretentiousness of southern yokels from a northern point of view.[16] The text shows once again the typical diptych structure common to romance (see Fewster, 1987:14-22, 139-41). The first and longer part mainly consists of boastful vows by the participants to the "tournament", including some incongruous descriptions of mock-heroic coats of arms (ll. 105-8, 123-6). It is in particular this device of inversion and incongruity that places this text far more obviously within the pale of burlesque than those discussed before.

Rather similar to the *Tournament* is the post-medieval *The Justing and the Debait up at the Drum* by Alexander Scott (c1525 - c1583), written in twenty-one ten-line bob-and-wheel stanzas. The recent editor of this text, Felicity Riddy, notices in this poem "a sustained element of literary parody after the manner of Chaucer's *Sir Thopas*" (Bawcutt and Riddy, 1987:269). Both the *Tournament* and the *Justing* make abundant use of the familiar romance phraseology, e.g. "*of þem þat were dughty / And stalworth in dede*" (*Tournament*, ll.8-9: 'of those that were brave and valiant in deeds') and "*Doutles wes nocht so duchty deidis ... / To se so stowtly on thair steidis / Tha stalwart knychtis steiris*" (*Justing*, ll.11, 15-16: 'Doubtless there were not such courageous deeds ... to see [performed] so valiantly on their horses that brave knights are directing the course of').

It is evident that both poems appeal to a familiarity with romance conventions, both stylistic and thematic. The butt of both poems is not so much the romance genre or the incongruity between

---

[16] Cf., for instance, the shepherds' reactions to Mak's "southern tooth" and boastfulness in *The Second Shepherds' Play* of the Wakefield mystery cycle.

chivalric ideals and practice on the one hand and the inferior classes (simple tradesmen) that aspire to them on the other. What the authors of *Tournament* and *Justing* set out to do is rather comparable to the way Henry Fielding mock-heroically describes the fights between villagers in *Tom Jones*. Fielding was not so much attacking the venerable genre of the epic as trying comically to upgrade the status of his novel (then still often considered an inferior genre) by facetiously claiming to compose in the epic tradition.

It is hardly conceivable that a brawl between peasants or tradesmen would as such be a subject of interest to a courtly audience (and Riddy informs us that Alexander Scott in particular was a composer of courtly lyrics, 1987:269). As will be argued presently, the romance was not yet considered a devalued genre near the end of the sixteenth century. The point was that, as with the literary epic in Fielding's time, the true thing could no longer be written. In Britain, Thomas Malory's *Morte Darthur* (more decisively than Chaucer's *Troilus and Criseyde*) was the romance to end all romances. The attitude to romance on the part of a courtly audience in Scott's days may well have been as ambivalent as that of Fielding towards the epic. This may have enabled Scott to incorporate romance elements into the lyric mode, and so to enhance the literary appreciation of what is essentially a comic motif: the mock-heroic fight *"up at the Drum"* between *"William"* and *"Syme"*, a contest which, after all the preliminaries have been arranged, fails to come off. In fact, Scott's *Justing* is excellent and accomplished "light verse". The *Tournament* appears to be somewhat more down-to-earth. In both poems, the humour is certainly "conscious and recognizable", but I doubt if it is primarily an indication of parody here.

A fourth little "group" of poems associated with romance consists of two lyrics, the anonymous late fifteenth-century "Sir Penny"[17] and William Dunbar's "Schir Thomas Norny" (c1505). "Sir Penny", consisting of 123 lines in what is basically the six-line tail-rhyme stanza of *Thopas*, describes the nature of money, allegorised as a knight, to whom, by way of comic reversal of the normal situation, popes, kings, emperors, bishops, abbots, dukes, earls and barons, in short, the whole social hierarchy, pay homage (ll.7-12). Part of the description of the romance knight reads like a travesty, as in the following stanza:

[17] The second poem of that name, edited as no. 58 in Robbins, 1952:51-2.

> Sir Peny ouer all gettes þe gre,
> both in burgh and in cete,
>   in castell and in towre;
> with-owten owþer spere or schelde
> es he þe best in frith or felde,
>   and stalworthest in stowre.   (94-9)

(Sir Penny has pre-eminence everywhere, both in borough and
city, in castle and tower; without either spear or shield he is the
best in wood or field, and the most valiant in battle.)

"Schir Thomas Norny", in only fifty-four lines in the same stanza-
form, is presented more like a telescoped version of a romance,
opening with the minstrel-like address to the audience ("*Now lythis
off ane gentill knycht*", [Dunbar, ed. Kinsley, 1979:98-9]: 'Now hear
about a gentle knight'). Sir Thomas, according to Kinsley's annota-
tion a fool at the Court of King James IV (1979: 300), is presented as
the son of a giant and a Fairy Queen, and is thus, as it were, a godson
to Sir Thopas. He is favourably compared to several personages who
may have been historical, as well as to the legendary Sir Guy and Sir
Bevis. The parodistic style of the poem is unmistakable, as in:

> This anterous knycht quhar ever he went
> At justing and at tornament
>   Evermor he wan the gre;
> Was never off halff so gryt renowne
> Sir Bevis the knycht off Southe Hamptoune;
>   (I schrew him giff I le).   (31-6)

(This adventurous knight, wherever he went, at jousting and in
tournament, would always win the prize; not of half so great renown was Sir Bevis, the knight of Southampton; I curse him who
says I lie.)

The techniques of the mock-tournament as well as of the stylistic parodies are echoed in Francis Beaumont's play *The Knight of
the Burning Pestle*, which was probably written and first produced
in 1607 (Beaumont, ed. Doebler, 1967:xi), and which first appeared
in print in a quarto of 1613. This play, roughly contemporaneous
with Cervantes' *Don Quixote*, pokes fun, among other things, at the
London citizens' enthusiasm for the Iberian chivalric romances that
enjoyed popularity in the early seventeenth century (Beaumont, ed.
Doebler, 1967:xiv; cf., for instance, Act I, ll.215ff). The citizen (a
grocer) and his wife, who are presented as emerging from the

audience of what was intended to be another play, throughout force
the players to adapt their plot to that of chivalric romances, and, as in
Don Quixote, the central idea is that everyday characters, objects and
events change quality when they are garbed in chivalric verbiage.
The citizen's apprentice, Rafe (was Beaumont thinking of the collier?), must play the part of a knight, and he instructs his fellow players to address him in terms of romance style, which he also adopts
himself, as in the following passage from Act II, describing the
arrival at a common wayside inn:

> Fair squire Tapstero, I a wand'ring knight,
> Hight of the Burning Pestle, in the quest
> Of this fair lady's casket and wrought purse,
> Losing myself in this vast wilderness
> Am to this castle well by fortune brought,
> Where, hearing of the goodly entertain
> Your knight of holy order of the Bell
> Gives to all damsels and all errant knights,
> I thought to knock, and now am bold to enter.   (ii.378-86)

Knight-errantry, courtly love, knightly battles, and the supernatural
are all debunked in this play, as are the form and style of the early
modern versions of romance, and it is clear that Beaumont no longer
takes the romance tradition and conventions seriously.

That such spoofing of romance conventions was by no means a
long-standing joke by the early seventeenth century is demonstrated
by my final illustration, Sir David Lindsay's *Squire Meldrum*, which
must have been written between 1550 (when the historical William
Meldrum died) and 1555 (the year of Lindsay's death).[18] At this late
date, Lindsay, no mean satirist, reverts to the ancient octosyllabic
couplet, and although the text is not devoid of humorous frankness,
in particular in the description of Meldrum's relation with the Lady
of Gleneagles, which is excerpted by Bawcutt and Riddy (1987), the
whole poem, running to a regular romance length of 1594 lines, is
written in a serious, "romantic" vein, which includes practically all
the standard features. As the editors put it, "the terms in which the

---

[18] Bawcutt and Riddy, 1987:248. For a complete edition of the text, see Hamer,
1931 and 1934. For a more detailed discussion of *Squire Meldrum*, see Riddy
(1974), who argues that Lindsay could no longer take the genre of romance seriously (1974:26), and that he "honours, laughs at, and in the end discards, romance" (1974:36).

'legend' of Meldrum's life is told presuppose an audience thoroughly familiar with the romance genre and alert to the poem's allusiveness" (1987:249). The poem was reprinted no fewer than seven times between 1582 and 1711. Meldrum is compared to the classical and medieval heroes celebrated in well-known romances, such as the Thebes legends, *Sir Firumbras* and *Eger and Grime* (ll.1309ff.).

Squire Meldrum is by no means a parody, but an homage to a contemporary worthy, in other words, a historical biography in terms of romance values. Inversely, one might say that this poem lifts traditional romance up to a very realistic level. The joust between Meldrum and Talbart, described in ll.370ff., is not comical, nor is the fact that in the various large scale skirmishes such modern phenomena as a gunfight at sea are introduced. That the feasts are not only sprinkled with wine and ale, but also with whisky (*"Gude Aquavite"*, l.886), may bring a smile to the face of the antiquarian, but it is evident that this detail is far from being meant as a ludicrous touch.

IV

If this essay has demonstrated anything at all, it is that even a super-ficial investigation into the parodies of Middle English romance brings to light the existence of a variety of literary texts, dating from Chaucer's time to the early seventeenth century, which in one way or another comment on the genre, or make use of its main features. It has, I hope, become clear that these meta- or intertextual comments are not always necessarily of a humorous or parodic nature. Mc-Knight ascribed the scarcity of humorous texts in Middle English to an inherent English puritanism (1913:xix-xx), a judgement which most modern critics, I suppose, will regard as too simple in view of later findings, such as those about the status of the fabliau. Fewster very recently, as noted above, has drawn our attention to the essen-tially self-parodic nature of romance in order to explain the relative difficulty of retrieving many clear-cut cases of humorous romance parody (1987:148). I think that the scarcity of humorous parody of romance can be ascribed to yet another, more general phenomenon. Parody is first and foremost an intellectual *divertissement*; it ex-presses, as Green has indicated (1979:393), at the same time an ex-treme *love* of the target, as well as envy and dislike .[19] Chaucer was the first and the last intellectual in whose own time "good" romances were still being composed and enjoyed (*Sir Gawain and the Green*

---

[19] Cf. the long quotation on pp.134 above.

Knight, *William of Palerne*, *Sir Launfal*, *Sir Eglamour of Artois*, the alliterative and stanzaic *Morte Arthure*, to mention only a few). He was therefore one of the few authors who could afford to criticise the genre which for him, entertaining as it may have been, had little or nothing to offer in the way of conveying his individual poetic spirit. At the same time, audiences of all classes of society delighted in these romances, and continued to do so for at least two more centuries, provided they were, as time proceeded, adapted to the changing outlook on life and morals. In as far as this happened, parodies were not necessary. On the other hand, the old chivalric ideals continued to appeal, even if—or because—the reality of everyday life had come to be more and more remote from them, a point subtly made in *The Knight of the Burning Pestle*. Not until the seventeenth century, when secular Renaissance drama had begun to fulfil the role previously performed by romance, did it become possible for Shakespeare and his contemporaries to show up the pitiful (and, moreover, imported!) remnants of the old convention for what they considered them to be, like the positive values they originally stood for: "a pretty fiction, i'faith" (*The Knight of the Burning Pestle*, V, 318).

REFERENCES

Abrams, M.H. (1981). *A Glossary of Literary Terms*. New York etc.: CBS Publishing Japan (1st ed., 1941).
Barron, W.R.J. (1987). *English Medieval Romance*. London and New York: Longman.
Bawcutt, P. and F. Riddy (eds.) (1987). *Longer Scottish Poems*. Vol. I: *1375-1650*. Edinburgh: Scottish Academic Press.
Beaumont, F. *The Knight of the Burning Pestle*. Ed. J. Doebler. London: Edward Arnold. 1967.
Beer, G. (1970). *The Romance*. Ed. J.D. Jump. The Critical Idiom, Vol. 10. London: Methuen.
Blake, N.F. (1977). *The English Language in Medieval Literature*. London: J.M. Dent.
Brewer, D. (1983). *English Gothic Literature*. London and Basingstoke: Macmillan.
Busby, K. (1982). Conspicuous by its Absence: The English *Fabliau*. *Dutch Quarterly Review* 12. 30-41.
Busby, K. (1988). *Dame Sirith* and *De Clerico et Puella*. In: Veldhoen and Aertsen, 1988:69-81.
Chaucer, Geoffrey. *The Complete Works of Geoffrey Chaucer*. Ed. F.N. Robinson. 2nd ed. Boston: Houghton Mifflin. 1957 (1st ed., 1933).
Chaucer, Geoffrey. *The Riverside Chaucer*. Ed. L.D. Benson. Boston: Houghton Mifflin. 1987.

Dane, J.A. (1988). *Parody. Critical Concepts Versus Literary Practices, Aristophanes to Sterne.* Norman, Oklahoma, and London: University of Oklahoma Press.
Dunbar, W. *The Poems of William Dunbar.* Ed. J. Kinsley. Oxford: Clarendon Press. 1979.
Fewster, C. (1987). *Traditionality and Genre in Middle English Romance.* Cambridge: D.S. Brewer.
French, W.H. and C.B. Hale (eds.) (1964). *Middle English Metrical Romances.* 2 Vols. New York: Russell and Russell (1st publ. 1930).
Gaylord, A.T. (1982). The Moment of *Sir Thopas*: Towards a New Look at Chaucer's Language. *Chaucer Review* 16. 311-29.
Green, D.H. (1979). *Irony in the Medieval Romance.* Cambridge: Cambridge University Press.
Kiernan, K.S. (1973). *Undo Your Door* and the Order of Chivalry. *Studies in Philology* 79. 345-66.
Kooper, E.S. (1984). Inverted Images in Chaucer's *Tale of Sir Thopas. Studia Neophilologica* 56. 147-54.
Lehmann, P. (1963). *Die Parodie im Mittelalter.* Stuttgart: Anton Hiersemann. (1st ed., 1922)
Lindsay, D. *Squyer Meldrum.* Ed. J. Kinsley. London and Edinburgh: Nelson. 1959.
Lindsay, D. *The Works of Sir David Lindsay.* Ed. D. Hamer. 3 Vols. STS. 1931-34.
Loomis, L.H. (1941). Sir Thopas. In: *Sources and Analogues of Chaucer's Canterbury Tales.* Ed. W.F. Bryan and G. Dempster. Atlantic Highlands, N.J.: Humanities Press. 486-559. (Repr. 1958)
McKnight, G.H. (1913). *Middle English Humorous Tales in Verse.* Boston and London: D.C. Heath.
Nykrog, P. (1973). *Les Fabliaux.* Genève: Librairie Droz. (1st ed. 1957)
Ramsey, L.C. (1983). *Chivalric Romances. Popular Literature in Medieval England.* Bloomington, Ind.: Indiana University Press.
Rice, J.A. (1987). *Middle English Romance: An Annotated Bibliography 1955-1985.* New York: Garland.
Riddy, F. (1974). *Squyer Meldrum* and the Romance of Chivalry. *The Yearbook of English Studies* 4. 26-36.
Robbins, R.H. (ed.) (1952). *Secular Lyrics of the XIVth and XVth Centuries.* Oxford: Clarendon Press.
Sands, D.B. (ed.) (1956). *Middle English Verse Romances.* New York : Holt, Rinehart and Winston.
Severs, J.B. (ed.) (1967). *A Manual of the Writings in Middle English 1050-1500.* Fascicule I: *Romances.* New Haven, Conn.: The Connecticut Academy of Arts and Sciences.
Smyser, H.M. (1932). *The Taill of Rauf Coilyear* and its Sources. *Harvard Studies and Notes in Philology and Literature* 14. 135-50.
Tigges, W. (1988a). *Sir Eglamour*: The Knight Who Could Not Say No. *Neophilologus* 72. 107-15.
Tigges, W. (1988b). *The Fox and the Wolf*: A Study in Medieval Irony. In: Veldhoen and Aertsen, 1988:83-95.
Tigges, W. (1988c). *The Land of Cokaygne*: Sophisticated Mirth. In: Veldhoen and Aertsen, 1988:97-104.
Veldhoen, N.H.G.E. and H. Aertsen (eds.) (1988). *Companion to Early Middle English Literature.* Amsterdam: Free University Press.

WOMEN AND ROMANCE

ELIZABETH ARCHIBALD

According to Chaucer's Wife of Bath, the representation of women in medieval literature was appallingly biased for the simple reason that all the books were written by men, and for the most part by elderly misogynist clerics[1]:

> For trusteth wel, it is an impossible
> That any clerk wol speke good of wyves,
> But if it be of hooly seintes lyves,
> Ne of noon other womman never the mo ...
>
> (*CT* III.688-91)

> (For you may be sure, it is impossible for any clerk to speak well of women, unless it is the life of a holy saint; but certainly never of any other woman ...)

The Wife of Bath is not exaggerating here. Romance may be seen as an exception in a literary tradition which was heavily misogynistic. Ecclesiastical literature made much of Eve's fatal influence over Adam in the Garden of Eden, and of the failings of all Eve's daughters: the Virgin Mary was hailed as a second Eve, the perfect opposite of the mother of humankind. The Wife of Bath tells us in her Prologue that her fifth husband, Jankyn the "*joly clerk*", owned a "*book of wikked wyves*" which contained arguments against marriage by Valerius, Theophrastus and St. Jerome, texts from which Chaucer quotes elsewhere in *CT* (for instance in the debate on marriage at the beginning of the *Merchant's Tale*); the Wife was so infuriated by Jankyn's enthusiasm for "*this cursed book*" that she tore out

---

[1] All references to Chaucer are taken from the *Riverside Chaucer* (1987); *Canterbury Tales* and *Troilus and Criseyde* will be cited as *CT* and *T&C* respectively. All references to *Emaré, Floris and Blauncheflour, Sir Degaré, Sir Launfal, Sir Orfeo, Sir Perceval of Galles, The Squire of Low Degree* are taken from French and Hale (1964); for more recent editions see the valuable bibliography in Barron (1987). References to verse romances are by line number, to prose romances by page number.

three pages, thus precipitating a violent quarrel which, according to
her, was the making of their marriage (*CT* III.627-827).

Authoritative criticism of women began with the Bible (see
for instance the comments in *Proverbs*, which were frequently cited
in the Middle Ages), but classical texts, both literary and philosophical, also supplied much-quoted evidence (Aristotle's view that
woman is an inferior version of man was accepted as scientific truth;
the cynical old bawd in Ovid's *Amores* served as a model for the
equally cynical and influential figure of La Vieille in the *Roman de la
Rose*). Christian writers naturally had much to say about the bad influence of women. St. Paul's grudging concession that it is better to
marry than to burn was often quoted; St. Jerome's *Adversus Jovini-
anum* was written as a defence of virginity and an attack on marriage, but in later centuries it was widely read and cited as an attack on
women.[2]

The references to the traditional anti-marriage and often anti-
feminist writings in Chaucer's work suggest that they would have
been very familiar to his audience too. The learned French writer
Christine de Pizan, a near-contemporary of Chaucer, described her
depression as she sat in her study surrounded by books written by
men criticising women. So many great scholars could not be wrong,
she felt; women must be an inferior species. But then three splendid
ladies, Justice, Reason and Rectitude, appeared to her and commanded her to build a metaphorical city of ladies out of the good deeds and
achievements of women through the ages. This scene forms the introduction to her *Book of the City of Ladies*, which is a remarkably
sophisticated and confident defence of women against all the classic
misogynist arguments (de Pizan, 1983:3ff.).

It might, therefore, be argued that romance is a major exception to the prevailing view of women to be found in medieval literature (though lyric poetry, of course, often celebrates love and
women). The Wife of Bath claimed that only women writers would
be well-disposed to women (ll.693-6), but romances were usually
written by men (or so we assume—most are anonymous). However,
we do know that many women read or listened to romances, and that
aristocratic women sometimes commissioned translations or original
compositions. Eleanor of Aquitaine, queen of France and then of
England in the late twelfth century, was an important patron of

[2] Miller (1977:399-473) gives selections from the misogynistic literature known
to Chaucer (including most of these authors); on medical and scientific views of
women in the Middle Ages, see Bullough (1973:485-501).

French poets and translators, and so were her daughters; much later, Caxton tells how Margaret Duchess of Burgundy, sister of Edward IV, encouraged him to translate *The History of Troye*, the first book printed in English, criticised his English on occasion, and rewarded him handsomely for the finished work (Caxton, 1973:97-8). Evidence for women as readers of romance is also to be found in some romance texts. For instance in *Ywain and Gawain*, as in its French source, the hero arrives at a castle where a young girl is reading a romance aloud to a knight and a lady (ll.3084-94). In Chaucer's *Troilus and Criseyde* Pandarus finds his niece listening to one of her women reading aloud (II.78-84). Chaucer frequently addresses the women in his audience—or at least pretends to do so; for instance, at the end of *T&C* he apologises to any women who may be offended by his portrayal of the faithless Criseyde, and emphasises his willingness to write about loyal women (v.1772-8). He returns to this subject in the Prologue to the *Legend of Good Women*, where he recounts in a dream that the God of Love accused him of heresy for having portrayed Criseyde as untrue, and ordered him to look in his books and find some Greek and Roman stories of *"wemen that were goode and trewe"* (G.268-77). The God of Love does not seem to be a reader, or at any rate an admirer, of medieval romance; it is striking that he expects Chaucer to use classical sources for his good women, and indeed all the following stories, written as the penance imposed on him by the God's consort, Alceste, are about classical heroines. (I will return later to the question of Chaucer's attitude to romance.)

Such passages should not be taken as evidence that English court ladies actually criticised Chaucer's presentation of female characters (it may be that Chaucer wanted to stir up discussion on this point); but they would be quite pointless if women were not reading, or listening to, *T&C* and other romances. There are certainly women present in the miniature of the poet reading his work to the court which accompanies the text in Corpus Christi College, Cambridge, MS 61 (frequently reproduced). What images of themselves did medieval women find in these narratives? What was the typical role assigned to the romance heroine, and what about the other female characters?

If epic can be defined in Virgil's terms as "arms and the man", romance would have to be "arms and the man and the woman". A very early statement of the romance principle that love and arms go together is found in Geoffrey of Monmouth's description of a tournament in his *History of the Kings of Britain*, the twelfth-century Latin best-seller which seems to have established King Arthur as a

major figure in European literature (1966:229). According to Geoffrey, women of fashion wore the colours of the knights they loved,
and refused to love any knight who had not proved his prowess in
battle three times: so the women became more virtuous and the men
more courageous. Of course in the world of epic too cowards cannot
be heroes. What is new in medieval romance is the concept that love
is ennobling and inspiring, both mentally and physically. Thinking of
your lady makes you braver and stronger, as Troilus finds :

> And this encrees of hardynesse and myght
> Com hym of love, his ladies thank to wynne,
> That altered his spirit so withinne.   (iii.1776-8)

> (And he acquired this increased courage and strength through love
> and desire to win his lady's gratitude, which altered his inner spir-
> it so.)

The main theme of many romances is the maturing of the hero as he
learns through experience about chivalry and about love (this is of
course not the case with established heroes like Lancelot or Gawain,
though in *Sir Gawain and the Green Knight* Gawain certainly finds
that he is not as experienced as he and the rest of the world believe).[3]
Ywain and Gawain is a particularly interesting example. Ywain, a
relatively unknown knight at Arthur's court, manages to kill a champion and marry his widow; but Gawain persuades him to go off on a
round of tournaments, and because he does not return after the
appointed year, his wife disowns him. Ywain goes mad for a time,
and then rescues a series of damsels in distress before his wife's maid
is able to effect a reconciliation between the offended lady and the
hero, now famous as the Knight of the Lion. One interpretation of
the poem would be that it is only after this change from seeking
personal fame in tournaments to helping others without thinking of
his own success that he is able to regain his wife's love.[4]
 This type of plot can only work with a male protagonist.
Heroines are not expected—or allowed—to show increasing ma-
turity, or to demonstrate a new and more socially considerate side to
their characters, by making the right choice in knotty moral dilem-

[3] Of course it is very dangerous to generalise about romance: for discussion of
possible definitions see Finlayson (1981-2). References to *Sir Gawain and the
Green Knight* are taken from Tolkien and Gordon, revised Davis (1967).
[4] For a stimulating discussion of the problems raised by Chrétien's plot see Hunt,
1984: 126-41.

mas or by acting altruistically instead of pursuing fame and fortune.
The hero can learn and mature as a knight because of his love, and
can demonstrate this by winning battles, but there is almost no room
in the plot structure for the heroine to grow, except in the realisation
that she is in love. What female activity or accomplishment is comparable to winning your first tournament, or rescuing your first
damsel in distress, or sending your first prisoner home to Camelot?
Heroines can only look forward to the return of their lovers and to
their weddings; their rite of passage is the transfer from a father's
control to that of a husband. Women do not become braver and more
generous because they are in love, or if they do the plot does not usually encourage us to notice. There is no question of ranking women's
activities in a hierarchy, no female equivalent of the best knight in
the world except the most beautiful lady, an entirely passive role (to
which one must be born). And the implication of this role is that the
lady will become the reward or prize for the hero's martial prowess.

A typical romance opening is a description of the hero and an
account of his departure from some court into the mysterious realms
of adventure, where his progress is continually charted; the lady, on
the other hand, usually waits in her castle for adventurous knights to
come her way. Once in love or even married, the heroine usually remains at home while the hero completes his quest; the nearest she
comes to adventure is being besieged, or threatened with an unwel-
come marriage, or abducted. In the ancient Greek novels or romances, the plot often consists of the travels and adventures of both
the hero and the heroine: they are separated for most of the time, but
the narrative follows them alternately, giving equal attention to
both.[5] In medieval romances the heroine very rarely travels with the
hero or without him (except when abducted): any lady who arrives
alone at Arthur's court or is encountered in a forest is very unlikely
to be the heroine, and may well be hostile to the hero, or at least sent
to test him. Romance heroines do not often set out in search of their
lovers, and it is very rare to find one disguised as a man, as sometimes happens in Renaissance romance and drama. The women who
do most of the travelling, and who seem to have the most liberty, are
the minor characters. In *Ywain and Gawain* the resourceful maid
Lunet travels to Arthur's court to denounce Ywain for deserting his
wife; in the same romance a young woman travels to the court to find
a champion in a legal quarrel with her older sister. In Malory's *Tale*

[5] On the Greek romances, see Hågg, 1983.

of Sir Gareth the heroine's sister Lynet summons the hero from
Camelot and travels with him, abusing him and treating him abom-
inably: it is all part of a test, and when Sir Gareth wins his lady the
sister marries his brother (Malory, 1977:177-226).

Many minor female characters in romance—maids, sisters,
enchantresses, religious recluses—are often powerful in some way,
knowledgeable, resourceful or enterprising: but the heroine must be
passive and weak, presumably on the age-old principle that men ad-
mire powerful women but do not want to marry them. The heroine's
characteristic role is absence: either the hero goes away from her
home, and the thought of reunion with her inspires him to great
deeds, as in *Ywain and Gawain*, or else she is abducted, like Dame
Heurodis in *Sir Orfeo* or Blauncheflour in *Floris and Blauncheflour*.
When a woman does manipulate the plot, either she returns immediately to passivity, or else she is not the heroine. For instance, in
King Horn the princess Rymenhild falls in love with the hero who is
living at her father's court; she sends for him and declares her love,
and he replies that he will go off and prove his knighthood before he
woos her (ll.241ff). After initiating his chivalric career and their
love affair, Rymenhild becomes quite passive; Horn returns in the
nick of time to save her from an unwanted marriage which she is
powerless to avoid. In *The Squire of Low Degree* the princess over-
hears the young squire complaining of his hopeless passion for her;
she sends for him and urges him to go off and prove himself in the
usual way :

> "For and ye my loue should wynne,
> With chyualry ye must begynne,
> And other dedes of armes to done,
> Through whiche ye may wynne your shone."   (171-4)

> ("For if you would win my love, you must begin with chivalry,
> and do further deeds of arms through which you may win your
> spurs.")

After taking the initiative here, she remains at home like Rymenhild,
vulnerable to the skulduggery of the villain until her lover returns to
marry her.

In *Sir Launfal*, the fairy who chooses the hero as her lover and
later saves him from Guinevere's unjust accusation is in a special
category. She is not human, and her activities constitute a criticism of
the degenerate Arthurian court, and especially of Guinevere (the
queen is presented in a typically misogynistic way as a nymphoma-

niac who brings a false charge against the young hero when he re-
buffs her). There may also be criticism of Camelot in another romance in which a woman takes the initiative in propositioning the
hero, *Sir Gawain and the Green Knight*. But here the propositioning
has very different purposes and results. By her skilful conversation
the Lady accuses Gawain of being uncourtly in not making love to
her, and also beguiles him into accepting the fatal girdle. This woman has too much power to be a heroine (in any case she is already
married), and indeed she turns out to be an enemy, and the agent of
the enchantress Morgan le Fay. It is striking that the traditional opponent of Arthur and the Round Table should be a woman, an educated woman who uses the magic taught her by Merlin to try to under-
mine the pride and renown of Camelot. Educated women are unusual
in romance, though not so rare as might be supposed. When they do
occur they are either especially threatening, enchantresses like Morgan, or else their education serves no useful purpose in the plot, as in
Floris and Blancheflour, where the fact that Blancheflour goes to
school with Floris emphasises his reluctance to be separated from
her, but is no help to her when she is carried off to the Emir's
harem.[6] The unconventional relationship between love and prowess
in *Sir Gawain and the Green Knight*, and Gawain's misogynistic outburst towards the end, when he compares himself with Old Testament heroes undone by the wiles of women (ll.2414ff), may encourage us to agree with those critics who argue that the poem is a parody, or a criticism, of the romance genre.

Gawain was well known in the romance tradition as a ladies'
man; like Lancelot he never marries, but unlike Lancelot he never
has a long-lasting affair. It is clearly not the case that courtly love
must involve adultery, as C. S. Lewis argued so influentially (1961:
1-43). But it is the case that it is hard to go on telling stories about a
knight once he is happily married, because the motive of impressing
or winning his lady is no longer effective. When James Bond got
married, Ian Fleming had to kill off his wife in the same book (*On
Her Majesty's Secret Service*), to free Bond for further adventures.
The same applies to medieval heroes: characters like Ywain or Launfal can only star in one romance, but Gawain, who never marries or
even has a permanent mistress, and Lancelot, who cannot marry
Guinevere, are ever-available for yet another adventure. There are,

---

[6] On educated women in romance, see Ferrante, 1980:30-4. See also Archibald
(1988-9:291-2).

of course, no female characters who star in a series of romances, since the happy ending for the heroine is marriage. Guinevere appears again and again only because she is Arthur's queen and Lancelot's mistress, and she is not the central character in the many romances in which she appears.

Unusually for romance, *Sir Gawain* does not end with a wedding or a coronation or a triumphant return from a quest; instead the hero returns in shame to Camelot, insisting on his inexpiable guilt. Ladies as well as lords are said to belong to the Round Table company who agree to wear green baldrics in his honour (1.2515), but in the next line it is described as a brotherhood, and that is a very dominant image in romance. It is a form of literature which idealises heterosexual love, but which often rates male friendship and camaraderie even more highly. This is particularly clear in *Amis and Amiloun*. Amiloun's selfish wife rejects him when he becomes a leper, but Amis sacrifices his own children (with his wife's consent) in order to cure his friend with their blood, and is rewarded by the miraculous revival of the children, and of course by the cure of his friend. The two men live happily together for the rest of their lives, but Amiloun's faithless wife is locked up on a diet of bread and water till she dies.

The significance and power of male bonding are also very clear in many versions of the Arthurian legend. Malory's Lancelot would have sympathised with Ywain's decision to leave his new wife and go off with Gawain to a round of tournaments, judging from his response to a damsel inquiring into his love life:

> "But for to be a weddyd man, I thynke hit nat, for than I
> muste couche with hir and leve armys and turnamentis,
> batellys and adventures."   (p.161)

> ("As for marrying, I prefer not to, for then I must sleep with her,
> and abandon arms and tournaments, battles and adventures.")

Although Lancelot is said to owe his great prowess to his love for Guinevere (p.149), Malory never tells us about their first meeting or the growth of their love; we see little of Guinevere throughout the *Morte Darthur*, and when she is shown with Lancelot in the penultimate tale, they are often quarrelling. In one reconciliation scene she asks his forgiveness for her unjustified anger, and he replies:

"Thys ys nat the firste tyme," seyde sir Launcelot, "that
ye have been displese with me causeles. But, madame,
ever I muste suffir you, but what sorow that I endure,
ye take no force."   (p.642)

("This is not the first time," said Sir Lancelot, "that you have been
displeased with me for no reason. But, madam, I must always put
up with you, and you take no notice of the sorrow I endure.")

Such scenes are far from offering an idealised picture of the relationship between the greatest knight of the Arthurian world and his
inspiration—the most beautiful lady of the court and Arthur's queen.
But Malory seems to be much more interested in the powerful camaraderie which unites Arthur's fellowship of the Round Table. Towards the end of the story, when Arthur learns that Lancelot has unwittingly killed Gawain's brothers while rescuing Guinevere, he recognises that the ensuing feud will be the end of his reign, and laments
in a famous passage not found in Malory's sources:

"Much more am I soryar for my good knyghtes losse
than for the losse of my fayre quene: for quenes I myght
have inow, but such a felyship of good knyghtes shall
never be togydirs in no company."   (p.685)

("I am much sorrier for the loss of my good knights than for the
loss of my fair queen; for I might have plenty of queens, but such
a fellowship of good knights shall never be gathered together
again.")

Guinevere retreats to a nunnery to atone for her part in the collapse
of the Round Table. Lancelot spends the rest of his life as a hermit—
but not alone, for the survivors of his old clan gather round him, and
they almost manage to recreate the spirit of male fellowship which
characterised the Round Table in its heyday (pp.721-5). For Malory,
as for other writers from the late twelfth century on, chivalry is
complicated by the presence of women, necessary though love is to
the medieval concept of courtly romance.

There are, however, a group of medieval romances which focus on women as protagonists, and which give a very different picture of women's experience, perhaps a more realistic picture in some
ways, and certainly a grimmer one. These are the Incestuous Father
romances, which are found in every western European literature in
the Middle Ages, and are related to the folktales of Cinderella and
Catskin: the example I shall discuss here is the Middle English *Ema-*

ré, written about 1400.[7] Emaré's father, an emperor, loses his
beloved wife, and later falls in love with his beautiful only daughter.
He decides to marry her, but she refuses; furious, he exposes her at
sea in a tiny boat. Here the female rite of passage, the transfer from
father to husband, is horribly perverted; parental power is presented
as sexual tyranny, and the innocent heroine has no male protector to
whom she can appeal. She arrives in a foreign land where a king falls
in love with her and marries her, but when she has a child during her
husband's absence his jealous mother sends word that she has produced a monster. Her husband's letter telling them to wait for his return is altered by his mother so asto condemn his wife and child to
exposure at sea. The heroine arrives in Rome, and is taken in by a
merchant. Many years later her husband comes to Rome on pilgrimage, and they are reunited; her contrite father also comes to Rome,
and she is reconciled with him too.

These Incestuous Father stories, which were written down
from the twelfth century on, are in no way the equivalent of a chivalric quest. The heroine does not set off to seek adventure, but has it
thrust upon her, so to speak. At the end she has not grown, changed
or learned anything except how cruel and unjust people can be, especially relatives. She is unable to seek out her enemies and take ven-
geance on them, but must wait for them to repent and come to her
(Mills, 1973:xiv). Her ordeals require patience and endurance, rather than strength or courage. There seems to be a considerable degree
of realism in these stories. I do not mean that many medieval women
spent years drifting round the Mediterranean in tiny boats; but the
isolation and vulnerability of women, particularly when married
into a foreign community or one far from home, were no doubt very
real problems as well as traditional literary themes. Confirmation of
this view can be found in Christine de Pizan's volume of advice to
women, *The Treasure of the City of Ladies*, which contains a section
on how a married woman should deal with hostile friends or relatives of her husband (1985:65-71). Love affairs are out of the question, according to Christine: the issue is self-preservation and survival, not pleasure (1985:90-105).

The picture of women's lives which is suggested by the Incestuous Father romances is very different from that in the male-
focused chivalric romances. It is striking that it is often in stories

---

[7] For discussion of the many analogues (among them Chaucer's *Man of Law's
Tale*, although it does not begin with attempted incest), see the introduction to the
edition by Rickert (1908), and also Schlauch (1927).

about incest—of which there are a surprising number in medieval literature—that other real-life problems also occur. Here the Monstrous Birth motif underlines the importance of producing an heir. Knights in romance seldom admit to marrying out of desire for a son, but the need for an heir clearly was a serious social issue, and it seems to be more openly acknowledged in the romances which have a woman as protagonist. In another kind of incest romance, represented by the Middle English *Sir Degaré* and *Sir Eglamour of Artois*, the heroine bears an illegitimate child who is exposed as a foundling, and later unwittingly marries his natural mother. The abandonment of unwanted children was certainly a common practice in the Middle Ages, and was no doubt very often the responsibility of the mother, to hide her shame (see Boswell, 1988).

    Being able to marry for love was no doubt an important fantasy element in a society in which so many marriages were dynastic, arranged for financial and political advantage, and in which betrothals in infancy were quite common. In the romances there is a suspicious number of unattached heroines, both wealthy and beautiful, who can marry as they please; either they are orphaned, or they have benevolent fathers or brothers who are happy to marry them off to a passing knight. In this respect a more realistic picture is probably painted by Marie de France in her Breton lays, which appealed especially to women, according to a near-contemporary.[8] Her heroines are often young women unhappily married to much older men chosen by their families; they are driven to commit adultery in order to find happiness (for instance in *Yonec* and *Guigemar*).

    We do not find the sisterly solidarity of Shakespeare's Rosalind and Celia in medieval romance. Heroines very seldom have mothers or sisters, though they sometimes confide in a maid (for instance in *Ywain and Gawain*); this isolation is particularly apparent in the case of Malory's Guinevere. Similarly Dorigen in Chaucer's *Franklin's Tale* has no other woman to talk to. But what is striking in Chaucer's tale is that much attention is paid to the heroine's experiences and her emotions: indeed they form the centre of the narrative. It may be significant that the source is said to be a Breton lay (*CT* V.709-15): as we have already seen, the lays retold by Marie de France often show the woman's point of view, and it may be that this popular genre was in fact more generous to women, and more inter-

---

[8] Marie de France, *Lais*, ed. Ewert (1978); translated Burgess and Busby (1986). Marie probably wrote at least some of her lays in England, though her identity remains uncertain.

ested in them, than chivalric romance. It might be argued, however, that Dorigen's central role is seriously eroded by the end of the poem. Although the plot centres on her rash promise to sleep with Aurelius if he can remove the black rocks which frighten her, and then on her dilemma when he apparently manages to do this, we are encouraged to empathise not only with her despair, but also with the more repressed emotion of her husband Arveragus, who insists that she must keep her promise, whatever the cost, and then begins to cry himself (ll.1479-80). Fortunately Aurelius is so impressed by this display of nobility that he frees Dorigen from her promise. The last scene of the poem, however, does not focus on the relief of Dorigen and Arveragus or on the renewal of marital bliss, as one might expect, but rather on the plight of Aurelius, the cause of all their troubles, who must still pay his debt of one thousand pounds of gold to the philosopher who has "removed" the rocks. When the philosopher hears how the adventure has turned out, he insists on being as generous as the others, and lets Aurelius off his debt. The Franklin's final question, *"Which was the mooste fre, as thynketh yow?"* (l.1622: 'Who was the most generous, in your view?'), refers to the three men; it seems to marginalise Dorigen, whose role was not to show generosity but to be the cause of it in others.

Even if the *Franklin's Tale* turns out to be less centred on the heroine than we might expect, Chaucer is a poet who is unusually interested in the woman's point of view; he can imagine (and conjure up for us) women whose attitude to love is not the conventional one described by most male authors of his time. Many critics think that Chaucer was not sympathetic to romance, and that the works of his which are usually called romances all contain some criticism of the genre, though it is seldom as explicit as in the parody *Sir Thopas* (see Windeatt, 1988:130, n. 4). Some of the changes he makes in the material he inherits are certainly very suggestive. For instance, whereas Boccaccio's Emilia in the *Teseida* prays to Diana that she may be won by the lover who loves her best, Emily in Chaucer's version of the story, the *Knight's Tale*, is not at all keen on marriage: *"Chaste goddesse, wel wostow that I / Desire to ben a mayden al my lyf, / Ne nevere wol I be no love ne wyf."* (*CT* I.2304-6: 'Chaste goddess, you know well that I desire to be a virgin all my life; I do not want to be a mistress or a wife.') But if she must marry, she says, let her husband be the one who wants her most. The fires she has lit go out, one of the torches drips with blood, and the goddess of chastity herself appears to say that her votaress shall be married to one of her suitors, though she does not reveal which (in fact it is Theseus, Emily's brother, who will choose her husband on the basis of a trial of strength between the two candidates). Chaucer's changes here make it hard to believe in the conventional picture of Emily's wedded bliss which the Knight blandly offers as a happy ending to his sinister tale.[9]

Emily's complaint includes fear of childbirth; ecclesiastical writers often described pregnancy and labour in lurid and horrifying terms to encourage women to stay chaste, but Emily's feelings do not seem to be swayed by religion. She simply does not want to be married. This view was highly unconventional in a society in which the only alternatives for a middle- or upper-class woman were marriage or a convent; yet Chaucer shows some sympathy with it not only here but also in *T&C*, where Criseyde (admittedly a widow) argues at first against a liaison with Troilus:

> "I am myn owene womman, wel at ese—
> I thank it God—as after myn estat,
> Right yong, and stonde unteyd in lusty leese,
> Withouten jalousie or swich debat:
> Shal noon housbonde seyn to me 'Chek mat!'"   (ii.750-4)

> ("I am my own woman, very comfortable—thank God—in accordance with my rank, very young, and free in pleasant pasture, without jealousy or any such quarrel. No husband shall say 'Checkmate!' to me!")

These lines have no parallel in Boccaccio. In fact, in the very next stanza Criseyde changes tack, asking why on earth she should not love if she wants to. But the idea of independence as a viable position is a very striking and unusual one in a romance.

It has been argued that "courtly love" and the fashion for the romance genre opened the door to emancipation for women. While it is true that romances often devote a great deal of space to the emotions and anxieties of the heroine, and to her important influence on the hero, the idealisation of passive beauty (always blonde) is hardly liberating, and there is little scope for feminine resourcefulness in the popular romance plots of an abducted or besieged heroine rescued by the hero, or the young knight inspired to great feats by the image of his absent lady. We have almost no information on the reactions of contemporary women to Middle English romances. Would

---

[9] Much more could be said about the presentation of women in the *Knight's Tale*, if space allowed; see, for instance, Aers (1986:76-82).

they have approved of stories in which heroines are totally over-
shadowed by lovers constantly away on chivalric pursuits? Or would
they have sympathised with the hero's mother in *Sir Perceval of
Galles*, who tries to keep her son away from the chivalric world so
that he will not be killed like his father and his brothers (ll. 161ff)?
What did they make of the strong religious tone in some later
medieval romances such as the Grail legends, where women are often presented as diabolical temptresses and the greatest knights are
celibate, like Galahad (e.g. Malory, pp.548-50 and 570-1)? If they
enjoyed Marie de France's lays, was it for the realistic picture of unhappy young *malmariées*, and the fulfilment of their desire to find a
lover? Christine de Pizan warns the wise lady against love affairs,
and the same advice is given equally firmly in *The Book of the
Knight of La Tour Landry*, a manual of behaviour written in the
fourteenth century for the education of the author's motherless
daughters, which was translated from the French by Caxton (1971:
163ff). It is ironic, then, that two of the most famous heroines of
romance were Isolde and Guinevere, both adulteresses, both destined
for tragedy.

It seems unlikely that romance either reflected or influenced
attitudes to women in medieval society. In his study of the later Middle Ages Huizinga devotes a chapter to "Conventions of Love", and
then sums up (1955:128):

> Indeed, medieval literature shows little true pity for
> woman, little compassion for her weakness and the dan-
> gers and pains which love has in store for her. Pity took
> on a stereotyped and factitious form, in the sentimental
> fiction of the knight delivering the virgin.

Malory's Round Table knights swear an oath not found in any of his
sources, which includes a commitment to behave courteously to
women and protect them (pp.75-6); at about the time that he was
writing, several orders of chivalry dedicated to the protection of
women were founded in France (Keen, 1984:186, 193). But chivalry
is an all-male club, and romance depicts male ideals of chivalric
prowess and male fantasies, as John Stevens has stressed (1973:43):

> It is a fascinating paradox that 'romance reading upon
> the book', which was arguably designed for female con-
> sumption in the first place, should so emphasize what
> goes on inside the *man's* head.

The Wife of Bath found it not so much fascinating as infuriating; her tale of an Arthurian knight and a Loathly Lady is eloquent testimony to the conventional privileging of male values in romance. There is much in her narrative which suggests a very cynical view of romance; for instance, the fact that the knight's quest is precipitated by his rape of a maiden, a very dubious action for a romance hero. The hero (who remains anonymous) is repeatedly humiliated by the crone, and is forced to yield the sovereignty of their marriage to her —but as soon as he does this, all his fantasies are fulfilled by her transformation into a young beauty who "*obeyed hym in every thyng / That myghte doon hym plesance or likyng*" (*CT* III.1255-6: 'who obeyed him in everything which might give him pleasure'). The focus of the traditional plot on the fulfilling of male fantasies is underlined by the sudden shift in the next lines to the brash voice of the narrator, familiar from her Prologue: "*and Jesu Christe us sende / Housebondes meeke, yonge, and fressh abedde, / And grace t'overbyde hem that we wedde*" (ll.1258-60: 'and Jesus Christ send us husbands who are obedient, young, and lively in bed, and grace to outlive those whom we marry'). The Wife is illustrating her earlier assertion about male writers in the context of romance. A traditional male-authored tale resolves the plot for the convenience of the hero, which means giving him a beautiful and obedient young wife. The Wife's final words remind us that a female writer might require a somewhat different ending.

We must remember, of course, that the Wife of Bath's comments were not written by a woman, but by Geoffrey Chaucer. The late fourteenth century seems to have been something of a turning point in terms of the representation of women in medieval literature. Half a century before Chaucer, Boccaccio had remarked in the preface to his *De Claris Mulieribus (Of Famous Women)* that there was a striking lack of writing on women's achievements; and during Chaucer's lifetime Christine de Pizan began her remarkable career as a professional writer and a defender of women's reputation.[10] Chaucer is never as explicit as either Boccaccio or Christine: he does not present himself as a committed defender of women, and indeed not all his female characters are defensible. But in his so-called

---

[10] Boccaccio, *De Claris Mulieribus*, trans. Parker (ed. Wright, 1943) [sixteenth-century translation]; trans. Guarini (1963). For a comparison of Chaucer and Christine, see Delany (1986); for a detailed study of Christine's life and writings, see Willard (1984).

romances, the ways in which he adapts his sources (or, in the case of
Sir Thopas, parodies them), the comments of his narrators, and the
presentation of the heroines, alert us to the fact that most medieval
romances are overwhelmingly concerned with male values, male
pursuits, and "what goes on inside the *man's* head".

REFERENCES

Aers. D. (1986). *Chaucer*. Brighton: Harvester.
Amis and Amiloun. Ed. M. Leach. EETS, OS 203 (1937).
Archibald, E. (1988-9). 'Deep clerks she dumbs': The Learned Heroine in *Apollonius of Tyre* and *Pericles*. *Comparative Drama* 22. 289-303.
Barron, W.J.R. (1987). *English Medieval Romance*. London: Longman.
Boccaccio, G. *Forty-Six Lives Translated from Boccaccio's* De Claris Mulieribus. Trans. Henry Parker (Lord Morley). Ed. H.G. Wright. EETS, OS 214 (1943; repr., 1970).
Boccaccio, G. (1963). *Concerning Famous Women*. Trans. Guido A. Guarini. New Brunswick, N.J.; Rutgers University Press.
The Book of the Knight of La Tour Landry. Trans. W. Caxton. Ed. M.Y. Offord. EETS, SS 2 (1971).
Boswell, John (1988). *The Kindness of Strangers: The Abandonment of Children in Western Europe from Late Antiquity to the Renaissance*. New York: Pantheon.
Bullough, V.L. (1973). Medieval Medical and Scientific Views of Women. *Viator* 4. 485-501.
Caxton, W. (1973). *Caxton's Own Prose*. Ed. N. F. Blake. London: André Deutsch.
Chaucer, Geoffrey. *The Riverside Chaucer*. Ed. L. D. Benson. Boston: Houghton Mifflin. 1987.
Delany, Sheila (1986). Rewriting Woman Good: Gender and the Anxiety of Influence in Two Late-Medieval Texts. In: *Chaucer in the Eighties*. Ed. Julian N. Wasserman and Robert J. Blanch. Syracuse, N.Y.: Syracuse University Press. 75-92.
de Pizan, C. (1983). *The Book of the City of Ladies*. Trans. Earl Jeffrey Richards. London: Pan (1st publ., 1982).
de Pizan, C. (1985). *The Treasure of the City of Ladies,or The Book of the Three Virtues*. Trans. Sarah Lawson. Harmondsworth: Penguin.
The Romance of Emaré. Ed. E. Rickert. EETS, ES 99 (1908; repr., 1958).
Ferrante, J. (1980). The Education of Women in the Middle Ages in Theory, Fact and Fiction. In: *Beyond Their Sex: Learned Women of the European Past*. Ed. P. Labalme. New York: New York University Press.
Finlayson, J. (1981-2). Definitions of Medieval Romance. *Chaucer Review* 15. 44-62, 168-81.
French, W.H. and C.B. Hale (eds.) (1964). *Middle English Metrical Romances*. 2 Vols. New York: Russell and Russell. (1st publ., 1930).
Geoffrey of Monmouth. *History of the Kings of Britain*. Trans. L. Thorpe. Harmondsworth: Penguin. 1966 (repr., 1978).

Hågg, T. (1983). *The Novel in Antiquity.* Oxford: Blackwell.
Huizinga, J. (1955). *The Waning of the Middle Ages.* Harmondsworth: Penguin (1st publ., 1924).
Hunt, Tony (1984). Chrétien de Troyes' Arthurian Romance, *Yvain.* In: *The New Pelican Guide to English Literature.* Vol. I: *Medieval Literature.* Part Two: *The European Inheritance.* Ed. B. Ford. Harmondsworth: Penguin. 126-41.
Keen, M. (1984) *Chivalry.* New Haven,Conn.: Yale University Press.
Lewis, C.S. (1961). *The Allegory of Love.* New York: Oxford University Press. 1961 (1st. publ., 1936).
Malory, Sir Thomas (1977). *Works.* Ed. E. Vinaver. 2nd edition. Oxford Standard Authors. Oxford: Oxford University Press. (1st publ., 1954; rev., 1971)
Marie de France. *Lais.* Ed. A. Ewert. Oxford: Blackwell. 1978 (1st publ., 1944).
Marie de France. *The Lais of Marie de France.* Trans. G. Burgess and K. Busby. Harmondsworth: Penguin. 1986.
Miller, R. P. (ed.) (1977). *Chaucer: Sources and Backgrounds.* New York: Oxford University Press.
Mills, Maldwyn (ed.) (1973). *Six Middle English Romances.* London: Dent.
Schlauch, M. (1927). *Chaucer's Constance and Accused Queens.* New York: New York University Press. (Repr., 1969).
Sir Eglamour of Artois. Ed. F.E. Richardson. EETS, OS 256 (1965).
Sir Gawain and the Green Knight. Ed. J.R.R. Tolkien and E.V. Gordon. 2nd ed. rev. N. Davis. Oxford: Oxford University Press. 1967 (1st ed., 1925).
Stevens, J. (1973). *Medieval Romance.* London: Hutchinson.
Willard, Charity C. (1984). *Christine de Pizan: Her Life and Works.* New York: Persea Books.
Windeatt. B. (1988). *Troilus* and the Disenchantment of Romance. In: *Studies in Medieval English Romances.* Ed. D. Brewer. Cambridge: Brewer. 129-147.
Ywain and Gawain. Ed. A. B. Friedman and N. T. Harrington. EETS, OS 254 (1964; repr. 1981).

LOVE AND MARRIAGE
IN
THE MIDDLE ENGLISH ROMANCES

ERIK KOOPER

The lovely young maiden Freine is nurtured in a convent at the doors of which she had been found as a baby.[1] One day she meets there a visitor, a spirited young knight, as yet unmarried, who has come to the convent attracted by rumours about her beauty. Sir Guroun, as he is called, is so much taken by *Her semblaunt and her gentrise, / Her lovesum eghen, her rode so bright* (ll.268-9: 'her outward appearance, her gentility, her lovely eyes and her bright complexion') that he falls in love with her. In order not to arouse the abbess's suspicion by an unexpected increase of interest in her institution, he cleverly contrives, by means of lavish gifts, to become a lay brother of the order. Soon his investment bears fruit:

> Oft he come by day and night
> To speke with that maiden bright.
> So that with his fair bihest,
> And with his gloseing atte lest,
> Hie graunted him to don his wille
> When he wil, loude and stille.   (287-92)

> (Often he came, both day and night, to speak with that beautiful
> maiden; so that by means of his fair promises and his flattery she
> in the end let him have his way in all respects.)

At his pleading she agrees to leave the convent and come to live with him in his castle. They live together exactly as if they had been married, and Freine endears herself to all, both '*more and lesse*', by her pleasant behaviour. However, theirs is an illegitimate relationship and so one day

> His knightes com and to him speke,

---

[1] One morning she was discovered by the porter of the convent, hidden in a hollow ash tree. After the tree she was called "le Freine" (OF *fraisne*).

And Holy Chirche comandeth eke,
Sum lordes doughter for to take,
And his leman al forsake;
And seid him wer wel more feir
In wedlok to geten him an air
Than lede his liif with swiche on
Of was kin he knewe non.   (311-8)

(His knights come and say to him, which Holy Church likewise
commands, that he should take [in marriage] the daughter of a lord
and give up his mistress entirely; and they said it would be much
better for him to beget an heir in wedlock than to lead his life with
someone of whose family he knew nothing.)

Though heartbroken, Freine accepts it all without a complaint, without a word of protest. On the day of the wedding she even decks the
bridal bed with her own costly '*pel*', the precious cloth in which she
had been found as a baby. This loving gesture prepares for a happy
conclusion: the mother of the bride, who also wants to inspect the
bridal chamber, on recognising the 'blanket' confesses that Freine is
not only her daughter but the twin sister of the bride at that. Sir
Guroun, Freine and the other guests hasten to the bishop, who immediately dissolves the marriage of Sir Guroun and the sister and marries him and Freine instead.[2]

To the modern reader the knights' advice must come as a
shock. Why may not Guroun simply marry Freine? And why does
not the Church show any pity? And to make it all even more start-
ling: why does not Freine herself show any sign of disapproval? To
answer these and other questions which the story raises we need to
know more about the medieval views on love and marriage.

In the course of the eleventh and twelfth centuries two models of
marriage developed, the aristocratic and the ecclesiastical. In spite of
some salient differences the two models tended in the same direction.[3] For the aristocracy safeguarding the patrimony, the ancestral
estate, was the main object. That could be threatened in several ways,

---

[2] The end of the story is missing in the one surviving manuscript, but it can be
reconstructed on the basis of the French original, the *Lai le Fraisne* by Marie de
France.
[3] Brooke (1989:126) has the same conclusion, Duby at first saw them as two
conflicting models (1978:15), but later limited this to the eleventh century and the
first half of the twelfth (1984:19, 185).

the most serious being an abundance of male heirs, which, were the latter all to claim part of the inheritance, would result in the disintegration of the estate. The solution was found in the protection of the children born in wedlock and in the adoption of the right of primogeniture: the patrimony could be inherited only by the eldest, legitimate son. A prerequisite for this system to work was the chastity of the wife, since adultery on her part would imperil the rights of any legal sons. Premarital sexual activity on the part of the woman was out of the question, as this would damage her reputation and take away the confidence that she would be a true and loyal wife. Another danger to the patrimony was of course the lack of a male heir. If a marital relationship failed to produce a child, the wife could be repudiated and replaced by a new and hopefully more fruitful bride. Marriage therefore, as Georges Duby put it, "regulated the sexual impulses, but only in the interest of a patrimony" (1978:7; see also 1984).

The introduction of the right of primogeniture had far-reaching consequences, although daughters were less affected by it than younger sons. After all, daughters had always been married off by their fathers as the latter saw fit, and this policy was simply continued, and became even more the rule. But where should the younger sons go? For the eldest son marriage provided stability and social and financial security, while also legitimising the fulfilment of his sexual urges. For the younger sons who wanted to attain to the same position only one course was open: they should strive to acquire a reputation of prowess that would make them a desirable match in the eyes of a rich and powerful lord with no other heir but a daughter. As a result these *iuvenes* or bachelors frequented the courts of the great lords, partook in all the tournaments and flocked to the houses of nubile heiresses. As Duby has pointed out (1978:11-5) they must have been a frustrated lot: tournaments had more losers than champions, while at least part of the fun of dalliance and flirtation with a beautiful heiress (who could marry only one of her many suitors anyway) and her lady friends was marred by the presence of numerous chaperones whose duty it was to preserve the reputation of their wards intact for future marriage. It goes without saying that in such a situation the lady's word is law, that even her smallest desire must be complied with and that she is likely to be idealised beyond recognition. In other words, we have here the breeding ground of the 'religion' of love, *amour courtois*.

In the ecclesiastical model of marriage two parts may be discerned which are complementary: a theological and a canonistic part.

The theologians see marriage as a sacrament instituted by God in Paradise with a specific purpose (to people the earth), and re-established after the Fall to remedy the sin of concupiscence. What is meant by this is that the power of the grace bestowed on the bride and the groom at their wedding through the blessing of the priest will remedy the damage done to the soul by the lust which is an inherent part of the marital act. (It follows that sexual intercourse before or outside marriage, even if it should have the intention of begetting an heir, is by definition sinful, lacking as it does the healing grace of the sacrament.) The nuptial blessing also turns the relation of husband and wife into a bond which is a reflection of—and by consequence as unbreakable as—that between God and the soul. Canonists, who approach marriage from a juridical point of view, look upon it as a contract, which establishes a legal relationship between two lawful persons and which becomes binding after the consent of both the man and the woman (Brooke, 1989:138).[4]

So far very little has been said about love. In the Middle Ages, as in any other age, various kinds of love were subsumed under this rather vague notion. Let us therefore briefly survey what kinds of love, both secular and religious, were discerned in this period.

We might commence this enumeration with the two extreme poles, to mark the boundaries: on the one hand perverted or unnatural love, and on the other mystical love. Perversion was caused, it was thought, by the abandonment of reason, resulting in such total surrender to bodily pleasure that one transgressed the laws of nature and sought to satisfy one's desires by unnatural means, such as homosexuality, or sodomy, as it was usually called. At the other end of the scale we find mystical love. By this term we should understand the striving after total conformation of the soul to God; it is an endeavour that can only be successful through a complete disengagement from all earthly attachments.

Love *par amour*, or passionate love, is the type most love poets are inspired by: its moving force, physical attraction, is of an emotive character, and its aim—however stimulating the conversations between the suitor and his lady may be—is the physical union with the beloved.

In the Middle Ages at least two further kinds of love are distinguished: natural love and rational love. Natural love springs from

---

[4] At least until the time of Thomas Aquinas (?1225-1274) many theologians maintained that it was the marital act and not the *consensus* that made a marriage irrevocable.

the laws of nature and results in such love as exists between parents and children. By rational love is understood the love that is based on reason rather than emotion: from it emanate both the love of God and the love of one's fellow-man as preached by the Church. The medieval Church condemned the passionate, erotic love celebrated by the poets because that was cupidinous and therefore irreconcilable with Christian teaching: it was detrimental to the soul and thus ultimately to one's salvation. Love, according to the Church's doctrine, should be based on reason, a requirement which also applied to love between spouses. Rational considerations which determine the moral suitability of the couple should have priority. Only after a provisional choice made on the basis of such criteria can considerations of a lower order be taken into account, such as physical or social attractiveness (d'Avray and Tausche, 1980:115). It goes without saying that the rational faculty should always remain in control of the inferior emotional forces (as also the husband, possessed with reason, should rule over his weaker wife, who was bound to be led astray by her emotions).

From such considerations it appears that the two models of marriage show a remarkable parallellism; although their motivations were far from identical, the Church and the property-owning classes were quick to realise that they had a common interest: both were in favour of a rational basis for marriage, of chastity for the spouses and particularly for wives, and eventually even of monogamy. Those who suffered from this were the young men and women, who may well at times have despaired of the compatibility of love and marriage. In many cases the official requirement of the Church for a marriage to be valid, the mutual consent of the partners, must have been a mere formality, and it is hardly to be expected that the brides and grooms of these arranged marriages should be romantically in love at the moment they made their vows.[5] Nevertheless, this should not lead one to conclude that no happy relationships could develop in such marriages. It is in the nature of an arranged marriage to assign a much less prominent part to sexuality, making it less remote from the Church's ideal of marriage, in which the spiritual aspect of the union between the spouses was emphasised. Thus it may well be the

[5] This is true for the land-owning classes, and for the aristocracy in particular. Kenneth McRobbie (1972) has shown that a few love-matches occur in Froissart's *Chroniques*, for instance between the Black Prince and the divorced Joan of Kent, in 1362, while Michael Sheehan (1971) has demonstrated that free choice occurred more often with members of the lower classes.

case that the ideal relationship as preached by the Church seemed less of an impossibility to medieval man than it may seem to us.

Let us now return to the *Lay le Freine*. The medieval audience will recognise that Freine and Guroun have started an affair which is illicit and that sooner or later the lovers will have to answer for that. Again, the knights' plea that Guroun marry a suitable wife, though perhaps morally not quite irreproachable, is not exceptional (Walter, the Marquis of Chaucer's *Clerk's Tale*, is faced with the same request). Under the circumstances, marrying a woman about whose family next to nothing is known is out of the question (yet the same Walter prefers the poor, lower-class girl Griselde to the daughter of a peer). The bishop who marries Guroun and the woman who turns out to be Freine's sister should have objected, for Guroun has already engaged in a valid albeit illicit relationship. However, he is not the first clergyman to gloss over the more subtle points of canon law when the social and financial advantages are visible to all. On the other hand, when it turns out that Guroun wants to have his first relationship raised to the status of an official marriage, there are sufficient grounds for the bishop to annul the second.

Is the poem a plea for a more serious consideration of the feelings of young persons? If it is, it somewhat overshoots its mark in the final lines where we are told that Freine's sister (by way of compensation or of consolation?), is soon after given in marriage to a knight of the country.

This giving away of girls in marriage is as common a feature in medieval romances as it was in real life. The marriages of the daughters of Henry II were well-considered dynastic alliances: Matilda became the wife of Henry of Saxony and Joan married William, King of Sicily. Few women would be strong-minded enough to follow the example of Elizabeth Paston, who refused to consent to the marriage arranged for her: she was locked up and beaten "*onys in the weke or twyes, and som tyme twyes on o day, and hir hed broken in to or thre places*" (Davis, 1976:ii.32: 'once or twice a week and sometimes twice a day, and her head was broken in two or three places'). She did not falter, however, and in the end, for a variety of reasons, the negotiations with her husband-to-be were abandoned. In the Middle English romances arranged marriages are imposed on— to mention only a few—Rymenhild (secretly engaged to Horn), Melior (in love with, and loved by, William of Palerne), and Melidor (fervently loved by Sir Degrevant). After her first dramatic experience Rymenhild moreover is abducted by Horn's arch-enemy,

Fikenhild, who forces her to marry him. Warned by a dream Horn
rushes to Fikenhild's castle where the wedding party is in full swing.
In the disguise of a minstrel he manages to get inside, slays Fikenhild
and marries Rymenhild. That he should rescue her on the day of the
wedding is of overriding importance: it means that the marriage has
not yet been consummated so that, in the first place, Rymenhild is
still a virgin, and, in the second, that the marriage can still be
declared null and void without any legal problems (of course
Fikenhild's death provides the easier solution). For Josian, the
beloved of Bevis of Hampton, no such rescue is possible as Bevis is in
prison; Josian preserves her virginity by means of a charm. Most
dramatic, of course, is the case of Tristram and Isoud: as a result of
the love potion that they have drunk they become lovers. When the
marriage between Isoud and King Mark takes place as planned, Isoud
sends her maid servant Bragwaine to the king during the wedding
night to conceal the loss of her virginity. It saves the day for her, but
King Mark soon becomes suspicious and because the marriage is not
dissolved Tristram and Isoud never experience more than brief
spells of happiness.

In order to preserve the ancestral estate a lord without male
heirs would carefully select a son-in-law. So too in the romances.
Many are the tales in which an unpromising young knight wins a
reputation that makes him worthy of the woman he loves. In *King
Horn* the eponymous hero is aware of his inferior status at the court
of Rymenhild's father (when still children he and twelve companions
had been set adrift in a small boat and washed ashore in the latter's
country); at first Horn rejects Rymenhild's marriage proposal, but
softened by her tears he asks for a delay: "*Mid spere I shall furst ride
/ And my knighthod proue, / Ar ich thee ginne to wowe*" (ll.548-50:
'I'll first ride out with my spear and prove my knighthood before I'll
woo you'). In *The Squire of Low Degree* the title is indicative of the
contents of the story, which with its hero's rise to fame parallels that
of *King Horn*—with one difference: here it is the lady herself who
requires proof positive of the squire's merits.

An original application of this topos in combination with that
of the forced marriage is found in *Havelok*. The kings of England
and of Denmark have, at their deaths, left their children in the care
of malevolent deputies. The Danish prince Havelok grows up in the
family of the fisherman Grim, who flees with him and his own family to England after he discovers who Havelok is. There Havelok, who
has developed into an exceptionally strong man, is employed in the
kitchen of the palace. He attracts the attention of Godrich, the regent

of England, by winning a stone throwing contest. As it happens,
Godrich had promised King Athelwold before his death that he
would give Athelwold's daughter, Goldeboru, in marriage to the
strongest man of England. He immediately seizes the opportunity to
fulfil his promise and simultaneously get rid of the girl, and arranges
for the marriage to take place. Both Goldeboru and Havelok enrage
him by refusing to consent, Goldeboru answering him with a splendid lofty air

> That hire sholde noman wedde,
> Ne noman bringen hire to bedde,
> But he were king or kinges eir,
> Were he nevere man so fair.   (1113-6)

(That no one should marry her or lie with her unless he were a
king or a king's son, however handsome he might be.)

The dialogue between Havelok and Godrich is of a completely different social register. On the day set for the marriage Godrich sends for
the kitchen boy, Havelok, and says, *"Maister, wilte wif?"* (l.1135:
'Master, do you want a wife?'). Apparently Godrich assumes that
such an insignificant servant will simply do as he is told, but Havelok
(who has no idea who is being offered to him) shows he is cast in the
right mould and replies bluntly: *"Nay, by my lif!"* (l.1136). What
can he offer a wife, he says; he can't house, feed or clothe her; even
what he is wearing himself is not his own. Godrich, however, is not
put off by such arguments:

> ... 'But thou hire take
> That I wole yeven thee to make,
> I shall hangen thee ful heye,
> Or I shall thristen ut thin eye.'   (1149-52)

('If you don't take her whom I give you in marriage, I'll hang you
high or gouge out your eyes.')

The same art of persuasion is practised on Goldeboru, and the couple
are married by the Archbishop of York. Left to themselves after the
ceremony, Havelok decides to take Goldeboru to Grim's house. During their first night together, when Havelok is asleep and Goldeboru
lies awake, feeling utterly dejected, she sees a light coming out of his
mouth and at the same time she is told by an angel that Havelok is the
son of a king and will be king of England and Denmark himself one

day. It is still a long way off, but there is a happy ending on the horizon for them.

In the romances discussed so far the role of love has been rather subordinated to that of knightly prowess. There are, however, a small number which do not combine the two and which concentrate entirely, or almost entirely, on the martial exploits of the hero: the Charlemagne romances might be mentioned in this context or *Gamelyn*, a romance with an all-male cast in the style of the later Robin Hood stories. Apart from these exceptions there are a few others in which the female contribution is next to negligible, but these belong to an altogether different category. These stories are mostly centred around the Holy Grail, a genre fairly rare in Middle English and represented by only one or two examples, such as the fragment of *Joseph of Arimathie*, or Malory's account of Sir Galahad's quest of the Grail. Love here is not the love between a man and a woman but the mystical love of God. Galahad, who has devoted his life to the service of God instead of to a lady, is allowed successfully to conclude his quest and to be granted the Sangrail as a sign of divine favour. Not long after that his soul is borne to heaven by a great multitude of angels.

Galahad's father is Sir Lancelot, the epitome of knightly virtue and courage. He too attempts to find the Grail and he comes very close: he reaches the chamber in which it is kept. He kneels before the door and prays God and Jesus to show it to him:

> And with that he saw the chamber door open, and
> there came out a great clearness, that the house was as
> bright as all the torches of the world had been there. So
> came he to the chamber door, and would have entered.
> And anon a voice said to him, 'Flee, Launcelot, and
> enter not, for thou oughtest not to do it.'
> *(Le Morte Darthur*, ii.355)

Divine interference stops Lancelot on the threshold of his greatest achievement: the knight has forfeited his right to win the Grail because of his adulterous love of Queen Guinevere, wife of King Arthur.

The vast majority of romances in some way or other combine love and arms, ending happily with the marriage of the hero and his beloved. Not so for Lancelot. His love of the Queen has an ennobling effect on him, it inspires him to great deeds of chivalry, but from the beginning it is bound to end in disaster. Arthur, after he has been publicly confronted with the truth, cannot let Lancelot go scot-free. The realm is split in two, and war, with ultimately the destruction of the kingdom, is the result.

There are a few other romances in which love triumphs over the socialising forces that normally lead to marriage—fortunately without the disastrous effect of Lancelot's passion. Sir Launfal becomes the lover of a fairy princess, Dame Tryamour, who makes him vow never to reveal their liaison to anyone. At the court of King Arthur the Queen accuses him falsely of homosexuality (when he has spurned her love). Launfal flies into a blind rage and he defends himself by bragging of his beautiful paramour, thus betraying their secret:

> 'I have loved a fairir woman
> Than thou evir leidest thin ey upon
>   This seven yere and more.
> Hire lothlokste maide withoute wene
> Mighte bet be a quene
>   Than thou, in all thy live!'   (694-9)

('I have loved a woman fairer than any woman you ever laid your eyes upon in the past seven years and more. Her ugliest maidservant would no doubt be more fit to be a queen than you!')

Tryamour does not respond to his pleas to show herself, and consequently Launfal cannot prove that his *leman* is more beautiful than Guinevere. When the hero is about to be sent into exile by way of punishment, Tryamour, in all her beauty, rides into the hall (a common practice in romances, cf. the first entry of the Green Knight in *Sir Gawain and the Green Knight*), vindicates Launfal, and takes him off with her to fairyland:

> Sethe saw him in this lond no man
> Ne no more of him telle I ne can
>   For sothe withoute lie.   (1034-6)

(Since that time no one has ever seen him again, nor do I know any more to say about him and that's the truth.)

Chaucer's *Knight's Tale* may be said to take up a middle position between the stories of Lancelot and Launfal. The destructive force of passion that we have seen at work in Lancelot here destroys the friendship between the two cousins and blood-brothers, Palamon and Arcite, who are simultaneously struck by an infatuation with Emelye (there is a reconciliation in the end). The two fight each other to the death, or, rather, would have done, had it not been for the intervention of Theseus, the Duke of Athens. Thanks to his authority and his command of the situation—and last but not least his willingness to listen to his wife's advice—the damage is limited to a few casualties in the tournament that was to settle the dispute about Emelye, together with the tragical death of Arcite (who had prayed for, and won, the victory in the tournament, but was killed by falling off his horse afterwards). On the other hand, love is victorious, as in the case of Launfal, for Emelye is given in marriage to Palamon, who loved her most.

The dramatic developments in the story of Lancelot are caused by a lack of self-governance: time and again his passionate love for the Queen proves stronger than himself. *The Earl of Toulouse* provides an interesting example of how Lancelot might better have behaved. Sir Barnard, the earl in question, falls in love with the wife of his lord, the Emperor of Almayne, who is described as being not only beautiful but also chaste (*"Of hyr body sche was trewe / As evyr was lady that men knewe"*, ll.43-4). He has grounds for hoping that his love is returned when the lady gives him a ring. Like Lancelot he acts as her champion when she is falsely accused of adultery, but unlike him he never makes any overtures. Eventually his patience is rewarded: after three years the Emperor dies, and the Earl succeeds him and marries the Empress. Barnard and Lady Beulyboon have fifteen children and since they live together for twenty-three years and no children are mentioned in relation to her marriage with the Emperor, this first marriage is apparently another case of a young girl-old ruler match.

The reverse would doubtless have occurred less frequently, but it is precisely from such an unusual situation that the *Wife of Bath's Tale* takes its poignancy. Men in the romances are always falling in love with supergirls—beautiful, chaste, well-behaved (and all this beyond comparison), young and of noble descent.[6] The 'loathly lady' clearly lacks a number of these qualities—if not all—and so the

---

[6] In recent years a beginning has been made with an examination of the other side of the coin, for example of questions like what it is that attracts women in men ("personality", Marie Collins concludes, which is "the sum of various moral and social qualities" [1985:28]), and what was the image of the ideal husband in the thirteenth century (N. Bériou and D.L. d'Avray, in an article as yet unpublished).

young man who is her husband finds himself, *mutatis mutandis*, in a
situation equivalent to that of countless brides (e.g. the young-but-
not-so-innocent May in the *Merchant's Tale*). This is the starting
point for the old hag's lecture on the virtues of true *'gentilesse'*, i.e.
the nobility of the soul, poverty and old age, which she ends with the
well-known question, whether he wants her

> 'foul and old til that I deye,
> And be to yow a trewe, humble wyf,
> And nevere yow displese in al my lyf;
> Or elles ye wol han me yong and fair,
> And take youre aventure of the repair
> That shal be to youre hous by cause of me,
> Or in som oother place, may wel be.'   (1220-6)

As in its parallel, *The Wedding of Sir Gawain and Dame Ragnell*, the
knight, having learned his lesson, leaves the choice to his wife who
rewards him by being young and beautiful as well as true and obedient.

One of the pervading themes in the Wife's *Prologue*, recur-
ring in the tale, is that of sovereignty in marriage. The superiority of
the husband over his wife (which has a sound biblical basis, in the
Old Testament in Genesis 3:16, where God says to Eve: '... and he
[your husband] shall be your master', and in the New in the repeated
admonitions of the Pauline Epistles), springs from the more general
conviction that woman was man's inferior. Yet a few medieval theologians tried to bridge the gap between the two. In the twelfth century both Bernard of Clairvaux and Hugh of St Victor stressed the
importance of the love between the spouses.[7] According to Bernard
this love relationship might lead to a harmony of wills in which the
inequality of the partners was no longer felt, and Hugh, commenting
on the story of the creation of man (Genesis 2:18-24), touches on this
idea of the equality or near-equality of the sexes when he says that
woman was made from the middle (i.e. from Adam's rib) and not
from his head or his foot—because she might then have been considered to be the equal of her husband.[8] These theological ideas found

---

[7] Bernard is referring to the mystical wedding of the soul, the bride, to God, the
groom, or that of the Church to Christ. His nuptial imagery makes his comments
relevant for the discussion at hand.
[8] The point Hugh makes here about the equality or near-equality of man and
woman and its impact on the medieval discussions on the hierarchical relationship

some support in the canonistic legislation on marriage (developed in the same period) according to which there was one moment, of crucial importance, at which man and woman had equal rights: they both had to give their consent. Without it the marriage was not valid and could be annulled at any time. As everyone is aware, it was to take centuries before the principle of the equal status of the spouses would win general acceptance, but a few authors were willing to stick out their necks and write in favour of equality long before that. Chaucer seems to have been one of them, if the *Franklin's Tale* is at all representative of his own convictions. In this tale the woman, Dorigen, accepts her suitor, Arveragus, as her husband and her lord. To enhance their bliss, Arveragus in his turn, of his own free will, swears that he will never *"take no maistrie / Agayn hir wyl"*, and will go on obeying her as a lover should his lady. The only request he has is that to the outside world he would have *"the name of soveraynetee ...for shame of his degree"* (ll.751-2). Dorigen's reaction is like that of the aged bride in the *Wife of Bath's Tale*:

> She seyde, 'Sire, sith of youre gentilesse
> Ye profre me to have so large a reyne,
> Ne wolde nevere God bitwixe us tweyne,
> As in my gilt, were outher werre or stryf.
> Sire, I wol be youre humble trewe wyf—
> Have heer my trouthe—til that myn herte breste.' (754-9)

A little later the Franklin comments:

> Heere may men seen an humble, wys accord;
> Thus hath she take hir servant and hir lord—
> Servant in love, and lord in mariage.
> Thanne was he bothe in lordshipe and servage.
> Servage? Nay, but in lordshipe above,
> Sith he hath bothe his lady and his love;
> His lady, certes, and his wyf also,
> The which that lawe of love acordeth to. (791-8)

Chaucer is at great pains here to show us that the future husband and wife, Arveragus and Dorigen, do not intend to give up their relation as lovers. It seems as if Chaucer is trying to strike a balance between two clashing types of relationship, that of a lover and his lady and

---

between husband and wife has been further elaborated in Kooper (1985:25-70; 1990).

that of husband and wife. The essential ingredient of the first is love, of the second reason. Another important difference is that in the first the lady rules, in the second the husband. We have already seen that both Arveragus and Dorigen have renounced any claim to superiority, which makes them in a sense equals. In his treatise on spiritual friendship, *De spirituali amicitia*, Aelred of Rievaulx (an English pupil of Bernard of Clairvaux) had already said that friendship consists in a combination of love and reason, and is possible only between equals.[9] If Chaucer is indeed presenting the relationship between Arveragus and Dorigen as one of friendship this would explain the otherwise rather unexpected praise of friendship that follows immediately on Dorigen's reply to Arveragus, quoted above:

> For o thyng, sires, saufly dar I seye,
> That freendes everych oother moot obeye,
> If they wol longe holden compaignye.
> Love wol nat been constreyned by maistrye.
> Whan maistrie comth, the God of Love anon
> Beteth his wynges, and farewel, he is gon!   (761-6)

"Friendship," Aelred says, "is that virtue by which the spirits themselves are bound by ties of love and sweetness, and out of many are made one.".[10] If our conclusion is right, Chaucer apparently subscribes to the view that the ideal marital relationship is based on friendship.

The hero of romance as he is best known to the modern reader is unattached at the outset, and when love enters his life it is the passionate love of a first infatuation with all its incertitudes, anxieties and physical side effects like sleeplessness and pallor. The safe haven of marriage he does not usually reach before the final lines, where it comes as the climax, the ultimate reward for his unflinching efforts. We might say that marriage in these romances marks the integration into society of the hero, who, as Elizabeth Archibald says elsewhere in this volume, matures as he learns through experience about chivalry and about love. In this sense the *Franklin's Tale* is an exception,

---

[9] I have argued elsewhere that Chaucer was acquainted with the basic tenets of the theory of friendship (Kooper, 1985). On friendship and marriage in the *Franklin's Tale*, see Wimsatt (1990).

[10] Amicitia igitur ipsa uirtus est qua talis dilectionis ac dulcedinis foedere ipsi animi copulantur, et efficiuntur unum de pluribus (*De spirituali amicitia* I.21).

but it is by no means unique. There are in fact quite a few romances which focus on the family and in which the disunion and, eventually, the happy reunion of all its members are the two poles between which the events take place. To judge by their numbers, such domestic romances were apparently very popular in the fourteenth century. The earliest example probably dates (at least in its English form) from the late thirteenth century; it is the story of Sir Orfeo, King of Traciens, and his wife Heurodis, and it is eminently suitable to round off this survey of love and marriage in the Middle English romances.

On a pleasant, sunny spring morning Lady Heurodis goes for a stroll in the orchard *"To see the floures sprede and spring, / And to here the foules sing"* (ll.43-4: 'to see the flowers grow and burgeon and to hear the birds sing'). Around noon she falls asleep under a tree. In her sleep something terrifying happens to her, and she wakes up quite hysterical. She is taken inside and put to bed by some attendants while others warn Sir Orfeo. He hastens to her chamber and, moved by pity, he says:

> O lef lif, what is te,
> That ever yete hast ben so stille
> And now gredest wonder shille?   (78-80)

> ('O my dearest, what is the matter with you who have always
> been so quiet and now cries out so shrilly?')

'Have mercy,' Orfeo beseeches her, 'and stop this pitiful crying!' Long ago, too, when he was wooing her and she was his beautiful lady, Orfeo, like any other courtly lover, would have asked for his lady's mercy, i.e. to grant him her favour. But now her beauty is destroyed, her pretty little fingers are smeared with blood and her lovely eyes *"Loketh so man doth on his fo"* (l.88: 'have the look in them of someone who sees his enemy'), and what Orfeo hopes for is pity. He begs his wife to tell him what has frightened her and how he can help her. His words have a soothing effect, but instead of revealing what caused her terror she says:

> 'Allas, mi lord, Sir Orfeo!
> Sethen we first togider were,
> Ones wroth never we nere;
> Bot ever ich have y-loved thee
> As my lif, and so thou me.
> Ac now we mot delen atwo.

Do thy best, for I mot go!'   (96-102)

('Alas, my lord, Sir Orfeo! Ever since we were first together we
have never quarrelled; on the contrary, I have always loved you as
my own life, and you me. But now we must part. Do the best you
can, for I must go.')

Heurodis wants to reassure Orfeo that whatever may befall she has
loved and always will love him, and if she should be made to go it is
not because she has stopped loving him—or loves someone else. To
certify that is more important to her than any other concern. Orfeo's
reaction is one of despair: 'Wherever you go, I will go as well!' But
it is all to no avail. Heurodis is abducted by the king of fairies to the
Otherworld, leaving Orfeo in such misery that he renounces his
kingship and departs to live as a hermit in the wilderness. Fortunately the story has a happy ending, for after a period of adversity Orfeo
succeeds in regaining both his wife and his kingdom.

The passage from which I have just quoted, with the terrified
Heurodis and her at first uncomprehending and then despairing husband, is realistic to a degree hardly met with in Middle English literature in emotional contexts.[11] What makes this scene especially attractive is its intimacy, the loving concern for the other and the confidence of mature and mutual love as it can only be displayed by a
couple who have been married for a goodly number of years and
have grown together towards a stable relationship. Such a picture of
marital love is rare in the world of romance. Let us hope that it was
less so for the men and women to whom it was read.

[11] A scene of comparable loving care and devotion occurs in *Floris and Blancheflour* when the two lovers stand before the Emir of Babylon and try to save
each other by (a) each accepting the blame for what has happened (Floris was
found in bed with Blancheflour in the Emir's harem), and (b) each passing a
protecting ring to the other.

REFERENCES

Primary Sources

Aelred of Rievaulx. *De spirituali amicitia*. Ed. A. Hoste, OSB. *Aelredi Rievallensis opera omnia*. I. *Opera ascetica*. CCCM I. Turnholti: Brepols. 1971.
Chaucer, Geoffrey. *The Riverside Chaucer*. Ed. Larry D. Benson. Oxford: Oxford University Press. 1988.
The Earl of Toulouse. In: Rumble (1965).
Floris and Blancheflour, Gamelyn, Havelok, King Horn, Lai le Fresne, Sir Launfal, Sir Orfeo, The Squire of Low Degre. In Sands (1966).
Malory, Sir Thomas. *Le Morte D'Arthur*. 2 vols. Ed. Janet Cowen. Harmondsworth: Penguin Books. 1966 (Repr., 1977).
Paston Letters and Papers of the Fifteenth Century. 2 vols. Ed. Norman Davis. Oxford: Oxford University Press. 1970, 1976.
Rumble, Thomas C. (ed.) (1965). *The Breton Lays in Middle English*. Detroit: Wayne State University Press.
Sands, Donald B. (ed.) (1966). *Middle English Verse Romances*. New York: Holt, Rinehart and Winston.
Sir Beues of Hamtoun. Ed. Eugen Kölbing. EETS, ES 46 (1885), 48 (1886), 65 (1894).
Sir Degrevant. Ed. L.F. Casson. EETS, OS 221 (1949).
William of Palerne. Ed. G.H.V. Bunt. Groningen: Bouma. 1985.

Secondary Sources

d'Avray, D.L., and M.L. Tausche (1980). Marriage Sermons in *Ad status* Collections of the Central Middle Ages. *Archives d'histoire doctrinale et littéraire du moyen âge* 47. 71-119.
Brooke, Christopher N.L. (1989). *The Medieval Idea of Marriage*. Oxford: Oxford University Press.
Collins, Marie (1985). Feminine Response to Masculine Attractiveness in Middle English Literature. *Essays and Studies*. 12-28.
Duby, Georges (1978). *Medieval Marriage. Two Models from Twelfth-Century France*. Trans. Elborg Foster. Baltimore/London: The Johns Hopkins University Press.
Duby, Georges (1984). *The Knight, the Lady and the Priest. The Making of Modern Marriage in Medieval France*. Trans. Barbara Bray. London: Alan Lane.
Edwards, Robert R. and Stephen Spector (eds.) (forthcoming 1990). *The Olde Daunce: Love, Friendship, and Desire in the Medieval World*. Albany: State University of New York Press.
Kooper, Erik (1985). *Love, Marriage and Salvation in Chaucer's* Book of the Duchess *and* Parlement of Foules. Diss. University of Utrecht.
Kooper, Erik (forthcoming 1990). Loving the Unequal Equal: Medieval Theologians and Marital Affection. In: Edwards and Spector.
McRobbie, Kenneth (1972). Woman and Love: Some Aspects of Competition in Late Medieval Society. *Mosaic* 5. 139-68.
Sheehan, Michael M. (1971). The Formation and Stability of Marriage in Fourteenth-Century England: Evidence of an Ely Register. *Mediaeval Studies* 33. 228-63.
Wimsatt, James I. (forthcoming 1990). Reason, Machaut and the Franklin. In: Edwards and Spector.

THE REAL AND THE IDEAL
Attitudes to Love and Chivalry
as seen in
*The Avowing of King Arthur**

DAVID JOHNSON

In what is perhaps the fairest assessment of this neglected Middle
English romance, J.A. Burrow (1987:109) has remarked that "the
Avowing could have been a masterly creation—if only the *Gawain*-
poet had written it." In a general way this is true of quite a lot of
Middle English poetry, but the double-edged force of Burrow's
remark is particularly applicable to the *Avowing*.[1] It suggests, of
course, that the substance of the *Avowing* would have been worthy of
the *Gawain*-poet's attention and talents, while at the same time it calls
attention to the presence of serious short-comings in the poem's ex-
ecution. The modern reader will indeed find both. The *Avowing*
stands out for its well-crafted structure, brilliant characterisation
and intriguing mixture of motifs from both courtly and more popular traditions. Here, too, one will find the most familiar characters
of Arthurian romance caught up in a narrative that is fast-paced,
forward-moving and which rarely flags. But the *Gawain*-poet did

---

* I should like to thank Prof. Winthrop Wetherbee for invaluable criticisms that
have shaped the final version of this paper, and Prof. Thomas D. Hill for reading
and commenting on an earlier version.
[1] The best and most recent edition of the poem is by Roger Dahood (1984); all
quotations are from this edition. A new edition is being prepared by Thomas
Hahn for Medieval Institute Publications of Western Michigan University; it is
scheduled to appear sometime in the latter half of 1990 under the title *Five
Gawain Romances,* and in addition to the *Avowing* will include the *Awntyrs,
Golagros and Gawane, The Marriage of Sir Gawain and Dame Ragnell* and *Sir
Gawain and the Carl of Carelisle.*
   The *Avowing* has also appeared in the following editions: John Robson,
1842:57-93; W. H. French and C.B. Hale, 1964:605-46; C. Brookhouse, 1968.
   Studies devoted either wholly or in large part to *The Avowing* are so few that
they may easily be listed here. Besides the editions cited above, there are three
philological studies: Luick (1914); Tihany (1936); Dahood (1971). Two studies
of its sources are found in Paris (1888) and Kittredge (1893). A pair of articles
focusing on the vows that feature so prominently in the piece are by Greenlaw
(1906), and Reinhard (1932).

not write it. It is a tail-rhyme romance, rather than an alliterative poem, and as such it is susceptible to the short-comings of its medium: what it gains in lively narration, it loses in descriptive richness; and the tendency to resort to stock expressions and tags must always have been a problem for poets working in tail-rhyme, especially the relatively rare sixteen-line stanza chosen by the *Avowing*-poet. Scribal corruption in the one extant manuscript has almost certainly resulted in metrical corruption as well, a fact which naturally has done little to recommend the work to recent readers. Yet the *Avowing* contains a number of incidental features which are reminiscent of *Sir Gawain and the Green Knight*, (for instance a boar hunt as well as a testing scene in a hunting context), and a more fundamental correspondence between the two poems is their subtle critique of the world which they portray and in which they participate: the world of Arthurian chivalry.

Roger Dahood (1984:79) has determined that the original dialect of the *Avowing* is somewhat more northerly than the West Midland dialect of *Sir Gawain and the Green* Knight (henceforth *SGGK*), though the two poems do share some linguistic features. The language of the manuscript is consistent with a South Lancashire provenance, which in turn strengthens the supposition that it was copied at Hale Manor, Lancashire, where it had certainly resided in the sixteenthth century (Dahood, 1984:11). This association with Lancashire is relevant to our purposes when seen in light of M.J. Bennett's work on courtly literature in Northwest England of the time. Bennett makes a convincing case for the positive effects on the literary arts of the careerist tendencies of Cheshire and Lancashire men, and his studies have yielded the most plausible explanation for the rather surprising mixture of language, form and courtly sophistication of *SGGK*. Travel, he points out (1979:74), whether on legal business, trade, or more significantly military service, would have brought such men into touch with new cultural influences. It goes without saying that there must have been more than a few poets and minstrels among these careerists, and it is one such, presumably a Cheshire man, who is thought to have been responsible for fusing courtly themes and values with provincial language and perspectives in *SGGK*. The following citation from Bennett (1979:74) takes us a step closer to the actual relationship of the *Avowing* to works like those of the *Gawain*-poet:

> If minstrels and poets had difficulty finding sponsorship
> in the households of the local gentry, there were lucra-

tive openings in the mansions and castles of Cheshire
men who had found their fortunes overseas or in other
parts of the kingdom. Whilst *Sir Gawain and the Green
Knight*, *Pearl* and other works of similar quality were
not in themselves the products of such hack songsters, it
is fair to assume that their sophistication was only at-
tained atop a groundswell of more popular culture.

It is among the "hack songsters", perhaps, that we must look for the
author of the *Avowing*; yet, as I hope to show, our poet succeeded in
his own way in juxtaposing two sets of values so as to create a tension
between them, and it is this success that renders it worthy of our
attention.

I

Since the *Avowing* is a relatively obscure poem, I will preface my
own observations by a short summary of its plot and structure. The
narrative falls into two evenly divided sections of 36 stanzas, or 576
lines, each.[2] These sections form in fact two distinct narratives which
are, however, firmly tied together by virtue of the characters who
appear in them and the unique use of their vows as a linking device.

Following nearly two stanzas of traditional introductory material, the scene is set (Arthur's court at Carlisle) and the action begins with Arthur's huntsman reporting the terrible ravages of a giant
boar. In a lively verbal exchange (such exchanges are a prominent
feature of the poem) the king takes in this report, asks after the
boar's whereabouts and determines to verify the huntsman's report
in person. For his expedition he chooses three knights to accompany
him: Gawain, Kay and one Baldwin of Britain. The hunter wastes no
time in leading the party to the boar, who demonstrates his ferocity
by killing a number of the dogs unleashed upon him. The narrator
informs us that the dogs have succeeded in tracking down the beast
and driving him into his den, but sardonically remarks:

> Butte witte ȝe, sirs, witturly,
> He stode butte litull awe.   (95-6)

---

[2] Burrow (1987:100, note 5) argues convincingly for this perfect division despite
the presence of a defective stanza (xviii), noting that the missing quatrain is most
likely due to scribal "eye-skip."

(But, Sirs, be absolutely sure of this: he had only little fear.)

This sardonic tone spills over into the words the huntsman addresses
to Arthur and his knights:

> Þenne þe hunter sayd, "Lo him þare.
> ȝaw þar such him no mare.
> Now may ȝe sone to him fare;
> Lette see quo dose beste.
> ȝaw þar such him neuyr more,
> Butte sette my hed opon a store
> Butte giffe he flaey ȝo all fawre,
> Þat griselich geste."   (105-12)

(Then the hunter said, "Look at him there. Don't seek him there
anymore. Now you can go to him at once; let it be seen who per-
forms best. Don't seek him there any more, but put my head on a
hedge stake, unless he skins all four of you, that horrible dangerous one.')

The hunter, clearly impressed by the destructive powers of the boar
and the seeming hopelessness of the situation, beats a hasty retreat.
No doubt inspired by the challenge inherent in the huntsman's words
and aware of the potential provided by the boar for proving his
knightly prowess, Arthur vows to lay low the boar, single-handedly,
before day-break. Having made his vow, he demands of his companions that they commit themselves to a similar quest; their assent is
spontaneous and seemingly unanimous. Gawain answers first, vowing to ride to the Tarne Wadling "*to wake hit all nyȝte*" (l. 132: 'to
guard it all night'). Kay vows to ride up and down the paths of Inglewood Forest and kill any who stand in his way. Baldwin responds
with three vows. The first is never to be jealous of his wife, the second never to refuse any man food, and the third never to fear death at
the hands of knight or king. At this point each character rides off to
perform his vow: Arthur turns to the boar, Gawain heads for the
Tarne and Kay begins his patrol of the woods. Of Baldwin, in a moment not unlike the earlier departure of the huntsman, we are told:

> Boudewynne turnes to toune,
> Sum þat his gate lay,
> And sethun to bed bownus he.   (155-7)

(Baldwin goes to the town, as his road lay, and then he goes to
bed.)

The reader is next treated to seven stanzas detailing Arthur's fight with (and vanquishing of) the boar, followed by five stanzas dealing with Kay's misadventures in attempting to free a damsel in distress from her would-be ravisher, one Menealfe of the Mountain. Gawain never encounters the supernatural foe both he and the audience have come to expect at the Tarne, for Kay (having been bested by the stranger knight in joust) has wasted no time in persuading Menealfe that Gawain will run a course with him in lieu of ransom. Stanzas 23 to 30 constitute a brilliantly entertaining encounter between Menealfe and Gawain, punctuated liberally by the typically brash boastings and taunts one has come to expect from Kay "the Crabbit". By contrasting him with both Kay and Menealfe, the episode explicitly establishes Gawain's superiority in two important facets of chivalric behaviour: martial prowess and courtesy. Having defeated the stranger knight twice (once to ransom Kay and a second time for custody of the damsel), Gawain charges him to report to Queen Guinevere as his prisoner and accept whatever punishment she may exact upon him. In the closing stanzas of the first half of the poem (ll.30-36), Gawain and the others respond to Arthur's hunting horn (Arthur awakes from a good night's sleep, but his horse has been killed by the boar) and the party rides back to Carlisle, exchanging reports of their exploits on the way. Once back at court, praise for Gawain abounds, and he in turn exhibits still greater generosity by pleading on behalf of his former foe, Menealfe. Guinevere defers to Arthur's judgement in such matters, whereupon a book of laws is produced and Menealfe is considered sufficiently rehabilitated to take his place among the other knights at the round table. Thus ends the first section of the *Avowing*.

The second section begins as Kay reasserts his boastful nature (he has clearly learned nothing from his humbling encounter with Menealfe), reminding the court,

> "Sire, a mervaell thinke me
> Of Bowdewyns avouying
> 3estureuyn in þe eunyng,
> Wythowtun any lettyng,
> Wele more thenne we thre."   (576-80)

("Sir, with regard to Baldwin's making his vows last night in the evening it seems to me a marvel, undeniably, indeed more than we three.')

It is Kay who initiates the series of events that will put Baldwin's "vows" to the test. He requests permission to take five knights on an expedition to try Baldwin's conviction never to fear death. Arthur grants the request, provided that Kay not do any real harm to his knight, but merely deny him passage on the way. Needless to say, Kay and his fellows are given a sound drubbing by the veteran knight. Baldwin returns to Arthur's court but, when asked, reveals nothing of the encounter to the king, thus impressing him both with his martial prowess and his humility.

Arthur next schemes to test Baldwin's vow never to refuse hospitality to any man. He despatches a minstrel to Baldwin's estate (stanza 45) and commands him to dwell there for a while and take note of how visitors are treated. The minstrel finds indeed that no one, of either low or high station, is refused any form of hospitality, be it food, drink or entertainment, at Baldwin's hall. Not only is there no porter to turn men away, but the lady of the house herself receives the minstrel graciously and takes great interest in him, for she "...*had myrth of his mouthe / To here his tithand*" (ll.747-8: 'was delighted to hear the news that he told her').

After an interval of one week, Arthur himself arrives at Baldwin's court and receives both his minstrel's testimony and first-hand experience of Baldwin's hospitality. Satisfied that Baldwin has made good his second vow, Arthur engineers the final test, that of Baldwin's claim never to be jealous of his wife. He commands Baldwin to go hunting for deer the next day, and bids his huntsman see to it that he stay out all day and night, to return at dawn the following day. In Baldwin's absence Arthur approaches his lady's chambers and demands she open the door and let him in. Stanzas 52 and 53 constitute another of the poem's brilliant, lively exchanges of dialogue, this time between Arthur and Baldwin's lady, who is not at all sure of Arthur's good intentions; nor, for that matter, is the audience—for a brief moment, at least:

> The kyng bede, "Vndo."
> Þe lady asshes, "Querto?"
> He sayd, "I am comun here, loe,
> In derne for to play."
> Ho sayd, "Haue ȝe notte ȝour aune quene here
> And I my lord to my fere?
> Tonyȝte more neȝe ȝe me nere,
> In fayth, gif I may!"   (821-28)

(The king commanded, "Open up." The lady asked, "For what
reason?" He said, "Look, I have come here to have some fun secretly." She said, "Have you not your own queen here and I my
lord as my company? Tonight you shall never draw closer to me,
truly, if I can help it.")

Arthur does in the end persuade her that she will come to no harm,
and he is allowed to enter, bringing with him a young knight who
will feature in his scheme. He commands the knight to undress and
climb into bed with the lady, but, on pain of death, not to touch her.
Having set up this tableau, Arthur sits down on the edge of the bed
and passes the hours till dawn by playing chess with a chamber-maid.
It is in this position that he confronts the unsuspecting Baldwin with
the seeming proof of his wife's infidelity. Returning from the hunt
(stanza 56) Baldwin is unmoved by the sight of his wife in bed with
another man. Arthur is amazed at this reaction, and Baldwin explains
that the knight could only have made it into her bed if she herself
willed it. Sensing that Arthur is hardly satisfied by this reply, Baldwin offers to explain all of his vows, and this becomes the occasion
for three tales of Baldwin's past exploits.

In brief, stanzas 58-72 contain the explanations for his previous "vows"; vows, it will now be seen, that are not proper vows at
all, but rather the expression of convictions arrived at on the basis of
past experience. During the reign of Arthur's father Baldwin had
been rewarded for his part in a campaign in Spain by the gift of a
large estate and castle, along with a garrison of 500 men. But tending
to the domestic and sexual needs of the entire garrison are three
women, two of whom become jealous of the third to the extent that
they slay her. When brought before the lord of the castle for justice
they plead for their lives, promising to do the work of three in fulfilling the needs of the garrison. Their request is granted. But one is
prettier than the other, and, jealousy getting the better of the home-
lier of the two, she cuts her companion's throat. The remaining
woman subsequently pleads for her life in much the same way as
before, promising to fulfil the needs of the entire castle on her own if
only they spare her life. Baldwin agrees to this arrangement, and the
matter ends there. Just how this experience can provide the basis for
Baldwin's conviction never to be jealous of his wife is less than clear;
I shall say more about it below, since there remain two tales to Baldwin's explanation.

Arthur is satisfied with Baldwin's answer on the score of jealousy:

"Butte of þo othir thinges þat þou me told
I wold wete more:
Quy þou dredus notte þi dede,
Ne non þat bitus on þi brede.
As euyr brok I my hede,
Þi ȝatis ar euyr ȝare!"   (1007-12)

("But about those other things that you have told me I would like
to know more: whydo you not fear your death or anyone who eats
your food. As I hope to live, your doors are always ready to receive visitors.")

The explanations for these convictions find their sources in two experiences at the same castle in Spain. His castle under siege by the
Heathen, Baldwin and his troops set out one day on a sortie, but one
of their comrades gets cold feet and decides to remain behind.
Having crept into a barrel to hide, he is struck and killed by an incoming projectile, while that evening Baldwin and his fellows return
from battle unscathed. When they discover their cowardly comrade's
fate, they realise how useless it is to fear death, and all swear an oath
never to dread it.

The siege is going poorly for Baldwin and his men, for supplies are running perilously low; they have only enough food and
water to last a couple of days when a messenger from the enemy
arrives in order to persuade them to surrender. Baldwin commands
his cooks, much to the dismay of his other men, to prepare a sumptuous feast for the messenger, and to spare no delicacies from their
supplies. The unsuspecting envoy enjoys himself immensely, returns
to his own camp and advises his king to lift the siege, for,

Þoȝhe ȝe sege þis seuyn ȝere,
Castell gete ȝe none here,
For þay make als mury chere
Als hit were Ȝole Day!   (1097-1100)

(Even though you continue the siege for the next seven years, you
will not obtain any castle here, for they behave as merrily as if it
were Christmas Day.)

Baldwin and his men rejoice at the sight of their enemies breaking
camp and lifting the siege for want of food and supplies. This experience convinces Baldwin and his fellows that the man who turns another from his table is a fool. At this point Baldwin concludes his account, and Arthur praises his integrity and urges him to love his lady

well. The poem ends with a very short prayer. Such are the essentials
of the plot of the *Avowing*.

II

The *Avowing* has often garnered praise for its well-crafted structure, and J.A. Burrow has taken criticism of this aspect of the poem a
logical step further by comparing it to a diptych. A.C. Spearing had
used this metaphor in his reading (1981:183-202) of the *Awntyrs off
Arthur at the Terne Wathelyn* to show how the two apparently unre-
lated narratives comprising that poem produce a meaning through
juxtaposition that is greater than the sum of their parts. Spearing
mentions the Middle Scots *Golagros and Gawane* as a further example of a diptych romance, and W.W. Ryding (1971) gives many more
instances from various literatures in his study of medieval narrative
structure. Yet neither scholar calls attention to the *Avowing* which,
as Burrow points out, better fits the model by virtue of its nearly
perfect numerical division and strong links between its panels. The
point made by all critics who apply the diptych metaphor to narrative
structure is that one panel reflects upon the other, and that meaning
results from their juxtaposition, a meaning that is absent from either
panel when viewed in isolation. Burrow (1987:108) expresses best
the probable rationale behind such a juxtaposition in the *Avowing*:

> Unlike the *Awntyrs*, in fact, the *Avowing* is held togeth-
> er by a strong and well-articulated plot: the two panels
> of the diptych are firmly hinged. The fact that the sec-
> ond half of the *Avowing* has already been set up by
> Baldwin's vows in the first distinguishes it from the
> looser kind of diptych structure to be found in the *Awn-
> tyrs* and in most of the instances discussed by Ryding.
> Yet it is true that the second half of the poem, like the
> first part of the *Awntyrs*, does offer something of a con-
> trast and a surprise, set off against the more convention-
> al Arthurian aspects of its facing panel. Indeed the chief
> interest of the *Avowing*, as of the *Awntyrs*, lies in the
> teasing relationship between its two parts: 'Look here
> upon this picture, and on this ....'

It remains a pity, however, that Burrow does not go on to elaborate
on the meaning evoked by the juxtaposition of these pictures; one

looks in vain for comment on why the author should have wanted his reader to "Look here on this picture, and on this" in the case of the *Avowing*.

Now it is invariably the section of the poem in which Baldwin features most prominently, in particular the *exempla* adduced as explanations for his vows, that has drawn the most criticism from past critics of the poem. Ralph Hanna, for example, objects to "the unchivalrous sentiments about women" revealed by Baldwin and the applause he receives for these sentiments (1974:34). Dahood, too, notes the thematic inconsistency of the Baldwin section (1984:34)— Baldwin's "receptive attitude toward murder and promiscuity does not accord with the morally superior character that he otherwise exhibits." In the end Burrow must concede that the *Avowing* poet failed to realise the potential of his scheme: by choosing an episode from the Murderous Women tradition to illustrate Baldwin's attitude toward women, he presents the reader with a most unflattering and unchivalric perspective on women—the "receptive attitude toward murder and promiscuity" just mentioned. Burrow's explanation for this inconsistency is simply (1987:108) that, "for once, the poet made a bad choice of story." Indeed, how are we to explain Baldwin's extraordinary behaviour? At first reading there is something singularly unchivalric about Baldwin's actions in Spain and his seemingly passionless attitude toward his wife and other women. Some explanation, it seems, is needed to account for the poet's use of the Murderous Women anecdote as the explanation for Baldwin's lack of jealousy. Yet how truly incongruous is this anecdote? To modern sensibilities, very; and if one measures the poem by the standards of the high-chivalric courtly-love tradition in medieval romance, Baldwin's tale (and the poet's choice) fares no better. But, as J.A.W. Bennett remarked (1986:175), "Chrétien might never have written for all this poet cares." The poem is decidedly "uncourtly" in tone, and this, it must be stressed, is particularly true where it concerns perspectives on women. One wonders whether the world of the poem is capable of entertaining any really enlightened attitude towards women. If Baldwin's apparently anti-feminist attitude has brought frowns to the brows of many critics, it bears pointing out that the ease with which Arthur's court exonerates Menealfe of any guilt in his own doings is hardly less "unchivalric" than Baldwin's failure to treat his three women like ladies; indeed, the treatment of the damsel by all concerned (Menealfe, but also Arthur, Kay and Gawain) as an object, as the spoils of war (she is carted off to Carlisle along with the meat of Arthur's boar, and disappears from the narrative after that) reflects an attitude towards women that is exactly paralleled by what we find in the Murderous Women anecdote—their traffic in women is no better, nor more chivalrous than Baldwin's dealings at his castle. A further irony is that Baldwin loves his wife very much, as is clear from his first response to Arthur in the final stages of the narrative. One is justified, then, in cautioning against placing too much emphasis, in any assessment of the poet's artistic intentions, on Baldwin's maltreatment of the women: it is the product of an attitude that is unsophisticated at best, and decidely anti-feminist at worst; it is also, one must admit, in keeping with much of what survives of Middle English Romance. When taken in this way, the supposed disruption of the *Avowing*'s thematic unity by Baldwin's behaviour may be seen to disappear.

Ultimately I think the poet is less concerned with celebrating Baldwin as a paragon of chivalric virtue than he is with pointing up some kind of contrast between two brands of chivalry with which he is familiar: the one deriving from the literary, fantasy world of Arthurian romance, the other being an expression of a view grounded in a more practical, real-world experience of the values treated in both. As I read it, the contrast produced by the juxtaposition of the two panels is characterised by an opposition of idealism *versus* realism; that is to say that the vows and adventures of Arthur, Kay and Gawain in the first panel are representative of a self-affirming, competitive and impractical kind of idealism, while the boundaries of the world delineated by Baldwin's vows and explanatory anecdotes in the second panel represent a real-world, socially grounded system of values. The two realms of experience are separated, of course, by the structural division into two panels; but their distinction, and the contrast between them, is further underlined by the fact that they are both precisely demarcated in time and place. The adventures of the Arthurians take place within the boundaries of the royal forest of Inglewood[3], and the action runs its course within the span of one night. Baldwin's explanatory accounts, too, are strictly defined in time and space: some time before Arthur's own, in far-off Spain. It is significant that Baldwin chooses not to enter the forest with the others, thus he never crosses into the "otherworld" realm of Arthurian chivalry

---

[3] Inglewood was an actual royal preserve, its exact dimensions known: sixteen miles long and ten miles wide; it features in two other romances, *The Awntyrs off Arthur at the Terne Wathelyn* and *The Wedding of Sir Gawain and Dame Ragnell*, where it also forms the scene for wondrous adventures; see Dahood, 1984: note to line 64.

portrayed in this panel; by the same token Arthur and his knights are
excluded from the realm of historical realism depicted in Baldwin's
campaign accounts. This structural separation of the two realms of
experience is an expression of the poet's awareness of the dichotomy
between the theory and practice of chivalry, between the Arthurian
model that was being promoted at this time, and the actuality of warfare as our poet might have known it.

Yet another feature suggestive of the contrast between the two
halves is a detectible difference in tone. The picture on the left-hand
panel of our diptych is painted for the most part in the colours of traditional Arthurian romance. The reader has no difficulty in recognising that the narrative elements of this panel have been "drawn out
of Arthurian stock" (Burrow, 1987:104). Among such stock features
are the pattern of first setting scene in Arthur's court, followed by
departure from it on quest or hunt, and the subsequent return to
court (cf. *Awntyrs* and *SGGK*); the all too familiar use of Kay as a
foil for emphasising Gawain's martial prowess and courtesy; the battle with a powerful foe, beast or giant, supernatural or otherwise; the
courtly custom of vowing on an animal. It comes as no surprise that
Gawain puts the terms of Menealfe's ransom (indeed his life) into
Guinevere's hands—Guinevere herself confirms Gawain's rank as
"her" knight (also seen in the *Awntyrs* where he is her guide on the
hunt). These are all common features of Arthurian romance. Yet the
vein of this first panel especially is largely humorous, and much of
that humour is created at the expense of the Arthurians' knightly dig-
nity: Arthur the practical joker, Kay, whose traditionally boisterous
behaviour is greatly exaggerated, and even Gawain, who is "jilted"
by the supernatural adversaries he had hoped to encounter at the
Tarne. The exchanges between Arthur and his huntsman, the latter's
challenging remarks and the narrator's comments, and the "undo
your door" scene with Arthur and Baldwin's wife are all good examples of where this humour is in evidence. As I mentioned at the outset, it is true that the tail-rhyme format is especially well-suited to the
creation of brisk and pithy oral exchanges; it is also true that tail-
rhyme poems usually stand out more for their swift-paced, forward-
moving narratives than for any extended and detailed description.[4]
Yet despite this inherent tendency, I feel that the *Avowing*-poet in-
tentionally strove for (and achieved) a lightness of tone that at times

---

[4] For a discussion of the Middle English tail-rhyme romance in general, see
Trounce, 1932:103ff.

is almost tongue-in-cheek. Besides its comic tone there is nothing truly original, as far as one can judge, about the entire first panel— nothing, that is, except the portrayal of Baldwin of Britain and his enigmatic vows, to which I now turn.

If the first panel has been painted in the colours of Arthurian chivalry (no matter how broad the strokes), the second panel appears in more rustic tones (the material for its events, as Burrow points out, is drawn from popular tradition). It is clear that the first panel shows the young knights acting out their ideals; and despite the fact that not all three vows are successful, they are attempted in the spirit of chivalry: Arthur bravely vanquishes the boar, Kay's intentions are good even if his skill does not match his boast, and Gawain is the nonpareil of knightly virtue and prowess. The first 300 or so lines of the second panel (i.e. the testing of Baldwin) maintain this spirit of chivalry, and may even be said to heighten it in as much as Baldwin's feats seem to exhibit to a remarkable degree his knightly qualities of courage, courtesy and self-control. But when the time comes for Baldwin to explain himself to Arthur one may notice a distinct shift in tone—Baldwin's expression of his somewhat piously pragmatic views on life is marked by a preponderance of proverbial utterances and a lack of comical undertones. The proverbs imbue this section of the narrative with a sense of real-world experience and concerns, while the fact that the previously noted comical tone of the first panel does not extend to the author's treatment of Baldwin may be an indicator of how seriously we are meant to take him.

From each one of his experiences at the siege in Spain Baldwin draws a lesson that becomes a part of his philosophy of life. Moreover, it is notable that, unlike most other stories that incorporate the motif of the Three Wise Counsels, Baldwin is neither presented with nor pays for the three "counsels" underlying his convictions: he acquires them the hard way, through experience. His first account has taught him, it would seem, to expect either good or evil from a woman, and his advice to others amounts to an exhortation to choose one that is *"meke and mylde atte hor mete"* (l.982: 'humble and gracious at dinner'). His own reaction to the severe test of his jealousy indicates that he had every reason to believe that his own choice had been a good one: *"For mony wyntur togedur we haue bene / And ȝette ho dyd me neuyr no tene"* (ll.901-2: 'for many years we have been together, and yet she has never done me any harm'). But more importantly both the testing episode and the Spanish anecdote are illustrations of Baldwin's self-control and noble forbearance.

His second explanatory account, the tale of the coward in the barrel, has about it the same aura of practicality rooted in a real-world experience. While Arthur's knights may fight for personal gain and glory, or to defend the rights of maidens and widows, Baldwin and his troops are faced with real warfare and the prospect of a very real and nasty death. When their cringing comrade is blown to bits by an incoming projectile, despite his efforts to avoid his fate, Baldwin and his men adopt an attitude toward death that is characterised by a real-life front-line fatalism: "when your number is up, it's up" seems to be their philosophy, and it is easy to imagine that under such circumstances, when he is confronted by death on a daily basis, a man might truly come to view it as Baldwin does: "*Welcum is hit. / Hit is a kyndely thing*" (ll.1044-5: 'It [i.e. death] is welcome. It is a natural thing.'). The chivalric virtue of courage in the face of danger is shared by both brands of chivalry presented here, but the difference between the kind of bravery that is implied in the first panel and explicitly illustrated in the second lies in the grounding of the latter in real-life experience. Surely the Arthur, Kay and Gawain of the first panel have never been in a grim fifteenth-century campaign, or seen guns; our minstrel, if we may reckon him among the careerists described by M.J. Bennett, would have had ample opportunity to see both.

The anecdote selected to explain Baldwin's incredible hospitality belongs to an ancient tradition, and it has many analogues. While the degree of his generosity is so great that it amazes even a king of Arthur's status and wealth, and while there can be no doubt that the presentation of this trait was meant to impress, at the heart of Baldwin's conviction there is a less grand and more simply human motivation for his actions, expressed by Baldwin earlier in the narrative in a proverbial utterance: "*Sir, God hase a gud pluȝe; / He may send vs all enughe. / Qwy schuld we spare?*" (ll.778-80: 'Sir, God has a good plough; he can send us all enough. Why should we refrain from using that?'). So long as God provides him with enough of the good things of this earth, he feels obliged to share them with his fellow man. Baldwin was able to apply this principle in a rather novel fashion and with happy results in the context of the siege, and the kind of excessive prodigality which he subsequently practised was a popular subject in romance[5], but ultimately it illustrates a more universal and everyday stance toward hospitality.

What is suggested by this presentation of Baldwin in his vows and actions, is that he is being offered to us as a *real* husband, a *real* soldier and a *real* burgher, as someone who has never really participated in the unreal world of Arthurian romance with its overly idealistic version of chivalry, as a figure who more closely reflects the values of a flesh-and-blood fifteenth century Englishman.

III

One of the unique features of the *Avowing* is its characterisation of the older knight, Baldwin of Britain. A reading of the *Avowing* as in any way critical of Arthurian chivalric ideals depends largely on one's interpretation of this character. Burrow (1987:109; see also Burrow, 1986:175-7) sees him as the older, mature knight, but prefers not to recognise the "strong tinge of cynicism" that Greenlaw (1906:377) detects in the man. He feels rather that Baldwin is the prototype of the "married lord of a great household", not the adventurous knight. His final assessment of Baldwin is: "It is not that he has given up the life of chivalry; but his sense of its values has been deepened and to some degree darkened by experience" (1987:109). There is little to disagree with here; Baldwin has not given up chivalry—his is a different strain, with different roots, as we have seen. Yet one cannot fail to detect in his words, and in the author's portrayal of him, a note of detachment, of impatience at the folly of the younger knights, and ultimately of cynicism toward the lofty ideals of the chivalric code as embodied in Arthurian romance. How else but as a sign of impatience are we to interpret Baldwin's own words at the

---

[5] The ultimately foolish consequences of such prodigality lie at the thematic heart of two other Middle English romances, *Sir Cleges* (French and Hale, 1964:877-95) and *Sir Amadace*. In both the protagonists pay the price for their exorbitant hospitality. The sentiment expressed by Baldwin and his comrades that "*He that gode may gete, / And wernys men of his mete, / Gud God þat is grete, / Gif him sory care*" (ll.1121-4: 'May the Good God, who is great, give wretched sorrow to him who can obtain property and denies people some of his food') is echoed by a similar phrasing in *Sir Perceval of Galles*. Perceval, having slain the terrible Red Knight, is resting at the hall of an old retainer when a messenger arrives asking for food and drink. The old knight bids his porter admit the man, for "*...it es no synn, / the man þat may þe mete wynn, / to gyffe þe travellende.*" (French and Hale, 1964:562, ll. 962-64: 'it is no sin for a man who can earn his living to give food to the traveller").

actual "avowing": "*Quod Baudewyn, "To stynte owre strife...*"
(l.137: 'Said Baldwin, "to stop our dispute ..." ')? The poet here casts
Baldwin in a role that distances him from the activities of the adventurous Arthurian knights; clearly, while Baldwin has not abandoned
chivalry, his version of it is quite distinct from that of the others; and
even if he has chosen to privilege the power of God and his grace
over that of chivalry, as Burrow suggests, that, too, implies a criticism of the pointless, self-affirming pursuit of its ideals by Arthur
and his knights.

We may turn elsewhere for a last possible indication that our
poet meant us to see Baldwin's cynicism as directed against the Arthurian world of the first panel. It seems that Baldwin of Britain's
star billing in the *Avowing* is unique in the extant romance literature:
in no other romance does he appear in this role, and nowhere is he
made the central figure of the story. Yet he does feature in the work
of an author who could conceivably have read the *Avowing*, or heard
some version of it, namely Sir Thomas Malory. As R.H. Wilson and
others have shown, Malory names a great number of minor characters in his *Morte Darthur* who remain anonymous in his sources.[6]
Such characters lend his work a greater sense of unity, and give "the
realistic effect that the world is more complex than can be indicated
in plots centered around a few individuals" (Wilson, 1943:378). One
of Malory's favourite minor characters, it appears, is Bawdewyn of
Bretayne. Malory first introduces Baldwin as Arthur's constable in
The Tale of King Arthur; this is an independent and original addition, for Baldwin does not appear in the source for this tale.[7] Baldwin returns in the same role in Book V, which scholars agree is based
to a large degree on the alliterative *Morte Arthure*. Here, too, Malory has changed his source; he gives to Baldwin the rank of regent
held by Mordred in the *Morte Arthure*. Also relevant for our purposes is the fact that Malory has Baldwin participate in a ceremonial
vowing similar to what we find in the *Avowing*.[8] In Book VII, the

[6] Cf. Wilson, 1956:566: "It is possible that Bawdewyn is introduced, and made
Constable [in books I-V, DJ], because Malory remembered in him an important
associate of Arthur's, a composite of Baldwin of Britain in the *Avowing of Arthur* and Bedoiers (sometimes constable, sometimes misspelled Bedoins) in the
Vulgate Cycle."
[7] See Vinaver, 1947:i.16, 18 and 19. The source for this section is given by Wilson (1943:369) as the Prose *Merlin* .
[8] See Vinaver, 1947:i.190. Baldwin vows "*unto the vernacle noble*"('to the noble
vernicle') to support Arthur in the imminent Roman war with 10,000 good

story of Gareth (for which no source is known), Baldwin again appears as Arthur's adviser. While Wilson (1943:366) feels that "presumably only a few touches here and there can be of Malory's invention" in this book, it is likely that his naming of Baldwin here is one of them. Thus far, then, Malory first introduces Baldwin where he did not feature in his source, after which he consistently casts him in the role of trusted knight, governor and adviser to Arthur; Malory's use of Baldwin as a minor character serves to strengthen the links between the disparate tales which he has culled from his sources. It is, in Wilson's words (1943:378), "to his credit as a literary artist." But there is more. Still more striking and suggestive for the present discussion is Baldwin's appearance in Book XVIII, *The Fair Maid of Astolat* (for which Malory is said to have drawn on the Old French *Le Mort Artu* and the English stanzaic *Le Morte Arthur*). Baldwin has undergone a significant transformation: he is now a hermit, yet one skilled in medicine, and it is to him that Lancelot, having just defeated the cream of the Round Table in a tournament, bids Sir Levayne take him to be healed of his wound:

> A sir Levayne, helpe me that I were on my horse! For
> here ys faste by, within thys two myle, a jantill ermyte
> that somtyme was a full noble knyght and a grete lorde
> of possessyons. And for grete goodnes he hath takyn
> hym to wylfull poverté and forsakyn myghty londys.
> And hys name ys sir Bawdwyn of Bretayne, and he ys a
> full noble surgeon and a good leche. Now lat se and
> helpe me up that I were there, for ever my harte gyvith
> me that I shall never dye of my cousyne jermaynes
> hondys.   (Vinaver, 1947:iii.1074)

We gain further insight into the *"ermyte"* Baldwin's character from the following:

> So the chylde wente in lyghtly, and than he brought the
> ermyte whych was a passynge lycly man. Whan sir La-
> vayne saw hym he prayed hym for Goddys sake of suc-
> cour.
>   'What knyght ys he?' seyde the ermyte. 'Ys he of the
> house of kynge Arthure or nat?'

---

knights. On the analogues for the ceremony of vowing in the *Avowing*, see Rein-hard, 1932:27-57.

'I wote nat,' seyde sir Levayne, 'what he ys, nother
what ys hys name, but well I wote I saw hym do mer-
vaylously thys day as of dedys of armys.'
　　'On whos party was he?' seyde the ermyte.
　　'Sir,' seyde sir Levayne, 'he was thys day ayenste
kynge Arthure, and there he wanne the pryce of all the
knyghtis of the Rounde Table.'
　　'I have seyne the day,' seyde the ermyte, 'I wolde
have loved hym worse bycause he was ayenste my lorde
kynge Arthure, for sometyme I was one of the felyship.
But now, I thanke God, I am othirwyse disposed. But
where ys he? Lat me se hym.
　　　　　　　　　　　(Vinaver, 1947:iii:1075; emphasis mine)

The relevance of the above to my reading of the *Avowing* should not
be overstated, yet I find the similarities in character development in
both works striking. Here Malory introduces a named character who
is elsewhere anonymous—for Baldwin of Britain appears entirely
without source authority—and transforms him from an active and
successful participant in Arthur's world of chivalric adventure, into
a hermit who has foresaken his previous worldly status, preferring
"*wylfull poverté*" to "*myghty londys*" and knightly adventure. In the
Avowing, as I read it, Baldwin shows the signs of an attitude toward
his former way of life (the life illustrated by Arthur, Gawain and
Kay) that could well lead him to choose the form of retirement represented by Malory's hermit. It is an attitude tinged with cynicism,
and marked by a distance from, and impatience with, the idealistic
games played by the Arthurian knight. That something of this attitude is present in Malory's Baldwin in Book XVIII is evident from
the words Malory puts in his mouth: "*But now, I thanke God, I am
othirwyse disposed.*"
　　There is of course no way of determining whether Malory
knew the *Avowing*. But the possibility is a real one that he might
have, or that both artists were drawing on an established characterisation of Baldwin of Britain in romances now lost. At any event the
correspondences in their treatment of Baldwin are too striking and
suggestive to ignore.
　　In the final analysis, *The Avowing of King Arthur* is a romance that offers more levels of meaning than one might at first suspect. It is first and foremost, perhaps, a good story well told. But
when one considers it against the background of fifteenth-century
careerist tendencies in the Northwest of England as detailed by M.J.

Bennett, the *Avowing*'s probable provenance and date, together with the atmosphere of realism inherent in the poet's choice and development of his materials in the second panel all lead one to include it among those poems that, "though rooted in a provincial dialect and style, ... like the alliterative *Morte Arthure, Winner and Waster, Sir Gawain and the Green Knight* and *St. Erkenwald*, seem to incorporate experiences derived from careerism, and perhaps can be shown to be addressing themselves to the concerns of men who had shared such experiences" (Bennett, 1981:74). Baldwin's vows and actions reveal and underline the contrast between idealised, fictional romance chivalry and reality—albeit a reality that parallels the Romance world but differs from it in essential ways. The "teasing relationship" between the two panels of the diptych is one that would give the more reflective listeners in the poet's audience pause to think about this contrast. In the broadest of terms, they would see in these two panels the courtly ideals of romance juxtaposed with a view of life at once more realistic and devoid of any idealism. This, I take it, is what the poet had in mind when he asked us to "Look here upon this picture, and on this..."

REFERENCES

Bennett, J.A.W. (1986). *Middle English Literature*. Ed. and completed Douglas Gray. Oxford History of English Literature, Vol.1, Part 2. Oxford: Oxford University Press.
Bennett, M.J. (1979). *Sir Gawain and the Green Knight* and the literary achievement of the north-west Midlands: the historical background. *Journal of Medieval History* 5. 63-88.
Bennett, M.J. (1981). Courtly Literature and Northwest England in the Later Middle Ages. In: *Court and Poet. Selected Proceedings of the Third Congress of the International Courtly Literature Society [Liverpool, 1980]*. ARCA 5. Ed. Glyn S. Burgess. Liverpool: Francis Cairns. 69-78.
Brookhouse, C. (ed.) (1968). Sir Amadace *and* the Avowing of Arthur: *Two Romances from the Ireland MS*. Anglistica XV. Copenhagen: Rosenkilde and Bagger.
Burrow, J.A. (1986). *The Ages of Man*. Oxford: Oxford University Press.
Burrow, J.A. (1987). *The Avowing of King Arthur*. In: *Medieval Literature and Antiquities: Studies in honour of Basil Cottle*. Ed. Myra Stokes and T.L. Burton. Cambridge: D.S. Brewer. 99-109.
Dahood, Roger (1971). Dubious Readings in the French and Hale Text of *The Avowyng of King Arthur* (MS Ireland-Blackburne). *N&Q* 18. 323-26.
Dahood, Roger (ed.) (1984). *The Avowing of King Arthur*. Garland Medieval Texts 10. New York: Garland.

French, W.H. and C.B. Hale (eds.) (1964). *Middle English Metrical Romances*.
2 Vols. New York: Russell and Russell. (1st publ., 1930).
Greenlaw, Edwin A. (1906). The Vows of Baldwin: A Study in Medieval Fiction. *PMLA* 21. 575-636.
Hahn, Thomas (ed.) (forthcoming 1990). *Five Gawain Romances*. Kalamazoo, Mich.: Medieval Institute Publications, Western Michigan University.
Hanna III, Ralph (ed.) (1974). *The Awntyrs off Arthur at the Terne Wathelyn*. Manchester: Manchester University Press.
Kittredge, G.L. (1893). *The Avowing of Arthur. MLN* 8. 502-3.
Luick, Karl (1914). Zur mittelenglischen Verslehre. *Anglia* 38. 269-348.
Paris, Gaston (1888). Les voeux de Baudoin. *Histoire littéraire de la France* 30. 111-13.
Reinhard, John R. (1932). Some Illustrations of the Medieval *Gab*. *Essays and Studies in English and Comparative Literature* 8. 27-57.
Robson, John (ed.) (1842). *Three Early Middle English Romances*. Camden Society 18. London: J.B. Nichols.
Ryding, W.W. (1971). *Structure in Medieval Narrative*. De Proprietatibus Litterarum, Series Maior 12. The Hague: Mouton.
Spearing, A.C. (1981). *The Awntyrs off Arthur at the Terne Wathelyn*. In: *The Alliterative Tradition in the Fourteenth Century*. Ed. Bernard S. Levy and Paul S. Szarmach. Kent, Ohio: Kent State University Press. 183-202.
Tihany, Leslie (1936). *The Avowynge of King Arthur: A Morphological and Phonological Study of the Words in Rhyme and of Certain Non-Rhyming Words*. Ph.D. diss. Northwestern University.
Trounce, A.M. (1932-4). The English Tail-Rhyme Romances. *Medium Ævum* 1. 87-108, 168-82; 2. 34-57, 189-98; 3. 30-50.
Vinaver, E. (ed.) (1947). *The Works of Thomas Malory*. 3 Vols. Oxford: Oxford University Press.
Wilson, R.H. (1943). Malory's Naming of Minor Characters. *JEGP* 42. 364-85.
Wilson, R.H. (1956). Addenda on Malory's Minor Characters. *JEGP* 55. 563-87.

NOTES ON CONTRIBUTORS

H. Aertsen is a Lecturer in English at the Vrije Universiteit, Amsterdam.

E.F. Archibald is Assistant Professor in English at the University of Victoria, British Columbia.

G.H.V. Bunt is Senior Lecturer in English at the University of Groningen.

F.N.M. Diekstra is Professor of Medieval English at the University of Nijmegen.

M. Gosman is Professor of Romance Languages at the University of Groningen.

D.F. Johnson is a teaching assistant at Cornell University, Ithaca, New York.

E.S. Kooper is Senior Lecturer in Medieval English at the University of Utrecht.

A.A. MacDonald is Professor of English Language and Medieval English Literature at the University of Groningen.

W. Tigges is a Lecturer in English at the University of Leiden.

N.H.G.E. Veldhoen is a Lecturer in English at the University of Leiden.